POPULATION PROBLEMS
OF THE AGE
OF
MALTHUS

POPULATION PROBLEMS

OF THE AGE

OF

MALTHUS

By

G. TALBOT GRIFFITH, B.A.

Sometime Senior Scholar and Earl of Derby Student of Trinity College
Adam Smith Prizeman, 1924

CAMBRIDGE
AT THE UNIVERSITY PRESS
MCMXXVI

CAMBRIDGE UNIVERSITY PRESS
Cambridge, New York, Melbourne, Madrid, Cape Town, Singapore,
São Paulo, Delhi, Dubai, Tokyo, Mexico City

Cambridge University Press
The Edinburgh Building, Cambridge CB2 8RU, UK

Published in the United States of America by Cambridge University Press, New York

www.cambridge.org
Information on this title: www.cambridge.org/9780521178631

First published 1926
First paperback edition 2010

A catalogue record for this publication is available from the British Library

ISBN 978-0-521-17863-1 Paperback

PREFACE

I am indebted to Mr G. Udny Yule, of St John's College, for a very careful criticism of the statistical portions of this essay and for many helpful suggestions which have enabled me, I trust, to improve these sections. Needless to say, the responsibility for any blunders in the substance and method of these sections that may still exist is wholly mine.

My attention was called by Mr Carlton Oldfield, of Leeds, to Adami's pamphlet, which was the basis of my information about Charles White.

I am particularly indebted to Dr J. H. Clapham, of King's College, who first suggested the subject and general scope of this essay to me and has given me invaluable assistance in all sorts of ways and at every stage of the work; and to my father, Dr T. Wardrop Griffith, of Leeds. I can lay no claim to technical medical knowledge, and therefore in the section dealing with the medical aspect of the subject my father's assistance has been most valuable; first, in putting me on to the relevant portions of the modern text-books and, secondly, in watching from a medical point of view the lucubrations throughout the essay of a mere layman on medical matters. He has, moreover, at all stages been an enthusiastic and indefatigable corrector of proofs. Without his continual help and encouragement the work would never have been finished.

G. T. G.

December 1925

CONTENTS

DIAGRAMS

CHAPTER I

The Figures of the Population

I

IT was not until the results of the first Census were available, unsatisfactory and incomplete though they may have been, that anything like an authoritative estimate of the population of eighteenth-century England became possible. So long as the estimates were based on inferences drawn from taxation returns, on the number of inhabitants to a house, or on the size of the family, matters on which no satisfactory conclusions could be reached, so long the estimates were worth little. These eighteenth-century estimates, moreover, were compiled in most cases by men with little statistical skill, whose chief object was as much to confound an opponent as to arrive at the truth. As Sir Ernest Clarke has pointed out, the professional avocations of the men who made the various estimates do not constitute the qualifications of a statistician. Gregory King was a map-drawer, a surveyor and a bit of a herald. Houghton was an apothecary, who dealt in tea, coffee and chocolate. Dr Price was a Nonconformist minister with a large following, and his great opponent the Rev. John Howlett was incumbent of Great Dunmow. It is interesting that these two protagonists should have been thus separated by religious difference, and possibly their asperities were rendered the more intentional by this fact[1].

It was in the writings of Dr Richard Price that the fear of depopulation received its most exhaustive mathematical treatment. His arguments were largely borrowed from earlier writers but were expressed with greater length and obstinacy backed up by his inflexible pessimism. His method, however,

---

[1] *Statistical Journal*, Feb. 1923, p. 265. Article on the "Population of England in the eighteenth century," in which the pamphlet literature of the century is analysed with great care and skill. I am much indebted to this article in dealing with the estimates of the population made before the Census figures were available.

will show the difficulties that there are in accepting as authoritative any estimate made before the Census.

His argument is based on returns of houses assessed and chargeable, taken at different periods; he argued that it followed from the decrease which these figures showed that the population had similarly decreased during the period.

There are various facts that may be urged against this main argument. First, there was confusion of houses and families. It was not clear whether the returns referred to houses as buildings or as the unit inhabited by a family. Secondly, the taxation returns were in any case likely to be very defective evidence on which to base a calculation without employing some factor of correction; this was done in 1777 by Howlett, but was neglected by Price. Thirdly, the character of the houses assessed changed in a suspicious manner; there was an increase in the number of the better class of house unaccompanied by an increase in the smaller houses, which suggests that the dwellers in smaller houses were getting more skilful at evading the tax collector quite as much as that the number of small houses was decreasing. Wales, writing in 1781, points out that the returns which were made by the window surveyors were by no means sufficient data on which to calculate the population, even where the chargeable houses were returned with the greatest exactness. Cottages, he added, were seldom returned and he was "very credibly informed" that the true numbers of cottages in parts of Yorkshire, in Nottinghamshire and other of the Midland counties were suppressed, as it was feared that the information was wanted with a view to further taxation[1]. Fourthly, there was the difficulty of the number of people that it was right to reckon to the house or to the family when the other difficulties had been overcome.

Price fortified his calculations as to the decrease of the population with three pieces of subsidiary evidence.

First: by taking averages over short periods he made out that the Hereditary Excise had decreased, from which he argued that the population had also decreased. Eden, however, by taking averages over long periods made out an increase; nor

[1] Wales, *An inquiry into the present state of the population of England and Wales*, 1781, p. 3.

does it necessarily follow that the decrease of the consumption of an excisable object is conclusive proof of the decrease of population. Wales was very sceptical of the argument drawn from the decrease of the Hereditary Excise, for he felt that its weight was very largely destroyed by the prevalence of smuggling[1].

Secondly: he declared that the inclosure movement was depopulating the country. This was a doubtful and contentious statement to make at the time, and Prof. Gonner in his elaborate work on *Common Land and Inclosure* has given the opinion that the inclosure movement of the century, though it may have caused local instances of displacement of the population, was not responsible for depopulation. Moreover, Price said that the rise in the price of meat was causing a decrease in the number of the people. Now, his complaint against inclosure is that it was converting arable land into pasture which would tend to lower rather than to raise the price of meat, unless indeed the rise in the price was caused by the increased demand due to an increasing population, which is not an argument that would have appealed to Price.

Thirdly: he argued from the Bills of Mortality for London that the population there was decreasing. This fact, if indeed it was a fact, which is more than doubtful, considered without reference to the country immediately surrounding the area covered by the Bills, was of very little value[2]. The general fear was that London—Cobbett's "wen" as it later became— was draining the rest of the country of men. If according to Price London was actually being depopulated or at any rate not increasing, then that source of drainage on the population of the rest of the country was not in operation.

It is with such criticisms and objections that one can meet the various estimates that were made of the population of this country in the period before the calculators had the comparative certainty of the first Census on which to work. With the exceptions of King's estimate for 1695 and Howlett's for 1777, which will be used in comparison with the series of figures finally adopted, these pre-Census estimates may now be left for those which were made after the introduction of the Census.

---

[1] *Ibid.* p. 4.   [2] *Econ. Journal*, Sept. 1922, p. 328.

II

With the first Census some definite figure was available on which to base calculations, and in the returns of the parish registers of baptisms, marriages and burials there was further available another source of information independent of the actual Enumeration Abstract. This information derived from the parish registers, used in conjunction with the Enumeration Abstract, was made the basis of an equation, which, with certain assumptions, would give an estimate of the population in the preceding years. Various series of figures, using these two independent sources of information in different ways, will shortly be examined.

The work in connection with the taking of the Census was in capable hands. John Rickman was a civil servant attached to the service of the House of Commons, and a statistician of considerable parts, a friend of Southey and Lamb, and, so far as one can judge, not open to the charge of being prejudiced in dealing with his figures in the way in which many of the earlier dabblers in population statistics certainly are. His work on the Censuses seems to have been largely a labour of love, for although he did receive some remuneration for his services, he declares that he was out of pocket on the whole transaction. He appears genuinely to have regarded the work on the Census as valuable for purposes of education and social improvement in which he was interested, and as the best contribution which he could make to the welfare of his country. He devised the methods which were to be employed, and prepared the Reports on the first four Censuses. In addition to the actual preparation of the Census returns, he indulged in, what are quite as important for our present purpose, elaborate calculations, based on the first Census and the parish register returns, as to the population of England in preceding periods[1].

Of these estimates based on the Census returns and the information derived from the parish registers, there are four series to be examined:

[1] For the life of Rickman see *Dictionary of National Biography* and Orlo Williams, *Life and Letters of John Rickman.*

(*a*) Rickman's first estimate, published in the early Census returns.

(*b*) Rickman's second estimate, published after his death in the Report on the Census of 1841.

(*c*) An estimate based on the excess of baptisms over burials.

(*d*) An estimate based on the excess of baptisms over burials, corrected to allow for the deficiency in the registrations of baptisms and burials in the period before the introduction of civil registration.

All these estimates are subject to two lines of criticism and equally so. First, the Census of 1801 was the first of its kind, the machinery was new, and it was probably regarded as the prelude to some new form of taxation or merely distrusted as an innovation. It is unlikely that it was as accurate as one would wish. In so far as the first Census was inaccurate as a representation of the state of the population in 1801, any estimates for other years will also be inaccurate. This will not affect the relative rate of increase during the period for which figures are based on this possibly defective information, but it will make a difference when the change is made from inaccurate to accurate Census figures. Secondly, these figures do not allow for any effect on the growth of the population that the relative amount of immigration or emigration may have had, except in so far as emigrants will cease to affect the returns of baptisms and burials; and immigrants, before they have been in the country very long, will begin to have an effect on those returns. This will not of course represent the full effect that any excess of immigration over emigration might have on the population, but in this connection it is fair to mention that official emigration figures did not start until 1815, and it is reasonable to suppose that if the movement had been one of any great size before that time, some attempt at official records would have been made[1]. Much of the immigration into England in the early part of the nineteenth century came from Ireland, and it is stated in Cornewall Lewis's Report on the Irish in Great Britain in 1836, that "in no part of England, probably, was there any very considerable number of Irish in the year 1795," and again that "the first

[1] S. C. Johnson, *A History of Emigration*, p. 14.

powerful impulse to the Irish immigration into Great Britain was given by the Rebellion of 1798."[1] It is thus possible that this is not a very serious objection to the figures.

Table I. TABLE OF POPULATION

Population of England and Wales calculated by Rickman on his corrected figure for the population given in the first Census, and the baptisms recorded throughout the eighteenth century and published in the parish register abstracts.

Observations on the 1801 *Census*, p. 9: "The existing population of England and Wales is taken at 9,168,000 in the following table; and the population therein attributed to the other years is obtained by the rule of proportion."

Year	Population	Increase	Percentage
1700	5,475,000	—	—
1710	5,240,000	− 235,000	− 4·29
1720	5,565,000	325,000	6·20
1730	5,796,000	231,000	4·15
1740	6,064,000	268,000	4·62
1750	6,467,000	403,000	6·64
1760	6,736,000	269,000	4·16
1770	7,428,000	692,000	10·27
1780	7,953,000	525,000	7·07
1785	8,016,000	—	—
1790	8,675,000	722,000	9·08
1795	9,055,000	—	—
1801	9,168,000	403,000	5·68

(*a*) In the first Census Report Rickman published figures for the population at every tenth year from 1700 onwards (Table I). These estimates are based on the enumerated population of 1801 and the average number of baptisms for the previous five years on the one hand, and on the other hand on the number of baptisms at the period for which the population is to be calculated with a sum in simple proportion. In this Report he also quotes, on similar grounds, estimates for the intermediate fifth year in the cases of 1785 and 1795, but these drop out in the recapitulation of the figures in the later Reports. For the compilation of the volume of parish register returns, the incumbents were instructed to render an account of the number of baptisms for every tenth year from 1700 to 1780 and thereafter for every year; this explains why the estimates for 1785 and 1795 were possible, and no other fifth year's estimate; it also shows that the estimates for the years previous to this more complete return of baptisms must have been based on the baptism

[1] *Reports*, 1836, xxxiv. pp. iv, v.

figures for a single year—as indeed is clearly stated in the explanation of the formula used, which Rickman gives in the first Census Report.

This method is, in effect, to take the birth rate or more correctly the baptism rate of 1801, and, with that rate as a constant and the number of baptisms taking place in other years, to calculate a population figure for each of those other years. Such figures are, therefore, open to the criticism that the assumption of a constant rate is unjustified. Without for the moment advancing any other objections to these figures, which are based solely on the baptism figures, the accuracy of the estimates of population which Rickman gives in this table is directly affected by the degree of steadiness which can be assumed to have existed in the baptism rate. The figures for baptisms are more likely to be defective than those for marriages or burials, but provided there is a constant degree of defectiveness the figure for the population will not be affected. So long as the calculation is made on a rate which is uniform in its degree of inaccuracy, the population figure may be uniformly correct. The baptism rate may deviate from the truth in two ways; it may appear to be steady though at a wrong level or it may appear steady when it should fluctuate. The criticism that the baptism rate is actually subject to considerable fluctuations is a much more serious challenge to the accuracy of the figures than would be the demonstration that a steady rate was actually at a wrong level.

There was as a matter of fact, as will be seen later, a steady rise in the birth rate throughout the eighteenth century. This means that the population of 1700, reckoned on the assumption of a constant birth rate at the 1800 level, which is the basis on which these calculations are made, would be represented as smaller than it actually ought to be on more perfect data. As will appear in the sequel, this estimate does show a population figure for 1700 smaller by 7·66 per cent. than the figure for the corresponding date in the series which is finally adopted.

In addition to this objection to these figures there is another which deserves attention. The natural increase of a people, that is the increase of a people apart from the effect on the population which may result from the excess of immigration over emigration, is the excess of births over deaths, each of which has an essential share in determining the increase. To calculate the population on one only of these factors is to ignore another equally important which ought to be considered. When the population has to be calculated from the data which are now at our disposal—that is, from figures for the baptisms and burials in a period and a population figure at the end of the period—the only safe way is to proceed by a comparison of the baptisms and the burials, and not by a reliance on a series of figures representing only one of these two equally important factors, which is the charge that may be brought against Rickman's first estimate. So long as the population is calculated on the figures for baptisms alone, that year which shows the greatest number of baptisms will show the greatest population and this may be an erroneous conclusion. If the population is only calculated at fairly long intervals it is probable that an increase in baptisms will almost necessarily be accompanied by an increase of population, but this increase is not the inevitable result of the increased number of baptisms. It is quite possible that an increased number of burials may outweigh an increase in the number of baptisms, in which case a correct enumeration of the population might show a decrease in numbers, whereas the population calculated in the manner adopted in this series of figures would show an increase. It is not suggested that the calculations on this method over a long period of years are not of considerable value as a confirmation of other estimates, in spite of their being based on an assumption which is not justified, for they only take account of one of the two essential factors which must be considered when dealing with the natural increase of a people.

(b) Towards the end of his life Rickman instituted some more elaborate calculations for determining the population in previous times. A circular letter was sent to all incumbents, requesting a three-year figure of the baptisms, marriages and burials in their parishes at six periods, namely 1570, 1600, 1630, 1670, 1700 and 1750. The population at these periods was then worked out in the three ways, using all three rates as constants, and then an average of the three was taken. This calculation was completed after Rickman's death[1] and published in the Preface to the 1841 Census Report—the first Census which Rickman had not personally supervised[2].

This series of figures is usually assumed to be the most satisfactory available. Sir Ernest Clarke says that he has little trust in any estimates made before the calculations of Rickman published in the Report on the 1841 Census, and Prof. Gonner states that there is no information as to how the figures for 1801 were obtained, and that for that reason Rickman had discarded the calculations based on them and had undertaken the new investigations, the result of which we have in this second estimate. So far as the value of the information is concerned, it seems to be a tenable view that the 1801 figures are not likely to be less satisfactory than the later figures[3]. The 1841 figures are derived from a circular letter to the incumbents, and are based on the parish registers, as are also the 1801 figures. Under the population act of 1800 the number of baptisms in 1700, 1710, 1720, 1730, 1740, 1750, 1760, 1770, 1780 and every subsequent year was required from "The Rector, Vicar, Curate or Officiating Minister." The sources of the 1801 and the 1841 figures thus bear a very considerable resemblance. The chief claim to greater credibility that the later figures possess, rests on the assumption that the better acquaintance with requests for Census information and the greater respect that would be paid to a demand of Rickman's in 1840 than in 1800 inspired the incumbents to prepare a more accurate return than it had been possible to elicit from their predecessors. This may indeed constitute a difference in degree, but it can hardly amount to a difference in kind.

[1] Rickman was born 22nd August, 1771, and died 11th August, 1840.
[2] Preface to the 1841 Census Report, p. 34.
[3] In the discussion of Gonner's paper, *Stat. Journ.* Feb. 1913, Prof. Gonner speaking of this second estimate of Rickman says, "figures are deduced...on what seems to be the assumption that population stood to the average of baptisms, marriages and burials in the same ratio at the respective dates as in 1841 or thereabouts." It is interesting to compare this with the following extract from the 1841 Census Report explaining these figures: "The results are arrived at by assuming in the years (for which the estimates are made) the same proportion of baptisms, burials and marriages to the existing population as in the years 1800 and 1801; in the last of which years the population was first actually enumerated." Preface to 1841 Census Report, p. 35.

There are two practical disadvantages in connection with this series of figures for the population when compared with the first estimate. They are only given at certain periods; instead of having a figure for every tenth year in the eighteenth century, we only have figures for 1700 and 1750. These figures, further, are derived from a threefold calculation which involves using as constants the marriage rate and the burial rate in addition to the baptism rate which alone is used in the first estimate. The result of adopting these figures would be not only to render any baptism or birth rate for the eighteenth century useless, which is done by the first estimate, but also to render the marriage and burial or death rates useless, and the only reward for this sacrifice would be the one figure for 1750. The use of the marriage or the burial rates as constants for the calculation of the population is open to criticism. In so far as the less serious fluctuations of the baptism rate in comparison with the other two rates is a justification for Rickman's first estimate, the greater fluctuations shown in the death and marriage rates constitute an argument against the use of the second estimate.

The actual difference in the two estimates for the year 1750 is almost exactly 50,000[1], the second estimate being the greater, and in any case the difference is very small considering the size of the figures dealt with. If, however, the three figures for the population in the second estimate from which the average figure is derived are examined, it will be seen that the one which brings the figure of the second estimate above the first is that based on the burials. Now in 1801 the burial rate was in the middle of a pretty steady downward movement, which was continued with only one slight intermission from 1780 to 1820. In 1750 the burial rate, using the population as given in Rickman's first estimate or using the figures which have been finally adopted, was considerably higher than it was in 1801; there was a general mean level of burial rate in the eighteenth century before the fall began in 1780, which was decidedly higher than the

---

[1] Rickman's first estimate   1750   6,467,000
                                    1700   5,475,000
   Rickman's second estimate   1750   6,517,035
                                    1700   6,045,008
   For fuller details see p. 12, n. 1.

burial rate in 1801 or than the general mean level of the rate in the early part of the nineteenth century. It is thus obvious that to use the burial rate of 1801 as a constant for calculating the population in 1750 or 1700 is unsound, and will give a population in those years in excess of what it should be if the other rate is the correct one; for if the rate in 1750 and 1700 was in reality higher than in 1801, the number of deaths registered in those years will be recorded in a society smaller than would be required, so to speak, to produce that number of deaths with a lower rate. The actual difference in the two estimates for 1700 is greater. In this case there is a difference of 600,000. But again it will be seen that it is the figure derived from the calculation based on the burials that is responsible for most of this discrepancy, as this figure is about 900,000 higher than the two derived from the baptism and marriage figures.

The figures derived from the marriage returns are open to the same objection as the death figures, though not in quite such a definite direction. The fluctuations are more erratic than in either of the other two rates, and there is no clear tendency displayed by these fluctuations.

The main criticism of this estimate of Rickman's is an extension of the criticism of the first; namely that it has done with all three rates what the first estimate did with the baptism rate, it has assumed them all as constants. It has been said that on the data we possess, the safest way to estimate the population is to compare the baptism and the burial figures at different periods; this is not done by calculating the population first on the baptism rate independently and then on the burial rate independently and finally striking an average. Such a method may work out and give a result which, like Rickman's first estimate, is valuable auxiliary evidence, but it is more by good luck than good management. The calculation based on the burial figures is even more obviously open to danger than that based on those for baptism, and for the same reason; by this method the year which shows the largest number of burials must also show the largest population, and although this may be true over a long period of years it is obviously an unsafe assumption on which to rest the estimates of a population. The result thus obtained may, however, be a fairly satisfactory estimate; in a year in which a bad epidemic had caused a large number of burials and consequently on these grounds a large population, a small number of baptisms might preserve the balance and the final estimate might approximate to the truth, but estimates based on such processes leave a good deal to be desired.

The second estimate of Rickman is valuable as being the only one which can in any way be regarded as an authoritative illustration of the growth of the population in the period before 1700; in this connection it is probable that it gains by being based on a threefold calculation, whatever the advantages or disadvantages of that system in the latter half of the eighteenth century may be. It is noticeable that the average and final figure given in the second estimate shows a population increasing, though not indeed at a uniform rate, throughout the period, and showing its slowest rate of increase where we should expect it, namely between 1630 and 1670. If the three component elements of that average result be examined separately it will be seen that there is not one of them that shows any regularity of increase. The baptism figure shows a decrease of population between 1630 and 1670, as also does the figure derived from the marriages, whilst in 1670 the figure derived from the burials shows the highest recorded population in the series[1].

Before leaving these estimates of Rickman's there is one other series which may be dealt with in conjunction with them. Finlaison, of the National Debt Office, compiled figures for the whole of the eighteenth century which received the blessing of Rickman in the Report on the 1831 Census. This series of figures deals with the eighteenth century, and, throughout, the

[1] Rickman's estimate as published in the Report on the 1841 Census (referred to as the second estimate).

Population of England and Wales, calculated from the figures given for baptisms, burials and marriages (three-year averages)

	Baptisms	Burials	Marriages	Average
1570	3,853,122	4,167,363	4,461,478	4,160,321
1600	4,883,059	4,364,637	5,187,458	4,811,718
1630	5,527,780	5,798,176	5,475,594	5,600,517
1670	5,256,700	7,199,693	4,864,546	5,775,646
1700	5,728,430	6,661,698	5,744,896	6,045,008
1750	6,377,574	6,717,858	6,455,672	6,517,035

figures are somewhat smaller than those given by Rickman, except in the case of the figure for 1800–1 which is larger than Rickman's figure (Table II). The greatest discrepancy occurs in 1750 when Finlaison's figure falls short of Rickman's by some 300,000. The two series of figures agree in showing a decrease in the first decade of the century, but from then on to 1760 the relative movement of the percentage increase shown by them varies. From 1760 the correspondence is greater; in the three decades from 1760 to 1790 the difference in their increase never amounts to 1·5 per cent., though in the transition decade 1790–1800 there is considerably more difference. The two series agree in showing that the increase in the decade 1760–1770 was the largest recorded in the century and that the last decade of the century was the smallest. They also agree in showing that the increase in the decade 1770–1780 was smaller than that of either of the adjoining decades.

Table II. TABLE OF POPULATION

Population of England and Wales during the eighteenth century compiled by Finlaison.

McCulloch, *Statistical Account of the British Empire*, 1839, 2nd ed. p. 402, says: "Mr Finlaison of the National Debt Office, availing himself of the returns as to births, marriages and deaths obtained under the population acts, as well as of various other sources of information, has framed the following statement of the population since 1700 which may be regarded as approaching as near to accuracy as the subject will admit of."

See also Rickman's remarks about the same series of figures, Preface to 1831 Enumeration Abstract, p. xlv.

Year	Population	Increase	Percentage
1700	5,134,516	—	—
1710	5,066,337	− 68,179	− 1·33
1720	5,345,351	279,014	5·51
1730	5,687,993	342,642	6·41
1740	5,829,705	141,712	2·49
1750	6,139,684	309,979	5·32
1760	6,479,730	340,046	5·54
1770	7,227,586	747,856	11·54
1780	7,814,827	587,241	8·12
1790	8,540,738	725,911	9·28
1800	9,187,176	646,438	7·56

(c) Both the preceding series of figures are open to the two criticisms that they assume constant rates, and that they do not rest on a satisfactory comparison of the information about baptisms and burials. In this series of figures, and in the series which follows and which has been finally selected, an attempt has been made to draw this comparison. At the outset it is well to state that these figures are subject to the same general criticisms that were applied to the first series, namely that the first Census may be defective, and that the figures make no allowance for the effect of immigration and emigration except in so far as these affect the baptism and the burial rates. The population figure of the 1801 Census as corrected by Rickman has been taken as the starting point. The figures for baptisms and burials are taken from the corrected version given in the Report on the 1811 and subsequent Censuses. From 1780 to 1800 there are figures given in the parish register returns of baptisms and burials for every year. It is possible, therefore, to calculate for those twenty years the excess of baptisms over burials with considerable accuracy. This has been done, and population figures have been calculated for the years 1780, 1785, 1790 and 1795 on this basis. Before 1780 the baptism and burial figures are only given every tenth year; therefore to do the same thing for the first eighty years of the century the figure for a given year has had to be taken as representative of the state of things for the ten years of which it is the centre; thus the figure for 1760 has been treated as the representative figure for the years from 1756 to 1765 inclusive. On that plan, by reckoning the excess of registered baptisms over burials, a population figure has been calculated for every tenth year throughout the eighteenth century. It is a very strong argument in favour of calculations of this kind that they do not assume any rate to have been constant throughout the eighteenth century, and that they do not calculate the population on one only of the essential elements but on a fair comparison of the two. There is however one serious objection, and an attempt has been made to overcome this in the fourth and last series of figures. The objection is that in this series the accuracy of the baptism figures as an indication of the number of births and of the burial figures as an indication of the number of deaths assumes an importance that it did not possess in Rickman's two series of figures. In the case of the earlier of these two series, the baptism figures, and in the case of the later, the burial figures as well, were used as constants to calculate the population from the known condition of the population at the time of the first Census and the numbers of the baptisms and burials at that time. Now the year 1801, so far as the baptism and burial figures as representative of the birth and death figures are concerned, was as much in the dark ages as the eighteenth century; therefore, although there may have been considerable leakages between births and baptisms and between deaths and burials, still, provided we can assume some constancy of omission, the population figure that results from that calculation will not be affected and herein lies the strength of using these figures merely as a ratio. In the series which we are now discussing they are used, or rather the difference between them is used, as an absolute figure to subtract from the population figure in one year to arrive at the population figure in a previous year. It at once, therefore, becomes obvious that it is important in this case that there should be no leakage between births and baptisms or between deaths and burials. This matter is complicated by the fact that the baptism and the burial figures do not deviate from those of the births and the deaths in the same proportion, and this means that no correction of the net result will be safe, but that in some way the baptism figures must be corrected to represent more nearly the births, and the burial figures must be corrected to represent more nearly the deaths. The population figures arrived at on this uncorrected plan do not, as a matter of fact, show any increase at all of the population in the first half of the eighteenth century, and in the second, third and fourth decades they actually show a small decrease, and a very much larger population for 1700 than is shown by any other series of figures.

(d) The fourth and final series of figures has been compiled on the same principle as the unsatisfactory series which has just been dealt with, but the figures for baptisms and burials have been corrected. Civil registration was introduced in 1837. The rate for the first five-yearly period after its introduction, namely that given for 1840, is suspect, as the figures for the first few years of the new method on which it is based are well known to have been unsatisfactory. By 1841, or thereabouts, the figures appear to be reliable and thereafter the rates show the results of the new system when it was in full operation[1]. In both the baptism and the burial rates there is a marked jump at the transition from the earlier unsatisfactory returns to the better information available under civil registration. An addition of 15 per cent. to the baptism rate before the introduction of civil registration (based on the rates for 1825, 1830 and 1835) disposes of the jump and makes it correspond to the birth rate after civil registration. Similarly an addition of 10 per cent. makes the burial rate before civil registration correspond to the death rate afterwards. These corrections have been applied to all the baptism and burial figures for the period for which we have to calculate the population, and on these figures, thus corrected and assumed to be representative of births and deaths, the population has been calculated for the eighteenth century, at every tenth year up to 1780 and thereafter at every fifth year. It may be well to emphasise the point that an addition of 15 per cent. to the baptisms and of 10 per cent. to the burials means much more than adding 5 per cent. to the natural increase; it means a very large increase indeed—in fact, in the first half of the eighteenth century almost creating an increase out of nothing. This correction of course opens up further possibilities of error and it is not contended that it is in the least likely to be entirely satisfactory; for instance, it is possible that a correction which may be reasonable and satisfactory in the early part of the nineteenth century is not the correction which should have been applied in the early part of the eighteenth century; and as a matter of fact the rates based on these corrected figures for the early part of the eighteenth century do differ from the rates based on the uncorrected figures by rather more than the mere difference in level before and after the introduction of civil registration. The extent of the possible error can be illustrated by the following example. If 16 per cent. be added to the baptisms and only 9 per cent. to the burials—a difference of + or − 1 per cent.—the population figure for 1780 goes down by 92,818 and for 1750 by 208,405. There is obviously a very large possible error as the result of a very small

[1] Census Report, 1851, p. cxxxi.

alteration in the percentage correction. Two other sources of error should be defined. First, the correction may be unsatisfactory because of a variation in the number of parishes from which no returns were received; this may be a constant source of error but is not necessarily so, especially in the case of a parish which was rural in 1700 and had been absorbed in an urban district by 1800. Secondly, the fluctuations in the prevalence of dissent may have had, and probably did have, some effect on the constancy of the error; what was a satisfactory correction for one part of the century may, with the increase of dissent, cease to be a satisfactory correction for a later part of the century. As a matter of fact some such error does seem to be traceable[1]. It is, however, suggested that with the imperfect data at our command the method is the one which is the most likely to give satisfactory results if the correction is approximately accurate. It is not likely that any series of figures for the population of the eighteenth century can withstand every attack, as all are at best but estimates. These corrected baptism and burial figures show a greater excess of the one over the other than do the uncorrected figures and consequently the estimate based upon them shows the population in the earlier years of the century as smaller than did the uncorrected figures. These figures show an actual decrease of the population in the third decade of the century, which was the middle of the three decades which showed a decrease on the other series of figures. An interesting fact about that decrease is that it comes in the middle of the gin-drinking period. Throughout the first half of the eighteenth century these figures show the increase to have been but small; it became greater in the first three decades of the second half of the century and, in the last two decades of the century, comparable in rapidity to the really great increase of the early nineteenth century.

These figures are those which have been finally adopted and on which the rates have been worked out. It may be as well, therefore, to summarise once again the considerations which tell against and for their acceptance (Table III).

First, any criticism that may be directed against figures which

_____
[1] See p. 29.

depend on the first Census for their origin may be directed against this series.

Secondly, the same may be said in regard to allowance made for immigration and emigration.

Thirdly, it may be said that the correction of the baptism and the burial figures is not satisfactory, and that a small variation in the corrections results in large variations in the ultimate figures.

Table III. TABLE OF POPULATION

Population of England and Wales during the eighteenth century, compiled as follows:

Rickman's correction of the 1801 Census figure for England and Wales taken as the starting point. The figures for the eighteenth century obtained by the excess of baptisms over burials working backwards from the figure for 1801. From 1780 to 1800 these figures are available every year; before 1780 only at the ten-yearly periods, during which period the figures given have been taken as representative of the decade of which they are the centre. To allow for the deficiencies in the baptisms and burials, the baptism figures have been corrected by the addition of 15 per cent. and the burial figures by the addition of 10 per cent., to make them the more nearly represent the births and deaths.

Year	Population	Increase	Percentage
1700	5,835,279	—	—
1710	6,012,790	177,511	3·04
1720	6,047,664	34,874	0·58
1730	6,007,638	− 40,026	− 0·66
1740	6,012,750	5,112	0·08
1750	6,252,924	240,174	3·9
1760	6,664,989	412,065	6·6
1770	7,123,749	458,760	6·9
1780	7,580,938	457,189	6·4
1785	7,826,032	—	—
1790	8,216,096	635,158	8·3
1795	8,655,710	—	—
1801	9,168,000	951,904	11·5

On the other hand it may be said:

First, these figures do not necessitate the assumption of any constant rate, and as a result there remains the possibility of arriving at rates for the eighteenth century.

Secondly, they take into account the two essential elements in the natural increase, the births and the deaths, and treat them in the comparative way which is the safe way to calculate a population figure on the imperfect data which are available.

Thirdly, a comparison of these figures and others that are available strengthens the contention that they form a fairly satisfactory representation of the movement of the population of

England and Wales during the eighteenth century, and this is encouraging and important in view of the fact that even now these figures are largely guesswork.

A comparison of these figures with others is interesting. The figure for 1700 falls very nearly half-way between Rickman's two estimates, which differ by about 600,000. It is within 100,000 of the correction of Rickman's second estimate which is accepted by Prof. Gonner, and it is within 30,000 of the correction which the same writer makes on the estimate of 1690, compiled from the Hearth Tax figures. For the figure at the beginning of the eighteenth century there is thus a considerable consensus of opinion. For 1750 this series of figures shows a smaller population than the other series; it will be remembered however that in this year Rickman's two estimates differed by almost exactly 50,000. Prof. Gonner adopts a correction of Rickman's second estimate which is lower than either of his estimates but is about 70,000 greater than the figure for 1750 in the series now under discussion. Between the highest and lowest of the four figures for 1750 there is thus a possible variation of about 265,000[1]. In 1777 Howlett formed an estimate of the population on the same data as those used by Price, but he took the trouble to arrive at a factor of correction to be applied to the number of assessed houses. In certain areas he ascertained by independent investigation the number of houses and compared that figure with the official assessment, thus arriving at a factor of correction which he applied to the whole country. His figure for 1777 was 6,630,000; this is undoubtedly a

[1] Population figures for 1750:
Rickman's first estimate	6,467,000
Rickman's second estimate	6,517,035
Gonner's correction of Rickman's second estimate	6,320,000
Estimate based on excess of births over deaths ...	6,252,924

After this chapter was written my attention was called to a paper by Dr Brownlee, *The history of the birth and death rates in England and Wales taken as a whole from 1570 to the present time*, reprinted from *Public Health* for June and July 1916. On p. 14 of that paper there is a table of various estimates for the population of England in the eighteenth century. One series gives a population figure derived in very much the same way as the series now under discussion—a factor of correction applied to the baptisms and to the burials—and it is encouraging to find that the greatest discrepancy between these two series of figures, which occurs in 1750, only amounts to 1·824 per cent.

serious under-estimate, but in connection with the series of figures under discussion at the moment it is interesting, for this series shows a slower rate of increase in the earlier part of the century, and a more rapid rate in the latter half of the century, than that shown by Rickman. The figure given by Howlett would tend to confirm this general movement, for, even allowing for a considerable degree of under-estimation, it still postpones the great increase in the century to the years between 1777 and the first Census, and it is in the last two decades of the century that the increase according to the present series of figures was becoming rapid[1].

There are also for the years 1780, 1790 and 1800 figures given by Malthus, "calculated from the excess of births above the deaths after an allowance made for the omissions in the registers, and for deaths abroad." These are isolated figures and therefore have not the authority or the value of a continuous series. The credibility of these figures may possibly be compromised by the fact that it was in accordance with the theory which Malthus was concerned to demonstrate, to show as rapid an increase in the population as possible. The figure which he gives for 1800 is decidedly in excess of Rickman's correction of the 1801 Census and presumably this must be put down to the correction "for deaths abroad." In connection with the series of figures now under discussion these figures of Malthus again go to confirm the rapid increase in the last two decades of the eighteenth century. Apart from the additional allowance made for deaths abroad they are compiled, so far as one can see, on much the same principle as that adopted in this series of figures, though they show higher estimates throughout; but in the last two decades of the century Malthus's figures show percentage increases of 8·98 and 10·30 as against 8·3 and 11·5 in this series of figures, a greater correspondence than is shown between this series and the increases as given by Rickman[2].

[1] *Stat. Journ.* Feb. 1913, pp. 284–5.
[2] Malthus, *Essay*, 1817 ed. III. p. 95:

1780	7,721,000
1790	8,415,000
1800	9,287,000

III

When the Census era is entered the figures which have been adopted are, for the first three Census years, those of the corrected versions of the enumeration given by Rickman, and after that the bare figures of the Enumeration Abstract (Table IV).

Table IV. TABLE OF POPULATION

(1) The population of England and Wales from the Enumeration Abstracts.
(2) The population of England and Wales from the same source, but with the corrections for absentees made by Rickman in the Preliminary Observations to the Population Abstracts. In 1801 and 1811 he added one-thirtieth of the population for these, in 1821 he added one-fiftieth, and in 1831 and 1841 no correction is made.
(3) The population of England and Wales as given in the Census Report of 1851 (*Accounts and Papers*, 1852–3, LXXXV. p. xxxiii). These figures are those adopted by Cunningham and Price Williams, except that in one of the two tables given by Price Williams the figure for 1841 is given as 15,909,132.

	(1)	(2)	Percentage increase	(3)
1801	8,872,980	9,168,000		8,892,536
1811	10,150,615	10,488,000	14·39	10,164,256
1821	11,978,875	12,218,500	16·39	12,000,236
1831	13,897,187	13,897,187	13·74	13,896,797
1841	15,906,741	15,906,741	14·46	15,914,148

Rickman corrected the Enumeration Abstract by the addition of one-thirtieth in 1801 and 1811, and of one-fiftieth in 1821. These corrections were chiefly needed in respect of the military conditions under which the first two Censuses were taken[1].

If divisions of the country are considered, the increase of London was greatest and practically the same in the decades 1811–1821 and 1841–1851. The greatest increase in the larger towns took place in the decade 1821–1831, and in the smaller towns between 1811 and 1821. The greatest increase in the rural parts of the country also took place in this second decade of the

[1] Preliminary Observations, 1801, p. 9: "The enumeration of 1801 amounts to 8,872,980 persons for England and Wales, and to this number an appropriate share of the Soldiers and Mariners is to be added. These appear to have been 469,188; and if (exclusive of them) the Total Population of the British Isles is 14,630,812, about a thirtieth may be added to the inhabitants to ascertain the Population of any distinct part." Prelim. Obs. 1811, p. xxv: "The Population of England and Wales in the year 1811 is taken at 10,488,000, for a similar reason as that of 1801 at 9,168,000." Prelim. Obs. 1821, p. xxxii: "To the population of Great Britain in the year 1821, no more than a fiftieth part is added, the Navy and Army having decreased since 1811."

century, while the increase in this decade over the whole country is the largest ever recorded.

In the ninety years from 1801 to 1891 the three places which showed the greatest increases were Bradford, Cardiff and Brighton, and in each case there is a pretty obvious cause at work.

The greatest individual increase recorded in the period is at Brighton between the years 1811 and 1821, when the town grew from 12,205 to 24,741, an increase of 102·71 per cent. A very slight acquaintance with the social history of the time suggests the cause[1].

IV

There are some interesting points to notice in this general movement. The period of decreasing population in the third decade of the eighteenth century was a period of peace, but, as has been said, it was in the gin-drinking period and the decrease was due to a rising death rate[2]. The decade 1760–1770 shows the greatest increase up to that time, an increase which is larger than that which took place in the decade following, and it is in this decade 1760–1770 that the Peace of Paris and the end of the Seven Years War fell. The effect of the American and the Napoleonic Wars on the growth of the population is not very clear. It may be that the slightly smaller increase in the decade 1770–1780 than in the previous decade was partially due to the American War, and very possibly the lull of peace between the end of the American War and the outbreak of the wars with France was partially responsible for the increase which began in the decade following 1780. The causes are too involved to allow much weight to be given to any generalisations of that kind, and it is very unlikely that wars in those days had anything like the same effect on people that they have to-day. Very many fewer people in proportion were engaged, the system of international interdependence was not so complicated as it is now and a war did not bring so inevitably the dislocations

[1] Prelim. Obs. 1801, p. 9.

[2] Hawkins, *Medical Statistics*, p. 18, speaking of the rate of mortality: " Its increase about the middle of last century has been attributed to the great abuse of spirituous liquors which was at length checked by the imposition of high duties."

that accompany it nowadays. It is interesting also that, on the showing of the final series of figures, the rate of increase went on growing throughout the period of the wars, and that the greatest increase ever recorded occurred in the decade in which the close of the Napoleonic Wars occupies the same position as was occupied by the Peace of Paris in the decade 1760–1770, a fact which is probably in part responsible for this. The Peace of Amiens in 1802 had some effect in this way also, for it did affect the marriage and the birth rates. It is worth noticing also that this series of figures does not give the very slow rate of increase in the decade 1790–1800 which is shown in Rickman's figures. This slower rate of increase was rather astonishing in view of the very much more rapid increases which took place in the two decades adjoining it, and in this series of figures that awkward and surprising check does not occur.

V

The estimates for the population in the eighteenth century do not deal, except very indirectly, with immigration and emigration, about which problems in the early part of the nineteenth century something may now be said. In the 1831 Census there is for every county and for the country as a whole an account of the number of baptisms and burials, showing the natural increase of the county during the decades since 1801 and also the actual increase of the county as shown by the Census enumeration. From these figures it is possible to see which counties increased more than they would have done had the only factor to be considered been the natural increase, and which counties lost population which they had acquired by their natural increase. For the whole of the country, also, it is possible to see how much of the increase recorded in the Census returns is due to the natural increase and how much is due to the other cause—the excess of immigration over emigration. With these figures, as with the calculation of the eighteenth-century population, there is a leakage between baptisms and births and between burials and deaths. Before, therefore, any very safe estimate can be arrived at as to the amount of the increase all over the country due in those three decades to the excess of immigration over emigration, allowance must be made for the deficiencies in the baptism and burial figures as was done in calculating the population. When this is done the result is that in England and Wales the following proportions of the increase are not due to the natural increase, that is they are due to the excess of immigration over emigration, unless the birth and death figures are still very far wrong. In the decade 1801–1811, 12·5 per cent.; in the decade 1811–1821, 11·4 per cent.; and in the decade 1821–1831, 7·4 per cent. It is interesting to note that this proportion got smaller as time went on. The probable explanation is that the fear of over-population which followed the taking of the early Censuses was sufficient to promote emigration to such an extent that it did something to swamp the increasing amount of immigration that was coming chiefly from Ireland, and, in spite of that factor working in the opposite direction, to decrease the influence which the excess of immigration had on the growth of the population. In these thirty years the great exodus from Ireland which resulted from the distress and famine in that country had not grown to the large proportions it afterwards assumed, although throughout the period there was considerable emigration from Ireland to this country.

In the case of the separate counties the same correction should be made for the deficiency in the baptism and burial figures, but this has not been done, and the following remarks are made on the figures as they are given in the Census returns. It is perhaps not so satisfactory to take the divisions of the country as to take the whole country, for it is probable that such errors as there are in the figures are more likely to affect these results than the result for the whole country; special local causes may give an erroneous result for one locality which would be very small when it was included in the general result. It is probable also that, using the uncorrected figures, some of the counties which do not show a very decided trend either way may show a wrong result, but those which either gained a large amount of population over and above their natural increase, or which lost a large part of their natural increase, are not likely to be put on the wrong side of the scale by the use of the uncorrected figures. Thus Essex, Kent, Middlesex and Surrey responded to the attraction of London and their growth was very much more than their natural increase. Similarly Cheshire and Lancashire responded to the growth of the cotton trade to such an extent that in the last of the three decades the immigration was greater than the natural increase. The West Riding, and in a minor degree the North Riding, show the same result, though not quite so pronouncedly as in the case of the cotton counties. Durham, Monmouth, Stafford and Warwick responded to the growth of the iron and mining industries but again not to the same degree as the cotton counties.

On the other hand Devonshire, Norfolk and Suffolk lost a considerable portion of their natural increase; in all three there were decaying textile industries and Suffolk was one of the worst counties from the point of view of Poor Law administration, being one of the six in which in 1824 the allowance system was said to be the most burdensome. Certain agricultural counties lost part of their natural increase, especially Wiltshire which lost more than one-half in the first decade of the century and about one-third in the third decade, although in the second decade its growth appears to have been rather more than its natural increase. This is a comparatively small increase, however, and might very easily be reversed on more perfect data[1].

The position that certain of these counties whose growth was more than their natural increase occupy in the general county increase of the kingdom will be seen from the following figures. Monmouth had the largest percentage increase of any county in three out of the first four decades of the nineteenth century. In the remaining decade Lancashire had the largest increase and it was second in two others and third in the remaining one.

[1] Counties which increased 1801–1831 more than their natural increase: Bedford, Cambridge, Cheshire, Cumberland, Derby, Durham, Essex, Gloucester, Hereford, Kent, Lancashire, Leicester, Lincoln, Monmouth, Middlesex, Northampton, Northumberland, Nottingham, Somerset, Sussex, Stafford, Surrey, Warwick, York; counties which lost part of their natural increase in the period: Berkshire, Buckingham, Cornwall, Devon, Dorset, Hertford, Huntingdon, Hampshire, Norfolk, Oxford, Rutland, Shropshire, Suffolk, Wiltshire.

Durham had the second largest increase in the last decade. All these three counties doubled their population in the forty years and Monmouth trebled its population[1].

---

[1] County Increase, *Stat. Journ.* XLIII. Price Williams.

	Lancashire	Durham	Monmouth
1801–1811	23·03 %	10·65 %	36·29 %
1811–1821	27·09	17·07	22·05
1821–1831	26·97	23·64	29·45
1831–1841	24·70	28·71	36·93

CHAPTER II

The Birth Rate, Marriage Rate and Death Rate

I

IT is essential to form a mental picture of the statistical background of an increasing population. Reduced to its elements the increase of the population of a country—or more correctly the natural increase—depends on the relationship between the birth rate and the death rate. The one rate without the other may be interesting and valuable, but can give no definite information as to the movement of the population. A steady birth rate with a steady death rate may mean either an increasing or a decreasing population according as the birth rate is higher or lower than the death rate, and similarly a falling death rate does not necessarily mean an increasing population unless the birth rate is falling more slowly or at any rate starts from a higher figure. A comparison of the birth rates and the death rates will therefore give a clear idea of the way in which the population is increasing; such a comparison also shows whether the rapidity of the increase is due chiefly to a rise in the birth or to a fall in the death rate, which is a very important distinction. When this question of primary importance has been settled by an examination of the two rates, they can then be further examined in relation to other ratios, for instance, the incidence of mortality—a very difficult question to investigate in this period—and the prolificness of marriage. In the case of the birth rate these ratios will be found to emphasise the important factors and act as a preparation for the discussion of the remoter causes of the increase, the economic, social and industrial causes which affect the birth rate and the death rate, the variations of which rates are the primary cause of the increase of the population.

II

A table has been given showing a birth rate from 1700 to 1846, based on a ten-year average where there is the necessary information available, with certain more modern figures for the purpose of comparison, together with an explanation of the method employed in constructing the table.

Table V. BIRTH RATES

The population figures for the eighteenth century are those given in Table III, based on the 1801 Census and the excess of births over deaths, as explained (d) on pp. 5 and 15 in the chapter on the figures of the population. From 1801 onwards the Census figures are used. (See Table IV, column 2.)

Before the introduction of civil registration (actually in the case of these figures up to and including the year 1840) the baptism figures have been corrected by the addition of 15 per cent. to make them more nearly represent the probable births, this correction being arrived at by a comparison of the rate before and after the introduction of civil registration if the correction is not made. Material is only available for rates based on the figure for one year before 1780.

The rates given for modern comparison are derived from the 64th Annual Report of the R.G. 1901, p. clxiii.

Births per 1000 living

1700	One-year rate	31·1	
1710	,,	27·5	A
1720	,,	30·5	
1730	,,	32·0	
1740	,,	33·3	
1750	,,	34·1	
1760	,,	33·3	
1770	,,	34·0	
1780	,,	34·4	
1785–1795	(11 year average)	35·44	B
1796–1806	,,	34·23	
1806–1816	,,	33·84	
1816–1826	,,	33·39	
1826–1836	,,	32·36	
1836–1846	,,	31·43	C
1851–1860	(10 year average)	34·13	
1871–1880	,,	35·42	
1891–1900	,,	29·87	

1700, 1710, 1720. Period *A*. A period of low rates.
1780, 1785–1795 and 1796–1806. Period *B*. A period of high rates.
1826–1836 and 1836–1846. Period *C*. Again a period of lower rates.

Comparison of period averages:

Period *B* shows a rise from Period *A* of 16·84 per cent.
Period *C* shows a rise from Period *A* of 7·069 per cent.
Period *C* shows a fall from Period *B* of 8·610 per cent.

See also Diagram I.

The 15 per cent. correction, which has been applied to the baptism figures, wipes out the jump which otherwise occurs when the rate changes from a baptism rate to a birth rate, and between that date and the middle of the eighteenth century this correction does not appear to have any greater effect on the rate than to raise it by about the amount of that jump. For the first half of the century, however, it appears to have the effect of slightly flattening out the movement of the birth rate. The birth rate worked on the baptism figures corrected by an addition of 15 per cent. does not show as great a rise from the rate prevalent in the first half of the eighteenth century to that in the second half as is shown by the rate worked on the uncorrected figures. This may of course be the correct result, but it may also be that in the early years of the century the correction does not work so satisfactorily as in the later period, or, as previously suggested, it may point to the fact that the increase of dissent during the century would have justified a larger correction during the later part of the century than in the earlier part and this would have given a bigger rise in the birth rate throughout the century. It is probable that the rate in the earlier part of the century gives a fairly correct general idea of the movement, but it would be unwise to draw any fine conclusions from figures which have been subjected to a correction like the above, and which, before the more complete information begins in 1780, are based on one figure every tenth year.

The change from a baptism rate to a birth rate shows a greater jump than the change from a burial rate to a death rate. This is exactly what we should expect; there is greater risk in assuming that every birth is recorded by a subsequent baptism than in assuming that every death is recorded by a subsequent burial. Baptisms of Nonconformists would escape registration in parish registers with greater ease and frequency than would the burials of the same class of people who were frequently buried in the parish burial grounds, and thereby appear in the register. Further, in the slum conditions which became intensified with the ill-regulated growth of the large industrial towns, the leakages in the baptismal register must have been considerable. It must also be remembered that, although before the introduction of civil registration the baptism figures have been corrected to make them the more nearly represent the birth figures, and although for purposes of argument it is convenient to speak of a birth rate throughout the period, the correction cannot convert baptism figures into birth figures; it can only correct the baptism figures so that they bear a closer resemblance to what the birth figures probably were.

The birth rate was low in 1710 compared with the rate in 1700 and 1720, and this might have been due to the war. From 1710 to 1790 the birth rate rose steadily and considerably, with the exception of a short check in 1760, which again might have been due to the war. After 1790—the last figure before the period of the war with Revolutionary France—the rate began a drop which persisted for the rest of the period with which we are dealing (i.e. up to 1840), to be followed by a rise in the middle of the nineteenth century. The last year or two of the eighteenth century, in addition to being years of war, were also years of epidemics and bad harvests and the marriage rate dropped considerably after 1790.

From the year 1700, when these figures begin, with the exception of 1730, the birth rate was always higher than the death rate and consequently was contributing effectively to the increase of the population. The extent of the importance of this rise can be judged by a comparison of three short periods. The birth rate was highest in the thirty odd years from 1775 to 1805. This period forms a peak in the rate which can be compared with a period of low birth rate before the eighteenth century rise—one comprising the rates for the years 1700, 1710 and 1720—and with a period of slightly lower birth rate at the end of the period—comprising the rates for the years 1826 to 1846. The period of high birth rate shows a rise of 16·84 per cent. from that of low birth rate at the beginning of the eighteenth century, and the period of lower birth rate from 1826 to 1846 shows a fall of 8·610 per cent. from the previous period of high birth rate from 1775 to 1805. It should be noted that the period of comparatively low birth rate from 1826 to 1846 shows a rise of 7·069 per cent. from that of low birth rate at the beginning of the eighteenth century.

This general rise in the birth rate during the eighteenth century and the first half of the nineteenth century and especially the period of high birth rate from 1775 to 1805 was contributing materially to the growth of the population, and must be reckoned with, though as will appear in the sequel it was not as spectacular as the contemporaneous drop in the death rate.

Table VI. TABLE TO DEMONSTRATE THE FERTILITY
OF MARRIAGE

The marriages in one year have been divided into the baptisms recorded five years later. A rate of this kind has been prepared for every year, and then ten-year overlapping averages compiled. These last are given in the table.
The dates given are those of the marriages.
The last three figures are based on birth figures (not baptisms).

1775–1784	3·6738	
1780–1789	3·7300	
1785–1794	3·6456	
1790–1799	3·6253	
1795–1804	3·6580	A
1800–1809	3·7252	
1805–1814	3·8260	
1810–1819	3·8766	B
1815–1824	3·8190	
1820–1829	3·7370	C
1825–1834	3·5957	
1875–1884	4·5222	
1880–1889	4·4414	D
1885–1894	4·2746	

Period B shows a rise of 4·660 per cent. from Period A.
Period C shows a drop of 5·837 per cent. from Period B.
Period D shows a rise of 14·899 per cent. from Period C.
See also Diagram II.

A table has been prepared to demonstrate the fertility of marriage throughout this period (Table VI). Marriages in one year have been divided into baptisms five years later and from these figures ten-yearly averages in overlapping periods have been given. All the figures in this table before 1834 are based on uncorrected baptism figures. Whereas it may be perfectly safe to trust these figures so far as they go for a comparison inside the period based on this defective information, the results given are much lower than they should be on more perfect data and it is not safe to use the figures for comparison outside the period. As a very rough test, figures for the years 1875 to 1894 have been compiled in exactly the same way, using in this case, however, birth figures in the Registrar General's Reports. An average figure for these twenty years shows a rise of 14·899 per cent. on the last two figures of the previous series, the figures for 1820 to 1834. In view of the fact that elsewhere, where it

has been necessary to correct baptism figures for the leakage between baptisms and births, a correction of 15 per cent. has been
made to the baptism figures, this test is somewhat reassuring
as to the degree of confidence which can be placed in the general
lines of the earlier series of figures, but it is only a rough test.

The general movement revealed by these figures is threefold.
A period of astonishingly low fertility from between 1785 and
1790 to between 1800 and 1805 is followed by a period of high
fertility lasting from about 1805, or slightly after, to shortly
before 1825, with a pronounced peak in the middle including
the figures for the years 1810, 1815 and 1820, followed again
at the end of the period by another period of low fertility. To
show the amount of this variation in fertility the period has been
divided into sub-periods. The figures for 1790, 1795 and 1800
form a period of low fertility; those for 1810, 1815 and 1820
a period of high fertility and those for 1825 and 1830 a second
period of low fertility. The period of high fertility shows a rise
of 4·660 per cent. over the period of low fertility which preceded
it, and the period of low fertility at the end shows a fall from
the centre period of 5·837 per cent. This period of high fertility
comes at an important point in the growth of the population as
it is the decade 1811 to 1821 which shows the largest decennial
increase ever recorded in this country.

There are one or two other interesting points to be noted in
connection with this fertility table. It has been noticed that the
period 1790 to 1800 or thereabouts was a period of astonishingly
low fertility. This decade is a period of high birth rate and high
marriage rate—the figure for 1790 being the highest recorded
for each rate during the period. The decade 1810 to 1820 is a
period of high fertility, and in that decade both the marriage
rate and the birth rate were distinctly falling. It is clear, therefore, that the increased fertility of marriage in the first quarter
of the nineteenth century was counteracting to some extent the
fall in the birth rate and in the marriage rate and was in consequence an important factor in the growth of the population.

This may probably be carried one stage further, and it may
be argued that the effort which the community put forward by
way of increased fertility to counteract the decline in the birth

rate goes some way to disprove the theory that, even apart from the use of modern contraceptives, fertility can be regarded as anything like a constant factor and to suggest that the view that before the use of these modern methods the procreation of children attained to the physiological limit is not true.

III

The figures for marriages are much less open to doubt than either the baptism or burial figures. The regulations for the registration of marriages were revised and affirmed by Lord Hardwicke's Marriage Act, after the passage of which, records of the number of marriages are forthcoming and are printed in the early Census returns. In the Preliminary Observations to the 1831 Census, there is a discussion of the value of the figures, and it is evident that the marriage figures are regarded as satisfactory.

It was not held that the marriages of Dissenters caused any serious leakage, as they had to be celebrated in the church, and when this regulation was relaxed provisions were made for securing their registration[1]. A possible omission of some few hundred marriages on a total number rising from 57,848 in 1760 to 122,483 in 1840 is not a very serious matter.

The swing in the marriage rate usually occupies some eight or nine years and it is therefore necessary to use long period averages which show the general movement but not the smaller fluctuations. A table which shows the smaller fluctuations conceals the general tendency of the rate. The course of the smaller fluctuations which are of some interest can be traced in a short discussion of the marriage figures themselves and the general tendency illustrated in a table of longer averages.

After the Peace of Paris there was a distinct rise in the number of marriages in 1763 and 1764; the numbers were low in 1780 during the American War, and rose again after the conclusion of peace. From about 1780 to 1805 the numbers were greater than either before or after that period, which corresponded roughly with that during which the birth rate was also high. A decline in marriages marked the first years of distress during

---

[1] Prelim. Obs. 1831, p. xxxiii.

the wars with France. The years 1794 and 1795 were years of
epidemics; in 1794 wheat began to rise rapidly in price, "the
price of provisions rose until 1795, which was a year of great
distress and scarcity, the winter of 1795 was excessively severe."[1]
The most remarkable fall and rise in the period occur from
1799 to 1804. With epidemics at the close of the century and
with soaring wheat prices from 1798 to 1801 the figures for
marriages go down with a rush. With the conclusion of the
Peace of Amiens and a slump in the price of wheat from 1802
to 1804 the numbers went up as rapidly as they had previously
fallen[2]. A similar rise is seen on the conclusion of peace in

Table VII. MARRIAGE RATES

The population figures are the same as those used in the compilation of
Table V.

The figures for marriages are taken, up to 1830, Enumeration Abstract,
1831, p. xxxi. From 1831 to 1841, 8th Report of R.G. *Reports*, 1847–8,
xxv. p. xxi. From 1841 to 1852, *Reports*, 1857, XXXII. p. 69.

The rates given for modern comparison are compiled from 64th Annual
Report of R.G. 1901, p. clxiii.

		Persons married per 1000 living
1758–1762	(5 year average)	16·70
1765–1775	(11 year average)	16·78
1775–1785	,,	17·20
1785–1795	,,	17·46
1795–1805	,,	17·30
1806–1816	,,	16·50
1816–1826	,,	16·16
1826–1836	,,	16·32
1836–1846	,,	15·78
1848–1852	(5 year average)	16·64
1871–1880	(10 year average)	16·21
1891–1900	,,	16·61

See also Diagram III.

[1] *Reports*, 1847–8, xxv. 8th Annual Report of the Registrar General.
p. x of the Introduction and onwards contains a very interesting discussion
of the marriage figures and the factors influencing them.

[2] *Reports*, 1847–8, xxv: "The marriages began to decline in 1799. A
sudden rise took place in 1802. The difference between the numbers married
in 1801 and 1803 is 54,182. It is a fluctuation of 40 per cent., and the greatest
on record."

"The winter of 1798–9 set in early and was extremely rigorous, vegetation
had no vigour, and the spring was unkindly, summer was cold, autumn wet,
all the crops were injured and some were destroyed. Half the crop of next
year (1800) was secured before Aug. 19th, when heavy rains set in which
made the wheat sprout."

"The seasons and crops of 1801, 1802 and 1803 were good."

1814 and 1815, again accompanied by a remarkable drop in the price of wheat. This rise is followed by a drop in 1817 in which year there was an epidemic of fever and of smallpox. The general movement of the marriage rate can be seen by taking longer averages. In Table VII the marriage rate has been worked on eleven-year averages from 1765 to 1846. The general movement on these figures is shown to be a steady rise until 1790 followed by as steady a fall—with the exception of a slight break in 1830—to a figure for 1836 to 1846 which is lower than anything recorded for the eighteenth century. Thus at a period when the population was increasing with its greatest rapidity the marriage rate was falling accompanied by a slight fall in the birth rate.

IV

The death rate during the period is the most important with which we have to deal (Table VIII). Up to 1780 the burials are only given for every tenth year in the Census Reports, and thereafter for every year. In the construction of the table for the period after 1780, eleven-year averages, overlapping by one year, centring round 1790 and afterwards round the Census years, have been given as well as five-year averages. The figures on which these rates have been based previous to the intro-duction of civil registration are burial figures which have been corrected for the purpose of this rate, as they were for the calculation of the population, by the addition of 10 per cent. which, on a comparison of the burial rate—uncorrected—before civil registration and the death rate afterwards, appears to be the appropriate correction. It must however be remembered, as in the case of the birth rate, that, although this correction makes the burials more nearly resemble what the deaths at the time probably were, no correction can really convert burial figures into death figures. This correction is not such a serious matter as in the case of the birth figures, the correction being 10 per cent. as against 15 per cent. This is what we should expect, for registration of a burial is more likely to follow a death than is registration of a baptism to follow a birth. As in the case of births, the leakages would be most likely to occur in the growing towns, and this view is adopted by Rickman in the Census Report of 1831 in which he states that many congregations of Dissenters have their own burial grounds, and gives as instances the Jews and Roman Catholics of London and

Table VIII. DEATH RATES

Population figures and figures for the modern comparisons as in Tables V and VII.

Before the introduction of civil registration the burial figures have been corrected by the addition of 10 per cent. to make them more nearly represent the probable deaths, this correction being arrived at by a comparison of the rate before and after the introduction of civil registration if the correction is not made. Material is available only for rates based on the figure for one year before 1780.

The burial figures are obtained—1700–1810, Prelim. Obs. 1811, p. xx; 1811–1830, Preface to 1831 Census Report, p. xxx; 1831–1850, Appendix to 1851 Census Report, p. cxxxi.

		Deaths per 1000 living	
1700	(1 year rate)	26·0	
1710	,,	26·7	
1720	,,	29·7	
1730	,,	33·4	A
1740	,,	31·7	
1750	,,	28·2	
1760	,,	26·7	
1770	,,	27·9	
1780	,,	28·8	
1785–1795	(11 year average)	25·65	
1796–1806	,,	23·14	
1806–1816	,,	19·98	B
1816–1826	,,	20·33	
1826–1836	,,	21·65	C
1836–1846	,,	20·80	
1851–1860	(10 year average)	22·23	
1871–1880	,,	21·38	
1891–1900	,,	18·21	

1720, 1730 and 1740. Period A. A period of high death rate.
1806–1816 and 1816–1826. Period B. A period of low death rate.
1826–1836 and 1836–1846. Period C. A period showing a small rise in the death rate.

Five-year figures

1785	26·6	1815	19·9
1790	25·9	1820	19·7
1795	25·3	1825	21·3
1800	23·7	1830	21·5
1805	21·8	1835	22·1
1810	20·8	1840	22·1

Comparison of period averages:

Period B shows a drop from Period A of 35·91 per cent.
Period C shows a drop from Period A of 32·91 per cent.
Period C shows a rise from Period B of 5·31 per cent.

See also Diagram I.

other places. This is clearly looked upon as a town phenomenon, and it is equally true that few Dissenters, even in towns, were buried elsewhere than in the usual parish burial grounds. Another source of leakage, pointed out in the same Report, arose from the fact that certain people from reasons of poverty were ready to inter their dead without religious ceremony, thus making possible the opening of cheap burial grounds as a form of speculation. This again is clearly a town phenomenon. The Report states that the annual number of these interments within the Bills of Mortality has been estimated at seven thousand. Burial grounds of this kind were also said to exist at Newcastle-on-Tyne and Manchester, but in these cases a register was kept and the figures were entered in the official returns. In so far as this habit prevailed in other places where these cheap burial grounds existed, their importance is diminished[1].

The death rate is the one of the three which shows the most definite trend during the period. From 1780 to 1820 the number of deaths is practically the same from year to year and the death rate falls, with one exception, throughout the period.

From the beginning of the eighteenth century there was a steady rise in the death rate until 1730, in which year it was higher than the birth rate. The rate forms a definite peak from about 1720 to 1750, which coincides with a period of gin-drinking. The rate then fell until 1760 and subsequently rose slowly until 1780. There are one or two factors to explain this rise. The golden age of the agricultural labourer is usually supposed to have ended somewhere about 1760 and there was an extremely dry season in 1764 which caused agricultural distress. The year 1773 was one of high fever mortality in London; during the eighties of the century there was a great deal of typhus in the country[2]; although there are few particulars, it is said that Oxfordshire, Gloucestershire, Worcestershire, Wiltshire and Buckinghamshire experienced much typhus from 1782 to 1785, which epidemic was more fatal than the epidemic at the beginning of the French wars[3]. From 1780 to

---

[1] Prelim. Obs. 1831, p. xxxiv.
[2] Creighton, *Epidemics*, II. p. 137.   [3] *Ibid.* p. 156.

1810 the rate fell from 28·8 per thousand to 19·98. In this movement the five-year averages show a slight check in 1795 to which there were many contributory factors. Among these we may mention the following: the distress resulting from the beginning of war and from war conditions; defective harvests in 1792 and 1793; bad harvests in 1794, 1795 and 1797 (which last year is included in the five years which go to form the 1795 figure); the first great rise in the price of wheat in 1795–6, and the period of epidemics in 1794 and 1795. It may be asked why the later and greater rises in the price of wheat and the later epidemics did not cause similar rises in the death rate. There were no doubt other factors at work, but it is probable that the conditions at the beginning of war, especially when accompanied by other distressing circumstances such as epidemics and bad harvests, following a period of peace, would have a greater effect in raising the death rate than the same conditions later in a war. Under these conditions a good many people would probably die who under more favourable conditions would have had their deaths distributed over the next few years; for a period of high mortality to some extent purges the country of its weakly specimens, and is therefore likely to be followed by a period of low mortality. This, at any rate, may have been contributory to the rise in the death rate in the middle of a period of general falling, but it would be dangerous to press it too far as there are many things that attack the strongest part of the community, and the conception of a period of high death rate as a purge is only acceptable within pretty narrow limits. From 1820 to 1840 the death rate rises; after the introduction of civil registration it continues to rise until 1850 when a steady fall begins.

The fall of the death rate from 1780 to 1810 or 1820, remarkable as it is, is shown to be practically the same in extent and general character on any series of figures which, in the course of writing this essay, have been used for constructing a burial or death rate, though, of course, the levels are different. The addition of 10 per cent. to the burials, as in the case of the baptisms, makes a slight difference to the character of the rate in the first half of the eighteenth century, but all the series of figures, with burials uncorrected or corrected, show this fall from 1780 to 1820.

The general level of the eighteenth-century death rate is clearly above that of the nineteenth in the period after the fall of the rate, that is after 1820 and during the slight rise, until the steady fall which begins after 1850. The figure for the decade 1851–1860, which is the highest recorded in the nineteenth century, only reaches a point between the figures for 1800 and 1810, by which time the drop in the death rate had been going on for quite twenty years.

The general movement of the rate is thus represented by a pretty well defined eighteenth-century level, followed from 1780 to 1810 by a great drop, followed again by a slight rise but by a general nineteenth-century level very much lower than the general eighteenth-century level.

The full extent of the fall in the death rate can be illustrated by a comparison of certain subdivisions within the period covered by the eighteenth and the first half of the nineteenth centuries. The period from 1720 to 1740 was a period of high death rate. The period from 1806 to 1826 was a period of low death rate, and the period from 1826 to 1846 showed a slight rise on the period immediately preceding it. The period from 1806 to 1826 shows a drop of 35·91 per cent. from the period of high death rate early in the eighteenth century, and although the rate again rises by 5·31 per cent. to the period from 1826 to 1846 that period shows a drop from the period 1720 to 1740 of 32·91 per cent.

This fall in the death rate is the most important fact which emerges from this discussion of the figures of the population. It becomes clear that the declining death rate was having a greater effect on the growth of the population than was a rising birth rate. The knowledge of this fact increases the importance of medical, scientific and sanitary improvements which are calculated to lower the death rate, and points to these improvements as the true causes of the great increase in the population. The comparative steadiness of the birth rate discounts the more sweeping statements that the industrial conditions and the opportunities of making an early profit out of children led to a rapid increase in the birth rate. What rise there was in the birth rate in the eighteenth century is not nearly so striking or so rapid as this fall in the death rate[1].

Contemporaries realised what was happening.

Rickman, writing in 1816, pointed out that the fall in the death rate was increasing the length of life, as indeed it must have done accompanied as it was by a steady birth rate. He also makes some interesting comments on the view that things in England were growing worse and worse in those years, an opinion which latterly has entirely eclipsed the fact of the fall in the death rate.

One thing I wish to say as to an opinion which you seem to entertain as to the well being, or rather ill being of the poor, that their state has grown worse and worse of late. Now if one listens to common assertion everything in grumbling England grows worse and worse; but the fact in question (the belief in it) is even a curiosity. Human comfort is to be estimated by human health, and that by the length of human life. Now I imagine I have proved in a very unexceptional manner that since 1780 life has been prolonged as 5 to 4, and the poor form too large a portion of society to be excluded from this general effect; rather they are the main cause of it, for the upper classes had food and cleanliness abundant before[2].

The Preliminary Observations to the 1821 Census emphasise the drop in the death rate and the increased length of life resulting therefrom, and the same emphasis on the "diminished mortality in England"[3] is seen in the more elaborate Report to the 1831 Census.

The annual number of burials, as collected in pursuance of the population acts, authorises a satisfactory inference of diminished mortality in England. The average number of burials not differing materially from the year 1780 to 1815; the first five years of that period, the last five, and the whole period of 36 years giving the same

[1] Since this thesis was written Mr Harold Wright has published a handbook on *Population* in the series of Cambridge Economic Handbooks. I am glad to find a reassuring confirmation of my views as to the parts played by a rising birth rate and a declining death rate in this period. On p. 107 he says, "Without going further into the evidence, it may be tentatively asserted that the tremendous increase in the population of Europe and America during the last century and a half is attributable far more to a diminished death rate than to a change in the birth rate."

[2] *Life and Letters of Rickman*, Williams, p. 182.

[3] Prelim. Obs. 1821, p. xxvi.

average result of 193,000 Registered Burials; the population having increased 3,300,000 in the meantime [1].

This last remark appears to be substantially true at the date at which this was written, though the rise was not maintained for long at that rate.

There is thus plenty of evidence that at this time it was known that the death rate was falling, and correct conclusions were drawn from that fact. For some time longer the fact was recognised; McCulloch, writing in 1847, said, "It appears probable, however, that the rate of mortality had been reduced to a minimum in 1815, and that it increased somewhat in the interval between that and 1830." [2] Actually the rate recorded for the five yearly period centring at 1820 is the lowest in the eighteenth and first half of the nineteenth centuries, and is not again equalled until the decade 1881 to 1890. It is true, however, that by that time the curve of the actual numbers of burials has taken an upward turn and, although this was not yet sufficient to send the five-year rate up, on the eleven-year figures the rate for the period 1816 to 1826 is slightly higher than that for the period 1806 to 1816. McCulloch looked upon the rise as temporary and due to the "distress resulting from the sudden transition from a state of war to one of peace," to the fall in prices, failures of county banks, and the shock which these events gave to "almost every species of industry." He began to detect a decline in the death rate in the "three years ending in 1845" though it was not for another ten years that the drop really began. The Hungry Forties do seem to have reflected themselves in the death rates.

This drop in the death rate from 1780 to 1810 or 1820 has been dealt with at some length, because it is very important in itself, and because it has been lost sight of by historians, who have been more concerned with the distress prevalent at the time. In spite of what may be said about distress, and in spite of the lurid stories which it is possible, and in many connections lamentably easy, to find, people were not dying faster and in greater numbers, for the actual numbers of deaths did not

---

[1] Prelim. Obs. 1831, p. xxiv.
[2] McCulloch, *Stat. Account of the British Empire*, p. 421.

increase in spite of the unprecedented growth of the population.

As the primary cause of the increase in the population in this period, therefore, we are confronted by a remarkable decrease in the death rate, which must be the main cause, backed up by a birth rate at a level distinctly above the death rate and rising steadily, except for 1760, from 1710 to 1790. This birth rate is an important contributing factor though not on the same scale as the drop in the death rate. When the birth rate begins to fall after 1790 the effect is somewhat counteracted by a rise in the fertility of marriage from about 1805 to 1825, which must be examined as a cause of the increase in addition to the great fact of the remarkable fall in the death rate.

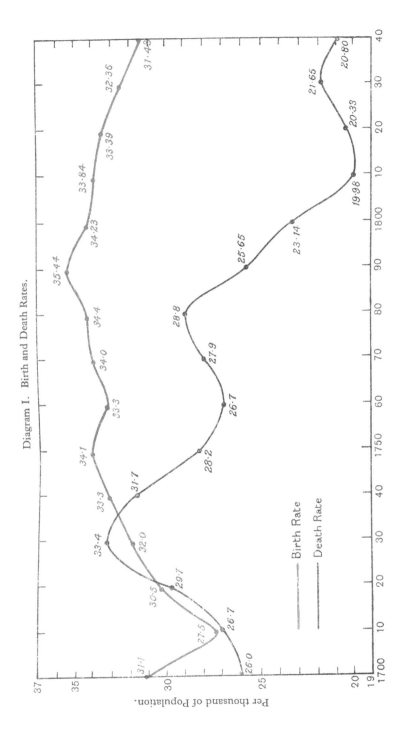

Diagram I. Birth and Death Rates.

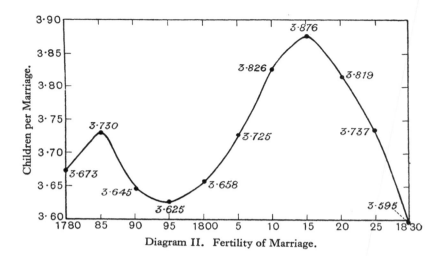

Diagram II. Fertility of Marriage.

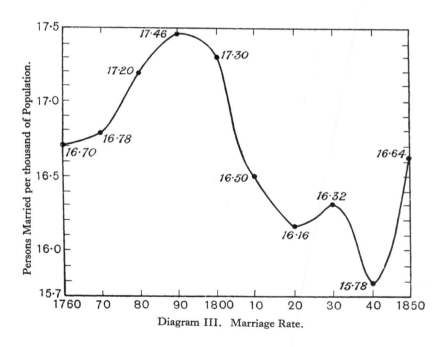

Diagram III. Marriage Rate.

CHAPTER III

Ireland

I

IF there are difficulties in determining the population of England in the period before the first Census, those difficulties are very much greater in the case of Ireland. In the first place no Irish Census was taken until 1821, so that we have to wait twenty years longer than in England for anything like reliable figures. Secondly, the question of the Irish population did not excite the same interest as that of England, and consequently there are fewer contemporary estimates and generally less writing on the subject.

Table IX. IRELAND. TABLE OF POPULATION

All the figures are taken from the table of population in the Irish Census Report, 1824, with the exceptions of the figure of Arthur Young's for 1779, the figure of McCulloch's for 1792, and the Census figures from 1821 onwards.

1695	1,034,102	Capt. South
1712	2,099,094	Thomas Dobbs
1718	2,169,048	,,
1725	2,317,374	,,
1726	2,309,106	,,
1731	2,010,321	Irish House of Lords and the established clergy
1754	2,372,634	Hearth Money returns
1767	2,544,276	,,
1777	2,600,556	,,
1779	under 3,000,000	Arthur Young
1785	2,845,032	Hearth Money returns
1788	4,040,000	Bushe
1791	4,206,612	Hearth Money returns
1792	3,747,000	McCulloch and Hearth Money returns
1792	4,088,226	Beaufort and Hearth Money returns
1804	5,400,000	*Reports*, 1825, VI. p. 7
1805	5,395,456	Newenham
1813	5,937,856	Incomplete Census and estimate
1821	6,846,949	Census
1831	7,767,401	,,
1841	8,175,124	,,
1851	6,552,385	,,
1861	5,764,543	,,

The scarcity of figures on which to form a reasoned decision means that the best has to be done with the various estimates that do exist; the one great point in favour of these estimates, which are derived from various sources, is that, allowing the whole phenomenon to be astonishing, there is only one estimate —and this an imperfect one—that is irreconcilable with the others. The time at which the great increase began is tolerably clearly marked, and is roughly that at which, on historical grounds, we might expect the increase to become rapid. With the year 1821 we pass from the period of estimates to that of the Census, and the figures have been continued for twenty years after the period at present under consideration (up to 1861), for no discussion of the population of Ireland during this time can be complete without some mention of the decline which took place in the decade from 1841 to 1851 and was subsequently continued[1].

In the Report on the Irish Census of 1821[2] a series of estimates for the population at various points in the period before the introduction of the Census is given. These are compiled in various ways and from various sources and are criticised both in that Report and elsewhere.

The figure for 1695 is an estimate made by Capt. South, and McCulloch says, "it is impossible to say what credit should be given to his statement." The estimates for 1712, 1718, 1725 and 1726 are taken from an essay on the improvement of Ireland by Thomas Dobbs, published in 1731, and do not appear to be commented on elsewhere. The estimate for 1731 was obtained through an inquiry instituted by the Irish House of Lords in that year. The Census Report says it was "far from satis-factory" as many places were not under the control of the established clergy by whose means the estimate was made and that the inquiry was not enforced by any Act, and McCulloch says that "this result is not believed to be entitled to much con-fidence."[3] The figures for 1754, 1767, 1777 and 1785 are based on the returns of the collectors of Hearth Money, reckoning six persons to a house, and these figures are adopted by McCulloch.

In 1779 Arthur Young gives the population at "something under three millions," but he only gives this as the "common idea," so it can hardly be considered as a serious contribution

[1] *Reports*, 1823, VI. p. 7.   [2] *Reports*, 1824, XXII. Prelim. Obs.
[3] McCulloch, *Account of the British Empire*, I. p. 436.

to the problem, though there is nothing inherently improbable about it[1].

Up to 1785, then, with the possible exceptions of the four estimates of Thomas Dobbs and the very vague figure of Arthur Young, which seems to be too high, there appears to be a very uniform general movement and a very steady if slow increase.

About that time the population began to increase at a phenomenal pace and there are many estimates for it. The series of figures in the Census Report quotes for 1788 an estimate formed by Gervais Parker Bushe, one of the Commissioners of Revenue, calculated on the returns of the collectors of Hearth Money, which he gives as 4,040,000. This estimate is adopted by Newenham in his *Inquiries into the Population of Ireland* published in 1805, where he states on the authority of Bushe that "there were about four millions of people in Ireland in the year 1788."[2] In the same work he adopts 4,200,000 as the figure for the population in 1791 based on a "very circumstantial, but not perhaps complete, return of houses made by the collectors of hearth money," early in 1792[3]. This estimate, given as from the same source, appears in the series given in the Census Report as 4,206,612.

In 1792 the Rev. Dr Beaufort published an Ecclesiastical Map of Ireland which, as the Census Report says, gave a "vague estimate of the population of each county." His estimate was 4,088,226. McCulloch says this was arrived at by estimating six persons to a house; he, on the other hand, reckoning five and a half to a house, gives the estimate at 3,747,000[4]. There is, therefore, in spite of variations, a considerable consensus of opinion as to the approximate population at the beginning of the last decade of the eighteenth century.

The great increase clearly began between 1780 and 1790. McCulloch quotes the estimates made from the returns of Hearth Money for 1754, 1767, 1777 and 1785, which we have already given. He then adopts for 1788 the figure given by Bushe, which is in the series given in the Census Report and

[1] Young, *Tour in Ireland*, II. p. 195.
[2] Newenham, *Inquiries into the Population of Ireland*, p. vii.
[3] *Ibid.* p. viii.   [4] *Reports*, 1825, VIII. p. 807.

quoted by Newenham. These figures place the great increase in the latter part of the eighties, and make the rate of increase between 1785 and 1788 quite amazing. This was recognised by McCulloch who says, "it is obvious from these statements that the population of Ireland increased after 1785 with extraordinary rapidity." The figures at the latter end of the period, at any rate, seem to be confirmed by the various estimates for the years 1791 and 1792 which we have examined. It is interesting that the sudden rise in the population, which these figures indicate, comes at a time when there is evidence of considerable prosperity in Ireland, prosperity which is lacking at other times when the population was increasing with as great and even with greater rapidity. It is possible that this prosperity started an increase in the population which hard times to come were powerless to stop.

A Report in 1823 which gives the same estimates for the population in 1695 and 1731 as those given in the Census Report of 1824, gives also an estimate of 5,400,000 for 1804[1]. The series of figures in the Census Report gives an estimate of Newenham's for the population in 1805 as 5,395,456. In making this estimate it is stated that Newenham had endeavoured "to correct the inaccuracies of the Hearth Money Returns, by a variety of ingenious calculations, formed on other bases." Between these two estimates there is no serious discrepancy.

In the abstract of the Census returns of 1821 estimates are published of the population in various districts of the country in 1813, but these results are incomplete as there are eight gaps. In the Report on the Census of 1821 a calculation based on this incomplete estimate for 1813 compared with the Census of 1821 is used to arrive at a population figure for the whole country for 1813. This estimate is 5,937,856. Judging from the general run of the figures this appears to be an under-estimate. An under-estimate is more likely than an over-estimate in the first Census; this would affect the figure for 1813, and it is very possible that the imperfect returns for 1813 are more imperfect than they appear at first sight, and that the imperfections are not confined to the definite gaps but that all the figures are more or less unsatisfactory.

---

[1] *Reports*, 1823, VI. Employment of the Poor in Ireland, p. 7.

From 1821 onwards we have the Census figures to guide us. The rate of increase in the population received a check in the decade from 1831 to 1841, and even between 1821 and 1831 people believed that the population was increasing faster than the Census of 1831 proved to be the case, for the Report on the State of the Poor in Ireland in 1830 says. that the population of Ireland might be safely estimated at that time to have reached 8,500,000[1]. The population in 1831, as a matter of fact, did not much exceed seven and three quarter millions. There was one very potent cause of check in 1822 when a failure of the crops was followed by the inevitable famine and fever, although the fever of 1822 was not as fatal or widespread as that of 1817. The check between 1831 and 1841 was probably due in great part to the growing emigration, for it is estimated that the emigration of Irish direct from Ireland and from the ports of the neighbouring coast of England was 403,463[2], and it will be seen that if this number of people had remained in Ireland, the rate of increase in the decade from 1821 to 1831 would have been only 3 per cent. greater than that in the following decade instead of 8·2 per cent.[3]

The great check to the population falls in the decade 1841 to 1851 which is not, strictly speaking, within the period with which we are dealing, but will be touched upon later.

These figures—except the Census figures—do not, in all probability, give more than a rough estimate of what the rate of increase in the population was, but they do give a result which is not inherently impossible, and in which there are not

[1] *Reports*, 1830, VII. p. 19.
[2] *Reports*, 1843, XXIV. Irish Census Report:

Direct emigration from Ireland	...	...	214,047
Irish emigration from Liverpool	...	...	152,738
			366,785
Add 10 per cent. for other English ports			36,678
			403,463

[3] Census figures

Census figures		1831	7,767,401 }	5·24 per cent.
,,		1841	8,175,124 }	
,,		1831	7,767,401 }	10·44 per cent.
,,	plus 403,463	1841	8,578,587 }	

The increase between 1821 and 1831 was at 13·44 per cent.

any very unlikely disturbances in the curve. For the remarkable sudden drop after 1841 we have the Census figures to keep us right.

Except as a point of academic interest it is not important to obtain estimates of the population before the Census more accurate than these in all probability are. The rise in any case is remarkable enough and sufficiently deserving of explanation even though before the Census the actual amount and course of it may be founded on figures that are open to some criticism and to some doubt.

That the increase is remarkable is shown by the following figures. If Young's estimate of the population for 1779 is taken, the increase in the sixty odd years from then until the Census of 1841 is 172 per cent.; the increase in England and Wales in the same period—from Rickman's estimate for 1780 until the Census of 1841—is 88 per cent., which is only slightly more than half the rate of increase in Ireland during the same period[1].

II

The reasons which have from time to time been put forward to account for this amazing rate of increase in the population, are, as was inevitable, very numerous. For the sake of clearness the causes given by three writers at different times in the period have been brought together, and they are found to supply three main heads for discussion. Other suggested causes, some of which find a place with these writers and others of which do not, have been considered later.

Arthur Young, writing in 1779, remarked that there were "several circumstances in Ireland extremely favourable to population, to which must be attributed that country being so much better peopled than the state of manufacturing industry would seem to imply." He then "particularises" five causes: "First, there being no Poor Laws. Second, the habitations. Third, the generality of marriage. Fourth, children not being burdensome. Fifth, potatoes the food."[2]

---

[1]
Ireland	1780	3,000,000	
	1841	8,175,000	Increase 172 per cent.
England and Wales	1780	7,953,000	
	1841	15,906,741	Increase 88 per cent.

[2] Arthur Young, *Tour in Ireland*, 2nd ed. 1780, II. p. 195.

Newenham, writing in 1805, gives expression to the pious opinion that "the principal, if not the only causes which conduce to accelerate the multiplication of the human species are plenty of food and frequency of marriages,"[1] which causes he then proceeds to apply to Ireland. The frequency of marriages in Ireland he puts down to five causes: First, the easily obtained and large amount of food which rendered children "little or no expense." Secondly, the fact that the "small farmers, the country artificers, have generally derived from their children the most important advantages." Thirdly, the readiness of the people to suffer privations and the absence of any ambition to possess "anything in the shape of a capital" before marriage. Fourthly, the absence of such restrictions as the Laws of Settlement. Fifthly, the scanty incomes of the Roman Catholic priests, which, "having been derived solely from marriages, christenings and confessions," gave rise to a natural presumption "that a considerable number of them have always been practically solicitous to promote matrimony."[2]

The two chief causes mentioned by these writers and which absorb most of the other causes they give, are the abundance of food and the frequency of marriages. Edward Wakefield in his *Account of Ireland* of 1812 repeats these two causes and adds "the minute division of land."[3]

There are thus three main causes to be examined, Food, Marriages, Land Organisation.

(*a*) The potato was introduced into Ireland at the end of the sixteenth or the beginning of the seventeenth century, and is a form of food which provides a subsistence—of a kind—with the expenditure of very little trouble in comparison with other and more usually cultivated staples. Adam Smith, judging from the state of health of the Irish in London, declared that the potato was a healthy form of diet as compared with the oatmeal of his native country and possibly with the wheaten bread of the English labourer[4]; nevertheless as the most important food of a people potatoes are far from ideal. The farmers of the

---

[1] Newenham, *Inquiries into the Population of Ireland*, 1805, p. 2.
[2] *Ibid.* pp. 13, 18.   [3] Wakefield, p. 690.
[4] *Wealth of Nations*, Everyman ed. I. p. 146.

south of Ireland were people of very little skill, nor did it require much skill to derive a livelihood from a crop which called for hardly any attention after it was once planted, and in a climate which upon the whole was good for growing potatoes. Very little land was required for the cultivation of potatoes, for we are told that less than a quarter of the land required to supply wheat sufficient for a family will maintain them on potatoes[1], and elsewhere it is stated that "two acres of good land would supply a family of five or six, or an acre and a half if the potatoes were good."[2]

The ease with which this food was obtained removed practically every check that the possible want of the means to purchase food might impose on the growth of the population in a country in which a higher standard of diet was maintained, and in which it was not the general thing for the great majority of the families to maintain themselves on food grown on their own plot of land and cultivated by their own hands.

Thus, so far as any expenses of food might place a prudential check on marriages, that check was lacking in Ireland, and similarly the ease with which large quantities of this food were produced made the rearing of children an easier and less burdensome business than in a country where "the common food of the poor is so dear as to be an object of attentive economy," and the difficulty of procuring adequate supplies of which will lead the children to "want that plenty which is essential to rearing them."[3]

"As potatoes are more easily procured than most other kinds of food, those who live on dear food must have considerable means of support before they have families."[4] This check at any rate was not in great evidence in Ireland, and it is freely

[1] Newenham, p. 14. This statement of proportions is Newenham's and has not been tested against modern calculations. Mr Yule tells me that in some calculations of his concerning food supply during the war, he reckoned that on an average in England potatoes would yield, at the pre-war rate of milling wheat, about twice the calories for human food per acre—not four times. Probably the Irish potato crop was a good one and the wheat crop a very bad one.
[2] *Reports*, 1825, VII. Lords Report on the State of Ireland, p. 123.
[3] Young, *Tour*, II. p. 198.
[4] *Reports*, 1825, VIII. State of Ireland, p. 373.

stated that the prevalence of the potato as the staple diet of the people was one of the chief causes of the great increase in the population[1].

But it was a perilous growth as the sequel painfully showed; there was no margin of safety, no resources to fall back upon; an increase built on such foundations was bound sooner or later to be shaken; there were several premonitory signs of the catastrophe that was to come, and though these may have had some slight effect, the warning was not taken. An increase built upon, and depending upon, such a hazardous source of supply, contained the seeds of its own destruction, and those seeds bore terrible fruit in the year 1846. It cannot be said that warning had not been given of what might happen, if that which was always realised as a possibility, and indeed under certain circumstances was recognised as inevitable, were permitted to take place in a sufficiently extensive form.

(b) The habit of early marriage which was made easier by the abundance of cheap food, was reckoned to be as great a cause of the rapid increase of population as was the plentiful supply of that food itself. As bearing on this there are first of all the general statements that the early marriages are increasing the population. Marriages are represented as being a man's "first thoughts" and as taking place "very, very young."[2] Then there are the rather more explanatory statements which connect the early marriages with the factors which cause them —such as "the facility of getting houses and the cheapness of provisions."[3] Those marriages are represented as being dependent on a short-sighted view of the immediate prospect of plenty of food to be derived from a small plot of land, with no regard to what may happen if the crop should fail[4]. In addition to being connected with the cheapness of the food supply, the

---

[1] *Reports*, 1823, VI. Employment of the Poor in Ireland, pp. 50, 121. *Reports*, 1825, VII. Disturbances in Ireland, p. 386. *Reports*, 1825, VII. Lords Report on the State of Ireland, pp. 76, 244. *Reports*, 1825, VIII. Commons Report on the State of Ireland, pp. 807, 819.

[2] *Reports*, 1825, VII. Lords Report on the State of Ireland, p. 244. *Reports*, 1825, VII. Disturbances in Ireland, p. 309. *Reports*, 1826–7, V. Emigration, Q. 2771.

[3] *Reports*, 1823, VI. Employment of the Poor in Ireland, p. 121.

[4] *Reports*, 1825, VII. Lords Report, p. 76.

early marriages are connected with the miserable standard of comfort thought sufficient by the Irish peasants in the matter of housing. Arthur Young's description of the cabins of the peasants[1], which he considered a "very evident" encouragement to population, is amply borne out by the testimony of the Reports half a century later, in which the two factors—food and habitations—are connected in their responsibility for early marriages[2].

The lamentable short-sightedness of all this policy is perfectly obvious; the whole system was based on imperfect foundations, and each step made the edifice more perilous than before. A population that was not increasing rapidly but which subsisted on potatoes would be in a sufficiently precarious condition. A population that was increasing at a rate that was remarkable in any circumstances, and was housed in a way which, instead of providing a check to the increase of marriage which might be expected to arise from the cheap and plentiful supply of food, simply increased the effects of that cheap and plentiful food supply, was in a still more dangerous position.

The fact that the poorer the people were the more inclined they seemed to be to contract these early marriages increased the dangers of the situation. Everything tended to reduce the already practically non-existent margin of safety. A witness before the Committee on the State of the Poor in Ireland in 1830 considered that the poorer they were the sooner they got married, many of them marrying before they were eighteen or twenty. The converse of this of course is that the practice was inclined to be checked as the standard of living was raised. The same witness thought that it was chiefly the prevalence of unemployment and loafing in the winter that promoted these marriages[3]. This practice does not seem to have been so prevalent among the better class Protestants in Ulster, but even

[1] Young, *Tour in Ireland*, p. 97.

[2] *Reports*, 1825, IX. State of Ireland, p. 96. *Reports*, 1830, VII. State of the Poor in Ireland, p. 6.

[3] *Reports*, 1830, VII. p. 351: If the men were not "idle and unemployed ...they would not be so fond of getting married...the great cause of these intermarriages is idleness, and forming those kinds of connections in the winter season; want of employment makes them really get married in many cases."

there the Moderator of the Ulster Synod does not set the level of providence very high; he thinks that in the farming districts and among "the rank of decent tradesmen" the principle of restraint operates, "but when you go below that, among actual labourers, no people can be much more inconsiderate."[1]

With this evidence from a Protestant the Titular Archbishop of Tuam is in agreement. He considers that anything which "has a tendency to augment the comfort of the peasant and to raise his condition in society, has also a tendency to check improvident marriages," and he says that "in general the females marry at 18 or 20; the males at 20 or 21."[2]

The causes promoting early marriages which have been dealt with hitherto may generally be put down to the ease with which food and habitations of an inferior kind were obtained, coupled with a great want of foresight which concealed the dangers that were involved in an increase of the population which took place under such conditions.

There are two other causes which are given as tending to early marriages which must be noticed.

First, it is stated that abduction led to the prevalence of the marriages. Major George Warburton in the Report on the Disturbances in Ireland in 1825 drew attention to the fact that in some of the disturbed districts abduction had been a very common crime, and the farmers had sometimes wished to marry their daughters as soon as they were old enough, so as to prevent their being forced from them into unpleasant marriages. He has, however, to qualify his remarks by acknowledging that early marriages were prevalent in districts where there had been no disturbances nor abductions[3].

In contrast with this testimony the Committee got a denial of the statement from John O'Driscoll, a Barrister in Cork, who said that he had heard[4] "that abduction has, in some parts of the country acted as a terror upon the people; has in fact driven the fathers of families to marry their daughters sooner than they would otherwise be disposed to do," but he did not think that this had "had any effect that could be spoken of."

---

[1] *Reports*, 1825, VIII. p. 361.   [2] *Ibid.* p. 247.
[3] *Reports*, 1825, VII. p. 151.   [4] *Reports*, 1825, VII. Disturbances, p. 386.

Another witness in the same report said that the crime of abduction escaped punishment so easily that it had caused alarm
among the people with the result that "the practice of marrying
young became general and a subject of imitation, and settled
into a fashion, so much so that it was a reproach to a girl to
exceed twenty before she was married."[1] Probably he put his
finger on the spot when he mentioned that the habit of early
marriage was "a subject of imitation"; the force of example is
a power which has to be allowed for. It is a force which is very
apt to be overlooked in discussing points of economic history.
Economic history which in its fundamentals is the history of
the kitchen and the stomach, and consequently intimately
connected with the daily lives of everybody, is apt to become,
when treated historically, a series of dull and ponderous descriptions of organisations of production and distribution. At
any time that is a great danger with which the subject is confronted, but it is more than ever a danger when, as in this
discussion, the economic problem is so nearly connected with
a moral and ethical problem, such as the question of the frequency and providence of marriage. It is often said that one
marriage in a family leads to another, and if in a family this may
also be the case in a country. It is possible that in Ireland,
where the problem was in essentials much simpler than in
England, this force of imitation may have had a greater power
behind it than it has in the larger country.

This is an interesting point, but it is not very likely that abduction had much real effect in comparison with the other, and
more obvious, incentives to early marriages among a people
proverbially happy-go-lucky and irresponsible.

Secondly, the Roman Catholic priests in Ireland were credited
with urging marriages among their flocks because their incomes
depended upon the fees which they derived from marriages
and christenings.

Here again the evidence is inconclusive; thus it is stated that
"there is no doubt that the priests live by fees only," and that
"the marriage fee is a large source of revenue to them," the
same witness also stating that he believes "it is known that the

[1] *Reports*, 1825, VII. p. 209.

priests avow that they do recommend early marriages."[1] On the
other hand it is stated by the priests themselves that the fee
"fluctuates, a Catholic priest in that diocese is permitted to get
one pound or one guinea for a marriage, but he cannot demand
anything over."[2] Still, even so, the more marriages the more
money. The Bishop of Kildare says that he does not "know
that in any diocese in Ireland, any person, of whatsoever rank
he may be, whether rich or poor, can be compelled by usage
to pay more than a guinea," and that "he can withhold all if he
pleases."[3] The Archbishop of Tuam says that it is common
for the priests to marry persons without demanding any fee at
all, and that in the province of Connaught there was at that
time no source of profit to the priest at the marriage beyond
the fee[4].

There is, however, no denial that the fees on marriages and
christenings formed a considerable portion of the stipend of the
priests. Duggan stated that his income was derived "from
Christmas offerings, marriages, baptisms, and when seldom I
get any, from offering masses and prayers for the dead." When
he was questioned as to the proportions in which his stipend
was made up of these various items he replied, "generally the
casual income of the year and that at Christmas and Easter are
at a par, if I get £100 at Christmas and Easter or £50, I consider that I get about the same for all the rest of the year in
general"[5]—a half of his stipend derived from fees.

There are other more or less vague statements that the priests
encouraged marriage. Wakefield thought they did; on the other
hand the Barrister at Cork, who has been quoted in another
connection, denied the accusation against them[6].

Again the force of imitation may come in; if it had been a
tendency for certain priests in certain parts of the country to

[1] *Reports*, 1825, IX. p. 41 (Frankland Lewis).
[2] *Reports*, 1825, VII. Lords, p. 127.
[3] *Reports*, 1825, VIII. p. 184. See also p. 394.
[4] *Reports*, 1825, VIII. p. 260.
[5] *Reports*, 1825, VII. Lords Report, p. 127.
[6] *Reports*, 1823, VI. Employment of the Poor in Ireland, p. 121. Sir J.
Anderson, p. 154. Gerard Callaghan says the priests did so after the war,
though not during it. *Reports*, 1825, VII. Disturbances, p. 151 (Warburton).
Reports, 1825, VII. Lords, p. 18. Wakefield, *Account of Ireland*, p. 690.
Reports, 1825, VII. Disturbances, p. 386.

encourage early marriages, it is very possible that, in a country where the priests have always exerted a great influence over the people, this encouragement, acting on the other circumstances making in the same direction, may have had some effect. It may very well be true that, as one of the witnesses said, the clergy had not done what they might to check a habit which was becoming a great menace to the country.

(c) The two main causes of the increase of the population which have been dealt with so far—the supply of food and the frequency of marriage—were rendered more effective and a greater menace by the minute subdivision of land, with which, for various reasons, they were associated. The possession of land gives to the holder a feeling of power and independence, which is apt to be dangerously misleading when that land is used to supply as large a family as it will maintain on the lowest form of food which has regularly been used by a civilised community, especially when that family has little or no other means of support. The evidence on this subject, as on many, is vague but plentiful[1].

This subdivision of the land and the increase of the population form a vicious circle; as the population increases so does the subdivision of land, for on the system on which that increase is built, it is necessary for each family to have its own potato patch; as the subdivision of land increases so does the population and as more and more subdivision takes place, more and more families are to be reckoned with in the growing of potatoes and in the maintenance of themselves on the scanty supply of potatoes that their land gives them.

The subdivision of land probably started "under the strong excitement of war prices, and of free trade in corn with Great Britain."[2] There was also a political motive at work, which in this case would have the same economic result. One witness went so far as to say that "the first impulse that was given to the population of Ireland was the act that gave to Roman Catholics the elective franchise; it became the object of great

---

[1] *Reports*, 1825, VII. Disturbances in Ireland, p. 322. *Reports*, 1825, VII. Lords Report on the State of Ireland, p. 214. *Reports*, 1825, IX. Lords Report on the State of Ireland, p. 181.

[2] *Reports*, 1830, VII. State of the Poor in Ireland, p. 6.

parliamentary interests to raise as many voters as possible."[1]
This was in 1793. Similar statements are also made in connection with the subdivision of land for the sake of creating
freeholders with the franchise, whether or not these subdivisions
are definitely connected with the granting of the elective franchise to the Catholics[2].

This increase in the population of Ireland, which has been
treated by a consideration of the various factors which operated
over a long period, may be treated more shortly in a chronological
narrative.

It has been seen that the great increase began about 1780.
It is suggested that the emigration, which in the decade before
had begun to assume considerable proportions[3], was checked
by the American War, and that thus there was in any case a
tendency for the population, so to speak, to be dammed up at
home. It has also been seen that it was from about this date
that the prevalence of abduction was said to have led to the
habit of early marriage. More important than either of these
causes was the industrial and agricultural prosperity which
Ireland enjoyed about this time.

In the session 1783–4 an Act was passed which granted
bounties on the exportation of corn from Ireland, and Newenham tells us that although the tillage of Ireland was greatly
fostered by this Act, its pasture land was not diminished but
actually increased. This he proceeds to prove by the increase in
the export of butter, which was so great as more than to counter-
balance the slight decrease in the export of beef, especially
as the increase in the size of the army in Ireland and the number
of ships revictualling there would cause a greater home consumption of beef than in former times[4].

McCulloch was of opinion that the first stimulus to population was given by the Bounty Acts of 1783 and 1784; on the
figures which he gives, some very definite and strong cause for

---

[1] *Reports*, 1823, VI. Employment of the Poor in Ireland, p. 154.
[2] *Reports*, 1825, VII. Disturbances in Ireland, p. 263. *Reports*, 1825, VIII.
Commons Report on the State of Ireland, p. 373.
[3] Newenham, *Inquiries into Population of Ireland*, p. 59. Emigrations in
1771–2–3, given as 28,600.
[4] Newenham, *View of the Circumstances of Ireland*, 1809, pp. 213, 218.

the increase of population in the few years following 1785 was necessary. This he considered was continued in consequence of the removal of the remaining restraints on the trade in corn between England and Ireland in 1806, which, combined with the high prices that prevailed during the war, maintained the impulse given by the Bounty Acts and caused fresh and great extension of tillage[1].

Between 1780 and 1792 or thereabouts the exports from Ireland of pork and butter increased considerably, and the exports of live stock increased enormously[2]. In the sphere of industry a similar increase of activity was evident. The Report of the Lords of Committee of Council on Trade in March 1785 stated that, although no soap and candles were officially admitted into Great Britain from Ireland, "great quantities are certainly smuggled into the western counties of England and Wales." The English trade in these same objects to the West Indies was in a poor way, and this was put down to "the possession the Irish have now got of that trade."[3]

Inland communications were improved; in 1784 the Grand Canal connecting Dublin and the Shannon was completed at a cost of more than a million pounds.

The textile trades which were making the wealth and the power of England, and which were later looked to as a possible salvation for Ireland, do not appear to have been very greatly concerned in this trade revival. The Continental demand for cloth was supplied more easily from England, and the one branch of the textile industries in which Ireland really excelled —the linen industry—supplied a material for which the Continental markets hardly looked to these islands at all.

The rupture with France and the disturbances of 1798 put an end to the period of industrial revival, but the agricultural prosperity appears to have continued for some time longer, and in discussing the population of Ireland it is the agricultural history that has the fatal interest. This agricultural prosperity continued owing to the high profits and the high prices that

[1] McCulloch, p. 439.
[2] Newenham, *View of the Circumstances of Ireland*, 1809, Appendix VI.
[3] Bryce, *Two Centuries of Irish History*, p. 102.

were realised during the war, and it was partially due to this prosperity that the unfortunate subdivision of land took place[1].

During this period, then, there were causes at work which would lead to an increase of population, which would probably have been a safe and healthy growth had these causes been continued. This increase was also partially due to causes that were not so sound, which would aid and abet the healthy growth, but would continue to operate when the healthy causes of increase had been removed. During the war period Ireland had enjoyed some measure of agricultural and even industrial prosperity, but this ceased with the termination of the war and the period of depression which followed it. The condition of Ireland at this time was calculated to make that depression as hard to bear as possible. A country with little reserve of capital to help it through a difficult time, and no opportunity for industry to repair the distress that was everywhere increasing, was likely to give way to the despair which, coupled with the other tendencies to an increasing population which existed, would cause the people to multiply heedlessly.

The solid foundations on which a healthy growth of population might have been founded ended with the period of war, but the unhealthy causes of increase, like a set of bad habits, continued to operate, and instead of being checked were probably increased by the growing misery which ensued. The increase continued, the warnings began and were but slightly heeded until a final disaster compelled people to turn in streams to that remedy which the earlier warnings had only been powerful enough to call into play to a limited extent.

III

Whatever circumstances be held to justify a large population in a country, the population of Ireland was excessive. When in 1833 it could be said that the standard of life of the agricultural labourer "was not as good as it formerly was"[2] and that oatmeal was now a thing he rarely saw; when in 1836 it could be said that "we thus find that there are in Ireland about

[1] Cunningham, *English Industry*, II. p. 588. *Reports*, 1823, VI. p. 7. *Reports*, 1825, VII. Lords Report, p. 18.
[2] *Reports*, 1833, V. Agriculture, Q. 10715.

five agricultural labourers for every two that there are for the same quantity of land in Great Britain"[1]; and when finally it is remembered what the standard food of the people was, it is not too much to say that the population had increased up to the limit of subsistence.

Arthur Young's theory that "population is proportional to employment"[2] would leave Ireland still in default. Various estimates are given as to the proportion of the population constantly out of employment, but in 1830 it was estimated at either one-fifth or one-quarter[3]. The population was thus enormously in advance of the available employment, perhaps we should say of the effective employment, for we find statements that unemployment was then a "Problem of Industry," and that there "are many districts comparatively barren, which might produce more than they do, if human labour were properly applied to them."[4] But the human labour and skill were not properly applied to them, the unemployment continued, and, so far as practical considerations were concerned, the "optimum density" of population was exceeded in Ireland.

The unemployment deprived the people of any resources in time of distress, it further made them rely at all times on the products of their own cultivation and threw them back more and more on the "infernal root" for their sole stay. The potato system was subject to the objection that a year's crop was usually finished within the year, and that in any case it was difficult to keep a supply for the next year. The crop was one in which there were greater fluctuations in yield than in most others, and a failure left the people without other resources upon which to fall back[5].

It was generally recognised that the population ought to be checked, but it was a very different matter when this had to be put into practice, for although this view is expressed it is also stated that it is unlikely that "persuasion will prevent people from marrying at an early age."[6]

[1] *Reports*, 1836, XXX. Poor in Ireland, p. 1.
[2] Young, *Political Arithmetic*, 1774, p. 86.
[3] *Reports*, 1830, VII. Qs. 2896, 5050. [4] *Ibid*. Q. 1930.
[5] Wakefield, *Account of Ireland*, p. 736.
[6] *Reports*, 1826–7, V. Emigration, Q. 3177.

A failure of the supply of potatoes brought into play one of the positive checks of Malthus. The oat harvest of 1817 was poor; the potato harvest had not failed and in places was even plentiful, but the season was wet and storage was difficult, and the wetness of the season exposed the people to hardships that would have been difficult to withstand even if the food supply had been good. Fever followed and the whole country was attacked at various times between March and August[1]. The Reports from the different parts of the country tell a wearisome and similar tale—usually only modified by the fever beginning at different times. The causes, to take one typical Report, are stated to be "unwholesome food in small portions, want of fuel, damp and comfortless habitations, and contagious influence greatly extended by travelling mendicants."[2]

Other witnesses and the second Report emphasise one or other of the numerous causes, all of them traceable to the growth of the population on what were insecure foundations. From Waterford we are told that "the want of employment arising from the change from war to peace, and the failure or deficiency of manufacture, contributed in a high degree to increase the distress."[3] In other portions of the same Report there are lurid accounts of the condition of the cabins and the state of perpetual dampness in which their unfortunate inhabitants lived and became ready victims for the ravages of an epidemic of fever. No class was exempt from the attacks, it was more general among the lower classes but more fatal among the upper.

There are three Reports on this epidemic of 1817–18, the first is in 1818, and is mostly narrative; the two Reports in 1819 contain practical suggestions. The former of the two recommends the setting up of town and district Health Officers, the second recommends that work be found in the form of improvement schemes, and the Committee directed their attention "to two most important departments of labour in Ireland, that employed in agriculture, and that of the fisheries," which were

[1] *Reports*, 1818, VII. Contagious Fever in Ireland, p. 53.
[2] *Ibid.* Appendix (Dungannon).
[3] *Reports*, 1819, VIII. State of disease and condition of the Poor in Ireland, pp. 373, 405, 425.

"likewise those to which the greatest extension may be given without hazarding reaction."[1]

The agricultural work was chiefly to be directed to the improvement of the bog-lands, of which it was said "there are of reclaimable bog-land in Ireland two million of Irish acres," and this was to be done with a twofold purpose. First, it was claimed that a scheme for clearing, lowering and embanking the different streams which had flooded so much low ground as, "in the opinion of eminent physicians," to form "a fruitful source of contagious fever," would improve the health of the country. Secondly, the prospect of raising a supply of grain that would render England "wholly independent of foreign countries for the food of its manufacturing population," was held out as an additional inducement to increase the employment in the country by a policy of agricultural improvement.

A favourable picture of the possibility of the development of the Irish fisheries was drawn. It was said that the coast of Ireland was the most favourable in the United Kingdom or in Europe for conducting the fishery, that herrings and cod were easily and surely obtainable, that the proximity of the English markets would render this occupation a profitable form of employment and that the indirect consequences which its development would have on the improvement of inland transport would further promote the object of the Committee—the increase of employment. The immediate decline of the fishery was attributed to the heavy taxes on the importation of salt which had been imposed about twenty years before, on account of which the numerous refineries which supplied the country with salt at a very low price were given up[2].

Another failure of the crop followed by fever, though not on quite the same scale, overtook the country in 1822; another Committee was appointed to inquire into possible means of employment for the unfortunate victims, and the *Annual Register*, though it had not mentioned the more serious visitation of five years earlier, published an article on this year's troubles. In this case the amazingly precarious condition of

[1] *Reports*, 1819, VIII. Second Report, p. 98.
[2] *Ibid.* p. 479.

the population seems to have been realised more than in the
previous epidemic, at any rate it was very clearly enunciated.
"In consequence of the heavy and incessant rains of the preceding year, the potatoes had decayed and perished in the
ground, so that a considerable part of the crop was lost."[1] In
this case it was a definite failure of the potato crop that was
the prime cause of the famine and subsequent epidemic, in
the former case it had been the impossibility of keeping the
potatoes under the unfavourable conditions which prevailed.
The suddenness of the outbreak of famine was said to astonish
people in England, where the condition of the food supply was
so different. The famine "appeared suddenly, because as each
peasant raised his own food on his own little piece of ground,
the deficiency of the supply was not indicated, nor the consumption checked in time, by an early rise in the market price."
The scarcity and consequent fever were less prevalent in some
parts than in others from the people being less exclusively
dependent on potatoes, as was the case in Ulster and Leinster.
In this case, although the potato crop had failed, the other crops
had not done so. The particular tragedy was that the narrow
margin of safety and the lack of resources which the potato
system in conjunction with a scarcity of employment left to the
people, deprived them of the possibility of benefiting by the
other crops which had not failed[2].

The Committee contrast the better condition of the north
"where the linen manufacture prevails" and join the Committee
of 1819 in urging the necessity of assisting any industry that
will increase the available employment in the south and west,
and in this particular case they recommend the extension of
the linen trade to those parts, and "concur in the opinion of the
Committee on the Linen Trade in considering it the duty of

---

[1] *Annual Register*, 1822.
[2] *Reports*, 1823, VI. pp. 4 and 5, Employment of the Poor in Ireland: "The
crops of grain had been far from deficient, and the prices of corn and oatmeal
were very moderate....The calamity of 1822 may therefore be said to have
proceeded less from the want of food itself than from the want of adequate
means of purchasing it; in other words from the want of profitable employment....When the produce of the peasants' potato ground fails, they are
unaccustomed to have recourse to markets and indeed they seem rarely to
have the means of purchasing."

the Linen Board by every possible means to extend this manufacture in the South and West, for wherever it has obtained a
footing, industry, moral habits, contentment and tranquillity
have followed."[1]

These positive checks had some effect and set on foot two less
drastic checks, namely the consolidation of farms and emigration,
though it required the much more terrible disaster that finally
overtook the country to secure that these measures were adopted
to anything like a sufficient extent.

The evidence that consolidation was going on is not very
satisfactory; thus in 1823 one witness, who was by no means
a tongue-tied individual, had not "heard of any."[2] Seven years
later it had made considerable progress, but the witnesses who
are emphatic that the landlords are turning to the consolidation of their estates to get rid of the surplus population, dwell
very strongly on the disadvantages of the system and emphasise the evil it is likely to create, and is creating[3]. The poor
people who were ejected and did not get employment went to
increase the overcrowding and the unemployment in the towns[4].

It was largely to secure this consolidation of estates that the
idea was mooted of introducing into Ireland Poor Laws of the
description that had existed in England before the wars[5]. The
state of affairs introduced by this consolidation, if the evidence
is to be believed, was not encouraging; it was quite as hopeless
to have people turned off their small potato grounds and
"wandering about the country as mere mendicants" in the
hope of picking up an odd day's employment as it was to leave
them on their old grounds[6]. If famine or fever came they
were in a worse position than ever. It might, however, make
them ready to accept the more drastic remedy of emigration.

In 1825 the Subletting Act was passed which, though it did
not entirely prevent subdivision of estates, rendered it less
prevalent, and probaby this Act is partly responsible for the
check in the increase during the decade 1831 to 1841. In 1838

---

[1] *Reports*, 1823, VI. p. 8.　　　　　[2] *Ibid.* p. 151 (Gerard Callaghan).
[3] *Reports*, 1830, VII. Q. 5453.
[4] *Reports*, 1825, VII. Disturbances, p. 361 (Rev. Michael Collins).
[5] *Quarterly Review*, XXXIII. p. 454. McCulloch's Evid. 1830, VII. Q. 6455 on.
[6] *Reports*, 1825, IX. p. 59.

the introduction of a compulsory provision for the poor made it clear to the landowners that, unless they could reduce the population of their estates to something like its economic limit, they would have to maintain the surplus at a heavy cost in workhouses.

Emigration did not have any very visible effect in checking the increase of the population until after 1831, but the amount of emigration during the decade 1831 to 1841 contributed very considerably to reduce the rate of increase of the population in that decade, in comparison with that which had taken place in the previous one.

In the Census Report of 1851 there are two estimates of the amount of Irish emigration in the preceding decade, which differ by close upon 50,000. One table is based on the assumption that nine-tenths of the emigration from Liverpool to North America, as well as all the emigration from Irish ports, consisted of Irish, to which was added the number of Irish emigrants conveyed from London and Plymouth in ships chartered by the Emigration Commissioners. From 1841 to 1845 the returns of the emigration from London and Plymouth did not distinguish how much of that was Irish, but this did not amount to very much, being in all only 2761. On this calculation the Irish emigration in the decade was 1,240,737[1]. For the same decade the Emigration Commissioners give a larger figure, but this discrepancy is probably due to the fact that the figures given in the Census Report proper did not include the whole of those for the year 1841. The figure the Emigration Commissioners give is 1,289,133[2]. The decrease in the population of Ireland in the decade was 1,622,739. In this decade, therefore, the emigration figure falls between three and four hundred thousand below that for the decrease in the population. There appear to be various possibilities to explain this. The Emigration Commissioners said that they "have little doubt that this estimate is below the truth, inasmuch as the emigration from Liverpool has in many years been almost exclusively Irish, and as no account is here taken of Irish who may have sailed from other

[1] *Reports*, 1856, XXXI. Irish Census Report, 1851, p. lv.
[2] *Ibid.* p. lvi.

ports, and especially from the Clyde." There may have been an enormous emigration to England, or the death roll from the famine may have been so great that, either alone or with the unrecorded emigration, it entirely swamped the results of the natural tendency in a population to put forward a special effort to recover from the effects of a great period of mortality. In any case the fact that is striking is the remarkable force of the check that must have been given which was capable of obtaining such results. Some measure of the shock inflicted and the effect it had in stimulating the check in so far as it took the form of emigration, is shown by a table of the registered emigration during the decade. The change in 1845–6 is remarkable[1].

In the following decade (1851–1861) the emigration, registered as permanent through the Constabulary Agents at Irish Ports, was 1,174,179, and in that decade the decrease in the population was 787,842. The Commissioners considered that to this "emigration may chiefly be attributed this decrease of the population, during a period when the country was remarkably free from any outbreak of famine, pestilence, or of the other social calamities which have occasionally retarded the growth of the population in this and other countries."[2]

It is noticeable in this latter decade that the net decrease in the population is considerably less than the recorded emigration, which leaves a considerable margin for the natural increase and recovery of the population. The remark of the Commissioners that this decade was particularly free from any famines and pestilences, bearing in mind the regular occurrence of these in the decades before, may be in some part an eloquent testimony to the success of the checks which had been in some degree supplied by, and in some degree stimulated by, the disaster of 1846 which came as the culmination of a series of

---

[1] *Reports*, 1856, XXXI. p. lv. Emigration figures:

1841	16,376	1846	105,955
1842	89,686	1847	215,444
1843	37,509	1848	178,159
1844	54,289	1849	214,425
1845	74,969	1850	209,054

[2] *Statistical Journal*, 1861, p. 402, Extracts from the Irish Census Report of 1861.

minor catastrophes of a similar kind, and a comparison of the decade before and after 1851 shows clearly the magnitude of the check that had been applied.

IV

The object of this inquiry into the growth of the population in Ireland has been to enable us to compare it with the contemporary growth in England with which this work is chiefly concerned, and to see whether it has any lessons to teach us which may help to explain the growth in England.

We have seen that the increase in the population of Ireland from 1779 to 1841 was practically twice as rapid as that which took place in England between 1780 and 1841. We are therefore in the position of setting out to discuss the causes of the increase in the population of England, an increase which has generally been represented as phenomenal during this period, and the first thing we find when we turn to Ireland is that the population there increased twice as rapidly as the population in England. The question therefore arises whether in reality there is any problem to explain in England at all. To test this the increase in England has been compared with the contemporary increase in France. The figures have been taken from and the discussion largely suggested by the very interesting chapter on the population of England in Porter's *Progress of the Nation*. Porter gives population figures for France in 1791—an estimate arrived at by a Committee of the Constituent Assembly—in 1817, when France had been reduced to her ancient frontiers and a comparison again becomes possible and reasonable, in 1825, in 1831 and in 1841. He then goes on to state that in the forty years previous to 1841 the rates of increase in the two countries are widely different and that the balance is greatly in favour of England, for he states that in this period "the increase in numbers in England and Wales was equal to 79½ per cent., showing an advantage in favour of England in the proportion of more than three to one." It is of course arguable that to compare France during any part of the war period with England in the same period is heavily to weigh the scales against France, that her losses in the Napo-

leonic struggle must inevitably have been much more serious
than those of any other country involved and that it is ridiculous
to expect her increase to compare at all favourably with that of
another country. It must however be remembered that most of
the European countries were pretty definitely involved and
that the enormous disproportion between the increase in France
and England would appear very much more than to swallow
up any allowance that should be made to France in view of the
greater effect of the war on her population. Furthermore,
Porter compares the increase in France from 1817 to 1841 with
the increase in England in the same period and says that "it
will be found that, while the increase in the French population
was 17·15 per cent. in 24 years, or after the rate of about three
quarters (·715) annually, the increase in the United Kingdom
was double that rate, or about 1½ per cent. (1·43) annually."
By United Kingdom, Porter appears in this connection to
mean England and Wales. It is not perfectly clear how he
arrives at the figure for the annual English increase of 1·43 per
cent. If the same period of twenty-four years is taken as in
France and the Inter-Censal figure for 1817 taken, the annual
increase between then and 1841 appears to average out at
1·36 per cent. On the figures given in the table of Population
for England and Wales the annual increase between 1831 and
1841 was 1·36 per cent., that between 1821 and 1841 was 1·29
per cent. and that between 1811 and 1841 was 1·40 per cent.
Whichever of those figures is adopted for the English increase
it still leaves that increase almost twice as great as the contemporary increase in France. If, moreover, any great stress is laid
on the fact that during the war period France probably had a
more severe time than the other countries involved, it should
further be remembered that a country generally puts forward
a great effort after such a period and this does not appear to
have been very evident in France[1].

[1] Porter, 1847 ed. p. 18:

Population of France:

1791	26,363,000	1831	32,560,934
1817	29,217,465	1841	34,230,178
1825	30,451,157		

Porter then goes on to point out that in both countries the increase was not due to a rise in the birth rate but to a fall in the death rate. In France he compares 1817 with 1834 and shows that between those two years the birth rate had fallen and the death rate had also done so. We have seen that the increase in England was chiefly due to the remarkable fall in the death rate, and, with the additional testimony now before us that the increase in France was due to a similar cause, we may possibly be justified in assuming that in other cases where it appears that the death rate was higher than in England the population in England will be increasing at a rate faster than that which is taking place in these other countries, though this conclusion is doubtful without a comparison of the birth rates. Porter goes on to quote some mortality figures for other countries in Europe on the authority of Sir Francis D'Ivernois, in which England shows much the lowest death rate, followed by Sweden and Denmark and then by Holland and Belgium, by France, the United States, Prussia and Wurtemburg. Although it is true that the rate given by this table for England is very much more favourable than any rate which appears on the table of mortality which has already been given for England and Wales, the death rate in this country did compare very favourably with that in any of the other countries[1].

On these grounds it is not unreasonable to assume that in spite of the somewhat surprising comparison of rates of increase afforded by a consideration of England and Ireland, there really is a problem to explain in England, and that the contemporary cries that the population was manifesting a sudden and unprecedented rate of increase were justified.

The increase, according to these statements, has amounted to,

In 50 years	1791–1841	7,867,178	$29\frac{5}{9}$ %
,, 40 ,,	1791–1831	6,197,934	$23\frac{1}{2}$
,, 26 ,,	1791–1817	2,854,465	$10\frac{3}{4}$
,, 8 ,,	1817–1825	1,233,722	$4\frac{1}{4}$
,, 6 ,,	1825–1831	2,109,747	7

[1] Porter, p. 20, Death rates, 1 in so many of the population:

England and Wales ...	1 in 59 (not accurate)	U.S.A. ...	1 in 37
Sweden and Denmark	1 ,, 48	Prussia ...	1 ,, 36
Holland and Belgium	1 ,, 43	Wurtemburg	1 ,, 33
France	1 ,, 40		

It would have been of value, in view of the remarkable increase in Ireland, if we could have shown that, as in the case of England, the increase was due chiefly to the decline in the death rate. Whatever the Irish figures might show would not alter the facts that in England there was a rising and then a falling birth rate, a somewhat declining marriage rate and a steady decline in the death rate during the important part of our period. A demonstration that the same thing was going on in Ireland would be an interesting commentary on the Malthusian controversy and would strengthen the conclusions that we drew from the English figures. It appears, however, that the Irish figures are not to be had. On *a priori* grounds this is not surprising. The first Irish Census was not taken until 1821, and it was in the first English Census that the first systematic study of the parish registers was undertaken; the work in Ireland would, therefore, in any case have taken place twenty years later than in England. Any figures received from the established clergy in Ireland would be very much less reliable than figures from the same source in England, as they would not include the Roman Catholics, who constitute the large majority of the people of Ireland, and Roman Catholic figures, if any existed, would in all probability be extremely unreliable. The Irish Census Report of 1824 says that as one of the objects of the Census was to ascertain the increase or diminution of the population it was unfortunate that no means had been taken to investigate the parish registers in the way this had been done in the English Censuses with such valuable results; it goes on to say that the "omission has doubtless arisen from a knowledge of the very defective state of Parish Registers in Ireland," and recommends that some more careful system of keeping them be imposed by statute. An elaborate discussion on the Table of Deaths in the Report on the Irish Census of 1841 contains an investigation of the figures available for the consideration of the health and mortality of Ireland in previous times. This Report says that the old Irish writers made no attempt to investigate the matter, that a certain incentive was given by the writings of Sir William Petty at the end of the seventeenth century, and that for some time, with more or less serious defects, there were Bills of Mortality for

Dublin. These Bills appear to have gone on until 1772, from which period the writer of the Report says that he had been "unable to obtain any account of their existence." He is convinced at any rate that they had not been kept since the beginning of the nineteenth century. These Bills, it must be remembered, applied only to Dublin, and the Report says that in no case had an attempt been made to draw up a general table of mortality for the whole country until the one contained in that Report, and that attempt was not retrospective[1].

These defects apply to birth and marriage figures as well as to death figures, and it therefore appears that any attempt to make tables similar to those which we have arrived at for England and Wales would not be successful in the case of Ireland for the period for which they would be valuable for our purposes.

The causes and conditions of the increase in Ireland focus our attention on certain factors that require investigation in England.

In discussing the question of population it is necessary to guard against appearing to argue that man lives by the amount of employment there may be at any given moment. Man lives by that which employment enables him to purchase—primarily food. Food obviously plays a large part in the increase of any population, and in Ireland the part played by food is made very clear indeed. The question may of course be one of quality or quantity or both, but in Ireland when the famine came and led to the huge wave of emigration and the decline in the population, it was certainly one of quantity. If we had better information as to whether the increase in Ireland was really due to the prevalence of marriage and a high birth rate, as the statements in the various sources of evidence unsupported by a statistical demonstration would lead us to believe, or as to whether it was due chiefly, as in England, to a decline in the death rate, it would be less difficult to determine to what extent the food supply on its qualitative side played a part in the history of Ireland. In any case, and this is the important

---

[1] For the relevant extracts in connection with this question see Appendix I, p. 261.

thing, the history of Ireland demonstrates clearly the importance
of the food supply, and our knowledge of the decline in the
death rate in this country will direct our attention to the qualitative aspect as well as to the quantitative side when we come to
discuss the question in connection with England.

In so far as the food supply in Ireland and in England was
either chiefly or considerably a quantitative question, the reliance on the easily raised and large supplies of potatoes in
Ireland, and the low standard of life involved in such reliance,
becomes increasingly interesting; and in so far as this aspect is
important it may well be that the determination evinced in
England to maintain a higher standard of life and not to become
dependent on potatoes was a considerable cause of the very
much slower rate of increase in England than in Ireland.

In England, at the period of scarcity in 1795 and 1796, a good
deal was heard about the use of potatoes. Schemes were on
foot to induce the people to make more use of this form of food.
There was in 1796 a pamphlet entitled, *Hints for the relief of
the Poor*, which declared that "The principal difficulty under
which the poor now labour arises from a scarcity of bread corn"
and then proceeds to recommend potatoes, "the principal diet
of the healthy and robust poor of Ireland."[1] The writer declares
that his object in the pamphlet is to overcome "the only difficulty which actually exists," which "arises from the unwilling-
ness of the poor to deviate in any degree from their accustomed
mode of living." He then urges "people of property, leisure
and reflection" to assist in inducing the poor to adopt his
suggestions and the pamphlet closes with a series of recipes of
the kind of "Pottages" which he recommends. Butter and
margarine among the poor in the late war correspond to the
wheat and potatoes of a hundred years ago, and in saying that
the poorer people were less inclined to take to margarine than
the wealthier classes, the same kind of complaint is advanced
that is made in this pamphlet. It is however fair to remember
that the instinct to preserve a standard of life is a natural and

---

[1] *Hints for the relief of the Poor*, 1795. See also *Annals*, 1796, xxv.
Report of Kensington Committee for reducing the consumption of wheat
flour.

good one, and in the case of the poorer classes the maintenance of the bare standard is at stake sooner than it is in the case of the wealthier classes. These classes may, possibly in face of some economic pressure, adopt some such substitutes as potatoes or margarine, but they only do this from among a great many other varieties of food. It is done more or less voluntarily, and their wages are not so closely connected with the standard of food they are accustomed to eat as are those of the poorer classes, who are generally much more dependent on the cereal staple in general use than are the higher classes, and if this is true nowadays it was probably much more universally true in the period with which we are now dealing. So long as the use of potatoes was loyally accepted as a substitute no great harm would be done, but the danger was, that, as in Ireland, it would become the regular diet of the people. With the history of Ireland in this period before us we may indeed be glad that, although the Poor Law may have demoralised the English labourer, it did so "in white wheaten bread,"[1] and that the determination of the people to maintain the standard of life they had been used to, avoided "the pernicious effect of introducing the habit of living almost entirely upon potatoes."[2]

In a recent work on the Population Problem the increase which began in England about 1760, and in other European countries rather later, has been described as "the response to increase in skill."[3] Now in Ireland the increase in the population became rapid about 1780, which marked, as we have seen, the beginning of a period of industrial and agricultural prosperity, but this prosperity is represented as having ended either during the period of the war or in the depression which followed.

The lack of skill displayed by the Irish is constantly being remarked upon in the Reports. The level of agricultural skill in 1823 is represented as being very low; "there is no regular, at least no beneficial rotation of crops adopted; implements are not only very scarce, but the few there are are extremely

[1] Fay, *Life and Labour*, p. 101.
[2] *Reports*, 1826–7, v. Q. 3214 (Malthus).
[3] Carr-Saunders, *The Population Problem*, p. 308.

defective."[1] Very much the same opinion is expressed of the south of Ireland in 1830. "The farmers in the South of Ireland have very little skill in agriculture; after a field or garden is put in fair condition they continue cropping it until it will not yield the seed again, and then let it go to grass naturally."[2]

The same remarks apply to the textile trades. All the schemes to increase the employment available in Ireland make some reference to the desirability and to the possibility of improving the textile industries, and contrast the superior condition of the inhabitants in the districts where these industries flourish with the unfortunate distress of the residents in places not so favoured[3]. In spite of all this the skill does not seem to have increased, at least not sufficiently to keep pace with the introduction of machinery into the industries with which those of Ireland would have to compete. "If the manufactures of Ireland," we are told, "are to be sustained, it can only be by the application of machinery. But this is impeded by the duty on coal. The direct practical result of these duties is to discourage the industries."[4] For the immediate purpose it does not matter that the decline in the industries is put down to an arrangement of tariffs; the point is that the increase in skill which was recognised as a necessity did not take place. In 1836 the emigration of Irish to England, where they were usually employed in the same occupations to which they had been trained in Ireland, is put down to the fact that they "have left their homes in consequence of the diminution of linen and woollen weaving in the North eastern counties, and in the County of Cork."[5] The work to which the Irish emigrants chiefly turned were "different kinds of coarse unskilled work, and especially several branches of the building trade."

Recommendations to improve the system of agriculture and industry occur with unfailing regularity, and there does seem to have been some improvement, but not much[6]. Finally, in

---

[1] *Reports*, 1823, VI. p. 132.   [2] *Reports*, 1833, V. Agriculture, p. 300.
[3] *Reports*, 1823, VI. pp. 1 and 13. *Reports*, 1825, VII. pp. 237, 312, 405–6.
[4] *Reports*, 1830, VII. p. 16.
[5] *Reports*, 1836, XXXIV. Cornewall Lewis's Report on the Irish in Great Britain, p. vii.
[6] *Reports*, 1833, V. Q. 388.

1830, one Committee bursts forth, and its bitter complaint shows the kind of result that followed the pious expressions of Committees that great improvements were necessary if disaster were to be averted. The Committee recapitulates the series of recommendations, notes the improvements that have resulted in Scotland from a good system of promoting public works, and records with satisfaction the beneficial results that have occurred in Ireland from these works "although not conducted on any permanent or well digested system." They then despairingly record the limit of their own achievements—a series of specific recommendations none of which have been acted upon[1].

On the whole, then, there does not appear to have been any very hopeful or consistent increase of skill in Ireland during this period such as would cause or maintain an increase in the population. It must be admitted that there was some increase, and that not an inconsiderable one in the early part of the period, and it is pretty certain that this improvement must have been partially maintained in spite of appearances and statements to the contrary. On the other hand, it must be remembered that in the sixty years from 1780 to 1840 the population increased almost twice as fast as it did in England, and that there was nothing like the increase of skill in Ireland to account for this that there undoubtedly was in England. It is of course very possibly true that it was the increase in skill in the early part of the period that gave the necessary stimulus to start the great increase in the population, and that once the increase had, as it were, got into its swing, it would take a great deal to stop it, and in this way the increase may have been indirectly due to an increase in skill.

If the increase in population anywhere in Ireland was due to and was firmly based on an increase in skill, it was in Ulster. "Protestant Ulster, stubborn and hard working, was laying the foundations of her industrial prosperity."[2] Here, if anywhere in Ireland, habits of prudence and restraint would exist; here certain of the possible stimulating causes that led to an increase in the Catholic parts of the country might be absent, and here, if anywhere, the growth in the population would be a healthy

---

[1] *Reports*, 1830, VII. p. 35. [2] Fay, p. 119.

and a safe growth. It is therefore interesting to see how the
population increased in Ulster, compared with the rest of the
country, between the years 1821 and 1841, when there are the
Census figures as a basis for the inquiry. In the decade 1821–
1831 the increase in Ulster is 14·2 per cent., which is the second
largest increase among the four provinces, Connaught having
an increase of very nearly double this, and Munster being about
1 per cent. lower than Ulster. In the decade 1831–1841, the
increases in all four provinces are much smaller and differ from
one another only by about 2 per cent. In this decade Ulster
comes third in the rates of increase. In both decades Connaught
has the greatest increase, and in both decades Leinster has the
smallest. If the increase in Ulster represents most nearly what
may be considered as a healthy increase, that in Connaught,
the most backward of the provinces, must have been very precarious indeed, and cannot have had any sufficient margin of
safety on which to rely. Leinster is the province which throughout the period has an increase smaller than Ulster, and it is
interesting to remember that this was the other province along
with Ulster which was mentioned as not being so seriously
affected by the famine of 1822. If the increase in the population
of Ulster is a healthy growth, that in the other provinces—with
the possible exception of Leinster—was not a healthy growth;
if the increase in Ulster was due to the increase in skill, the
other provinces increased as rapidly or more rapidly in spite
of the absence of the same degree of skill[1].

The whole history is, however, sufficient to make us suspicious of the theory that the increase in this period was merely
the response to the increase in skill as is represented. Undoubtedly it played its part, but it obviously does not apply in
anything like the same degree to different places, and it is
obviously unsatisfactory as a general and all-embracing theory.
The increase in skill in England was very much greater than in

[1] Percentage increases in the Provinces of Ireland:

	1821–31	1831–41
Connaught	27·5	5·5
Munster	13·5	5·2
Leinster	6·9	3·4
Ulster	14·2	4·3

Ireland and the increase of population was very much greater in Ireland than in England.

We have seen that in England the increase was not due to a rapidly rising birth rate backed up and rendered possible by a rising marriage rate; for the birth rate and the marriage rate both fell after 1790. It was, however, seen that a certain rise in the fertility of marriage took place towards the end of the period, which checked the fall in the birth rate in spite of the declining marriage rate. The increased prevalence of marriage, in the absence of statistical proof, may have played a large part in the growth of the population of Ireland, and in this connection it is interesting to note that the system of apprenticeship, the breakdown of which will have to be examined in England as a possible cause of the increase, never existed in Ireland, and therefore in Ireland could never have acted as a check on early marriages. To some extent also the absence of minute subdivision of land and the lack of cottage room may have had the effect of checking early marriages in England[1].

V

There is one important point of connection between the population problems in England and Ireland during this period. The immigration of Irish into England was a considerable if secondary factor in the increase of the population in the latter country, and goes a long way to explain the excess of its actual over its natural increase.

This immigration does not seem to have begun seriously until the beginning of the nineteenth century and on *a priori* grounds this is what we should expect; the population of Ireland did not begin to increase rapidly until about 1780, and it would not be for some time that emigration would present itself as a necessary or desirable source of relief. We are told that there were in all probability no very considerable numbers of Irish in England in the year 1795 and that it was the rebellion of 1798 which gave the first stimulus to the movement[2].

---

[1] *Reports*, 1826–7, v. Q. 3361 (Malthus). *Reports*, 1834, XXIX. p. 329. Malthus, *Essay*, 1817 ed. II. p. 344.

[2] *Reports*, 1836, XXXIV. pp. iv, v.

This immigration of Irish into England was of two kinds.

There was, first, the time-honoured and temporary immigration of the harvesters and summer labourers. So far as the increase of the population is concerned this kind is of very little importance, except indirectly; no doubt some people who had migrated temporarily will have been caught in a Census registration and recorded as permanent residents, especially as the Censuses during this period were taken at a time of year when there were many Irish of this class in the country[1], and no doubt certain of those who came over intending to return made a more permanent stay, and possibly induced others to join them. Among this class of short time immigrants the same people came year after year; they generally left Ireland about the middle or near the end of May, after they had planted their potatoes, and returned in October or November[2]. In 1836 these Irish wanderers are compared to other classes of migratory labourers and are evidently looked upon approvingly[3]. They are compared to the Welsh reapers, to the Welsh women in the market gardens near London and to the inhabitants in Craven, who used to get in the harvest in the plain of York, though it is suggested that latterly they have been ousted by the Irish[4]. The wanderings of these Irish people were considerable; in 1826 we get a definite mention of them in the harvest in Sussex[5], and in the following year we are told that the great majority of Irish who came over in harvest time did not remain in Lancashire or Cheshire, but went on to other parts of the country, and seemed to prefer the longer tour[6]. This system was upheld because it was said to enable work to be done for which the native workmen were inadequate without disturbing the

---

[1] Before 1841 the Census was taken on the day indicated and subsequent days if necessary, from 1841 onwards on one day only:

1801, 10th March	1831, 30th May
1811, 27th May	1841, 7th June
1821, 28th May	1851, 30th March

[2] *Reports*, 1828, IV. p. 9.

[3] See also *Reports*, 1833, V. Q. 8448, Hereford: "The Welshmen do come into the county very much at harvest." "I say a good many Welshmen are employed in harvest."

[4] *Reports*, 1836, XXXIV. p. xlvii.

[5] *Reports*, 1826, IV. Q. 1176.

[6] *Reports*, 1826–7, V. Q. 2295.

ordinary rate of wages or giving a stimulus to population. The statement that they do not reduce wages does not go unchallenged, but this charge is more definitely made against the permanent settlers.

The other kind of immigration was that of people who came with the intention of settling down in the country and finding permanent work; it was prompted ultimately in the main in Ireland by the same feeling as influenced the promotion of the emigration movement in England—fear of over-population—though in Ireland and to the ordinary man it would present itself chiefly as a favourable opportunity of getting work with better pay. This movement of people from Ireland to England caused widespread fear which is very generally expressed in the Emigration Reports of 1826 and 1827 with their dread of an influx of Irish filling up any "vacuum" that may be caused by a successful encouragement of emigration from England unless measures are taken to prevent this[1]. To guard against this result it was suggested that emigration should be accompanied by a system of destroying the cottages of those who had left the country[2]. In Ireland itself the tendency to fill up a gap in the population from its natural increase was emphasised by Malthus, and it was suggested that a redistribution of lands accompanied by a destruction of cabins might prevent this[3]. This fear of the influx was particularly urged in the case of Lancashire by the Bishop of Chester, who said that if a certain proportion of the weavers from Lancashire were removed to increase the wages and comforts of those that remained—the economics involved are a little doubtful—their places would immediately be filled by Irish who were accustomed to work for much smaller wages, and that already this was happening.

This fear that their efforts to lessen the menace of over-population, of which they were so afraid, were being thwarted

[1] *Reports*, 1826–7, v. p. 7, Second Report: "It is vain to hope for any permanent and extensive advantage from any system of emigration, which does not primarily apply to Ireland; whose population, unless some outlet is opened to them, must shortly fill up every vacuum in England or in Scotland, and reduce the labouring classes to a uniform state of degradation and misery."
[2] *Reports*, 1826–7, v. Third Report, p. 234, Qs. 1184, 2308.
[3] *Ibid.* Q. 3231 (Malthus).

GPP 6

by an influx of improvident Irishmen, was intensified at this
time because it was said that the immigration was increasing
and was becoming more composed of people who intended to
remain[1]. In 1834 the immigration of Irish is regarded as a
"subject of the very greatest importance from the influence it
must have in counteracting all efforts for checking a redundant
population."[2]

The question of removing the Irish to their own country was
dealt with by an Act of 1819[3]. Before the passing of that Act
the Irish were considered as casual poor having no settlement,
and were therefore relieved by the parishes in which they were
found, from which they could only be removed on committing
certain definite acts of vagrancy[4]. Before the Act of 1819 the
evil was being realised, and it was reported by the Stipendiary
of Manchester that in the course of two years, unless the influx
of Irish was checked, "the relief afforded to Irish poor would
at least equal the whole rental of the town of Manchester."[5]
The difficulty of avoiding this result was seen, as it was said,
"there is no place to which they can be removed." Under the
new Act it was possible to remove an Irishman who merely
became chargeable though he had committed no act of vagrancy.
This opened the possibility of great injustice, though at any rate
in London a reasonable interpretation seems to have been
adopted[6]. The Act was looked upon as a great improvement, as
a salutary check on the Irish immigration and it was praised
not so much for what it did as for what it prevented[7]. The
number of Irish passed to Ireland in certain years under this

---

[1] *Reports*, 1826–7, v. Third Report, pp. 227, 229: "In point of fact, the
numbers removing from Ireland to England, have infinitely increased, and
the character has been changed from one of labourers leaving their small
farms and cottages, to which after a temporary absence they were in the
habit of returning, into an emigration of vagrants, who neither have the ties
of home, nor the hope of obtaining provision to induce them to go back."
See also *Reports*, 1825, VIII. p. 428.

[2] *Reports*, 1834, XXXVII. p. 67.

[3] 59 Geo. III, c. 12.

[4] *Reports*, 1821, IV. p. 4.   [5] *Reports*, 1818, v. p. 245.

[6] *Reports*, 1821, IV. p. 59.

[7] *Ibid.* p. 19: "The number of those who have been passed bears no proportion to the thousands of Irish and Scotch paupers who were previously
receiving parochial relief in England. The value of that Act is to be estimated
not so much by what it does as by what it prevents."

law gives some idea of the scale on which the question of the Irish in England had to be considered. These figures do not of course in any way represent the number of Irish in the country, but only that portion of them who had failed so badly that they had had recourse to the Poor Laws and had been removed. In the seven years from January 1814 to January 1821, 39,413[1] persons were passed from Liverpool to Ireland, and of course Liverpool was the outport for a good many northern and midland counties. In the same period 5753[2] were passed from Bristol, and in the five years from 1823 to 1827 inclusive, 20,418[3] were passed from Lancashire. For purposes of rough comparison it may be recalled that in the decade from 1811 to 1821, in which the actual gain in population above the natural increase was greater than in either of the adjoining decades, the excess was 198,171. If we combine all the three series of figures given above and take it as a rough estimate that they represent the enforced passages for a period extending over seven years, we can then say that if, in the decade, for every one Irishman that was removed to Ireland between two and three were allowed to remain, this would account for the excess of the actual increase over and above the natural increase, and although there may be no means of proving this it does not sound inherently improbable.

The attraction to the Irish is represented as being the higher wages which they could earn in England[4], and this gave rise to opposition to the Irish immigration as being likely to reduce the condition and the wages of the English labourer to the level of those of the Irish. At this particular period the question was, of course, involved with that of expanding industry and the necessity of getting more workmen. In 1825, although it was generally agreed that the effect of the Irish immigration would be to reduce the level of wages in England, it was also said that the increase in the cotton trade had been so great that the immigration might not have had much effect in that particular

---

[1] *Reports*, 1821, IV. p. 83.   [2] *Ibid.* p. 110.
[3] *Reports*, 1828, IV. p. 206.
[4] *Reports*, 1830, VII. p. 49: "The main cause which produces the influx of Irish labourers into Britain is undoubtedly the higher rate of wages which prevails in one island than in the other."

trade and that it could not have been extended without the additional labourers[1]. The apparent reluctance on the part of men from different parts of England to migrate to the growing industrial districts and the obvious satisfaction of the Poor Law authorities with the progress their migration schemes had made, all render more probable the theory that the immigration of Irish had no very serious effect on the wage level, especially as in the state of expanding trade a large and increasing number of hands was essential. The proximity of Lancashire to Ireland and the fact also that it was the county which was particularly concerned in the expansion of one of the chief industries, enhance the importance of the Irish immigration as a phenomenon of the industrial development. The theory of wages does not concern us; in this controversy the view is expressed that, if the Irish had not come, the manufacturers would have instituted more successful measures to get English labourers to migrate to the new districts and that it was the "state of the manufactures" which regulated the wages paid[2]. On the other hand, in certain places, the Irish influx is looked upon as an "unlimited supply" which can be used to prevent or break strikes[3].

The effect of the Irish on the manners and habits of the people is probably not clearly marked in any one direction. They are represented at this time as being in their own country a people given to early marriages and large families; if they carried these habits to the manufacturing districts to which they migrated, as is likely, they are in part responsible for the somewhat higher birth rate in those districts. On the other hand, the habits of the Irish were anything but good for the general health of the towns in which they lived; with their indifference to filth and the overcrowding which always seemed to be associated with them, they were very liable to fever and to all the evils of the growing and unregulated towns[4], and if they did not entirely keep those evils alive, their influence on the population cannot have been beneficial, though it may have been damaging only from the qualitative aspect and not from the quantitative[5].

---

[1] *Reports*, 1825, VIII. p. 691.
[2] *Reports*, 1836, XXXIV. p. xxxiv.   [3] *Ibid*. p. xxxvi.
[4] *Ibid*. p. xlii.   [5] *Reports*, 1844, XVII. p. 29.

The occupations of the Irish, apart from agricultural pursuits which have been noticed in connection with the temporary migrants, seem to have been divided chiefly between the textile industry, especially in Lancashire, and various kinds of heavy unskilled work.

It was natural that the Irish should be employed in the cotton industry in Lancashire; the trade was expanding, the Irish were near, they habitually landed in Lancashire and had had some experience of weaving at home, and in 1833 we are told that there are "a great many Irish weavers in Lancashire."[1] In spite of this the Irish do not seem to have been welcomed in the industries; in 1835 manufacturers "agree that they prefer English labourers from a purely agricultural district to Irish from a similar source."[2] Few, if any, Irish were ever employed in the superior processes in the factories in Aston, Staleybridge and Hyde; they were almost all to be found in the lowest grades of work, a certain number were employed in the card rooms, and few ever attained to the rank of spinners[3].

In Scotland, owing to the prejudice on the part of the inhabitants against factory labour, the Irish seem to have firmly established themselves in the factories.

On the whole, their skill was not equal to the more difficult processes of industry. It was in the heavy and manual labour that the Irish were chiefly engaged, just in those trades which, apart from any new conditions and breakdown of restrictions following the new organisation of industry, were likely to afford the maximum reward early, and in which there were no obstacles to early marriage, the habit of which the Irish labourers brought from home. In these industries also they did not penetrate to the more skilled branches; "even among the inferior kinds of artisans, as carpenters, masons, bricklayers,"[4] there were few Irish and they were not successful. It was as "bricklayers' labourers and in the lower and harder kinds of employment of that description" that they excelled and appeared to have secured some particular descriptions of labour exclusively to

[1] Reports, 1833, v. Q. 3714.
[2] Reports, 1835, xxxv. p. 295.   [3] Reports, 1836, xxxiv. p. v.
[4] Ibid. p. xxxi.

themselves[1]. In 1833 they are mentioned in the building trade in "carrying bricks, making mortar, taking down and erecting of scaffolds, and all those employments connected with the building trade, which we can get done by them in preference to the journeymen tradesmen,"[2] though we are particularly told that they are not employed as bricklayers. They were also said to have increased of late in Liverpool as "the docks appear generally as full since the new ones have been made as they did before."[3] The same description of their occupations is given in 1835[4].

It is not easy to give any figure which will represent anything like an accurate estimate of the number of Irish in the country, or the share that the Irish immigration played in contributing to the odd half million by which the population appears to have grown beyond its natural increase in the first three decades of the nineteenth century. If we may assume that most of the Irish who are recorded as being in the country in the twenties and the thirties came after the beginning of the century, the contribution will appear very considerable, and it must be remembered that, towards the end of the period at any rate, there was some emigration going on and that therefore there must have been more immigration to secure the net gain of population.

In 1826 it was reckoned from the baptismal registers of the Roman Catholic chapels in London that the Irish population which was connected with these places had risen from 71,442 in 1819 to 119,799 in 1826, so that by the end of the period there were probably a good many more Irish in London than appears from this figure, though it is also probable that a larger proportion of those were old inhabitants than would be the case in many other places[5]. In 1835 it was estimated that in Manchester "the Irish and their immediate descendants" amounted to about 60,000, in Liverpool to about 50,000, and

[1] *Reports*, 1826, IV. Q. 2344.
[2] *Reports*, 1833, VI. p. 106.   [5] *Ibid.* p. 294.
[4] *Reports*, 1835, XXXV. p. 296: "Among the workmen employed in the building trades of Lancashire are an immense number of Irish, but I am informed they are chiefly employed in the inferior and worst paid occupations."
[5] *Reports*, 1826–7, V. p. 591.

to between 30,000 and 40,000 in the rest of Lancashire[1]. This makes a total for Lancashire of about 150,000. We are told that in 1836 "altogether there are not 100,000 Irish in Lancashire."[2] The London figures, being based on Roman Catholic baptism figures, may represent an Irish migration older than the other figures. These figures for London, together with the figures for Lancashire, account for about half the excess of actual over natural increase in the years 1801 to 1831. There were also other parts of England to which the Irish had migrated. Their general diffusion over Scotland and England was said to be more remarkable than their numbers, and they were to be found in every manufacturing town from Aberdeen to London[3].

On the whole, then, in dealing with the Irish we are dealing with a people who from the peculiar circumstances of their life at home were in a favourable position to take advantage of the industrial opportunities of England during this period. They were impelled by the necessity of doing something to relieve the distress at home[4], and in the proximity of Lancashire they were fortunate in the accessibility of a county which was more likely than most to provide them with work; the amount of their immigration must have formed a considerable percentage of the excess of actual over natural increase.

VI

To review the ground that has been covered up to this point, we have determined that the increase in the population in England and Wales was primarily due to a decline in the death rate. We have compared that increase with the increase that took place in Ireland in the same period, and were somewhat surprised to find that the increase in the latter country was almost twice as rapid as in the former. In spite of that fact, however, we have satisfied ourselves, by comparing the increase

---

[1] *Reports*, 1835, xxxv. p. 295.   [2] *Reports*, 1836, xxxiv. p. vii.
[3] *Ibid.* See also *Reports*, 1826–7, v. Q. 2096.
[4] *Reports*, 1826, iv. Q. 2341 : "Has the number of Irish flowing into London very much increased within the last three years?"
"With the exception of the influx in 1822 I do not think it has."
1822 was a year of famine and disease in Ireland.

in England with that in France and by comparing the death rate with that in various other countries, that there really is a problem to investigate in England.

We have learned from a consideration of the causes mentioned for the increase of the population in Ireland that the question of food is very important, although absence of statistical information in Ireland blurs the point whether the quantitative or the qualitative aspect is the really important one.

We have received a warning against attributing too much of the growth of the population to the increase of skill which undoubtedly took place, though this contributed in various ways, directly and indirectly. The Industrial Revolution has been blamed at some time or other for most of the things which happened in the early nineteenth century; this warning will possibly in some degree absolve it from being credited with the increase of the population on insufficient grounds.

We have also received rather vaguer hints that the breakdown in the economic restrictions on marriage imposed by the apprenticeship system may have been conducive to an increased universality of marriage towards the end of the period, and that the lack of cottage room in England which did not exist in Ireland may have served to prevent a rate of increase as rapid in England as that which took place in Ireland.

CHAPTER IV

The Position of Malthus

DURING the reign of Queen Elizabeth there began in England a system of aggressive economic nationalism which later developed in all the growing nation states of the Continent and was known as Mercantilism. The compelling motive behind that system was the desire for power, which involved the capacity for self-support in industry and food supply, in so far as this was possible, and an abundant supply of man-power to carry the scheme of national power into effect. Under the painstaking and detailed administration of Burleigh in this country, the armament industries and the "key industries" were stimulated by the beginnings of the monopoly system. Foreigners were brought in to revive the mining and metallurgical industries of the country with a view to supplying the deficiency in the ordnance requisite for the national defence, culminating in the company of the Mines Royal which was incorporated in 1568. To ensure the supply of gunpowder for the guns constructed under the stimulus of the mining and metallurgical patents, monopolies were given for the working of saltpetre and sulphur. The important item of the navy was attended to; regulations were made in restraint of the felling of trees with a view to preserving the necessary supplies of timber for the shipyards and the smelting trade was restricted in those neighbourhoods where shipbuilding was likely to take place. Harbours were improved, often by forced labour. All these developments required men, and this is most obvious in the efforts to stimulate the navy. Burleigh had his eye on the importance of a seafaring life to the strength of England, and his "political Lent" and the "increase of fish and navy days," decreed in 1563, bear witness to this. This policy of fostering the navy was maintained by the Stuarts when other things were going wrong[1].

[1] For this general description of the early rise of the mercantile system in England, in so far as any definite source can be given that source is Cunningham, vol. II.

The growth of the great nation states on the Continent created the same kind of phenomenon that was seen in England under Elizabeth. With the Peace of Westphalia and with the rise of Colbert to power in France the system began to enjoy a hundred years of uninterrupted sway among the nations of Europe. To secure national strength and growth under this system a large and increasing population was necessary; the dependence of each country on its own resources, which was involved in the system, also demanded a large population, for the larger the population the greater the production. Indeed it came to be believed, with a fervency that bordered on the fanatical, that a nation's strength depended entirely on the number of its inhabitants, to the exclusion of limiting conditions of welfare that seem obvious to us nowadays. Populousness, national wealth and popular welfare came to be regarded as entirely interdependent.

This theory that an increasing population was in all cases desirable and necessary became an axiom which continued for some centuries, and discussions were always taking place as to the various means of securing this. Towards the end of the eighteenth century, when, in point of fact, the population was increasing with a rapidity hitherto unapproached, there was, owing largely to the failure to take a Census, a great feeling that the population was decreasing.

It was into such an atmosphere that Malthus's *Essay on Population* burst. The continued absence of any reliable and official figures of the population heightened the surprise effect of the essay, and when in 1801 a Census was taken, it confirmed what Malthus had said about the increase of the population up to that time. The *Essay*, backed up by the Census, killed the axiom that under all circumstances an increasing population is desirable.

In view of the population figures which we have discussed for England and Wales, and the rates which went to make them up, it is arguable that Malthus has put the emphasis on the wrong phase of the population problem. If this is the case, that wrong emphasis has been perpetuated, because Malthus's book is by far the most famous in the controversy, because at the time of its publication it caused a very great sensation, and because in later days the parts of Malthus's book that have been quoted or misquoted, and the views which have been attributed, not always fairly, to Malthus, have continued to place the emphasis on the wrong side of the problem.

Malthus spoiled the vision of the land of promise. He intended so to do; the occasion of the *Essay* was an argument with his father in which the elder Malthus upheld the doctrine of human perfectibility of Godwin which the younger Malthus attacked. To the world at large, or at any rate to the inhabitants of a healthy country, it is more natural and pleasant to look forward to an increase of the population as a right and proper part of the progress of the nation—and if conditions are such that this increase is also a national requirement, as it was being represented, so much the better—than it is to be told that the population is already too big and that any further increase is bound to result in one or more of a series of unpleasant consequences. Yet this was the message which Malthus had to give.

Unlike Adam Smith, Malthus did not tell people the kind of things they wanted to hear. Adam Smith may have been the father of Political Economy, but many of his views had been anticipated—though that applies also to Malthus—and he realised so imperfectly what was to be the nature of the movement that secured the triumph of his doctrines that cotton and steam, two of its chief agents, are only incidentally mentioned in the *Wealth of Nations*. But, on the other hand, the world was getting tired of the old mercantile government control, and the optimism of the eighteenth century was pronouncing in favour of individual independent action in place of spoon feeding. This independence was the basis of Adam Smith's teaching and flattered the somewhat self-satisfied people of his time. The optimism, however, had to be broken and it was Malthus who did the felling of the image; all was not well with the world and it was not possible for each to go his own sweet way and for that way necessarily to turn out best for him and for everybody else in the long run.

The *Essay* was, therefore, a shock and an unpleasant one. It was more than that, it was unanswerable. Under the existing conditions, the truth of the main proposition was so clear and strictly relevant that it was hopeless to argue against the author, much as one might rail against him. If ever a country is likely to find its population pressing against the means of subsistence, then an island with limited possibilities of growing its own food and defective means of transport is in a bad position to start with, and when it is added that the country thus situated was engaged in a European war with the greatest military genius of modern times, the situation is obviously in a fair way to becoming desperate. It may not be far-fetched to see a reflection of the fear which the *Essay* caused, in the figures of inclosure by private bill. The decade 1790–1800 was almost as much one of war as was the decade 1800–1810, yet the inclosure bills in the latter decade were over nine hundred as against something under six hundred in the former decade. Partly, no doubt, this would be due in any case to the prolongation of the war and the economic contest which Napoleon started by the Berlin Decrees, but, on the other hand, in those days England was chiefly self-supporting, and it may well be that the warning which Malthus gave with such emphasis, following the period of placid optimism in reference to population, gave an extra fillip to the inclosure movement.

The fact that Malthus lived in the country may have had an effect on the growth of his theory of population. He saw the limitations and the possibilities of agricultural improvement; for him society was predominantly agricultural, and it is in such a society that, with an increasing population, the truth of the "principle" becomes most manifest. It was through the activity and enterprise in the new towns, whereby our manufactures commanded a market that enabled us to purchase our food from foreign countries and created and improved the means of transport which brought that food, that the immediate threatenings of the principle were warded off. With modern transport facilities the problem has become world-wide and—provided organisation is adequate—a crisis postponed for many generations. With all the fertile waste and semi-cultivated land that there is in the world it must obviously be a long time before there is any need for the world to find itself in the position that England was in when Malthus began to write.

In addition to the checks to the population arising from vice and misery, which were regarded as inevitable in the first edition of the *Essay*, Malthus recommended in the later editions another check, namely, moral restraint by which he meant postponement of marriage, and this, he said, if it did not lead to vice was "undoubtedly the least evil that can arise from the principle of population." This may have been a correction that was in any case bound to follow the careful revising and consideration of what in its first form was little more than a magazine article, or it may have been done in response to the outcry that the first edition caused. In any case it very much strengthened Malthus's position; it left the original proposition as unanswerable as it was in the original *Essay*, but it rendered the means whereby the inevitable catastrophe was to be warded off less offensive. But the *Essay* ceased thereby to be an answer to those who claimed the perfectibility of the world; once admit a sentiment of moral restraint which is allowed to improve the lot of man, and the road to perfection is opened. Had not the principle of moral restraint been admitted into the later editions, it is very likely that Malthus would not have continued to occupy the place in the discussions on the problems of population which the first edition had given him. Vice and misery as the only factors with an influence on the subject could not have held the field indefinitely, and by introducing moral restraint Malthus re-established his position. It is, however, probable that the general meaning usually attached to the word "Malthusian" and some if not most of the attacks on Malthus are the indirect outcome of the admission of this moral restraint, for such attacks have usually attributed to Malthus measures of birth control which he never once entertained and which so far as one can see he would have condemned. This arose from a perversion of the ideas he did intend to inculcate in the kind of moral restraint which he advocated.

The check that Malthus advocated, as he clearly stated, was "a restraint from marriage, from prudential motives, with a conduct strictly moral during the period of restraint." Once marriage has been contracted Malthus has no idea of any further check. "Mr Malthus never carried his anxiety as to children further than the marriage contract. He seems to have thought (as will certainly in most cases happen) that the marriage once made, children must come as they may."[1] Moreover, he expressly denounces any of the more direct checks which have been dubbed neo-Malthusian. In replying to an accusation that he "recommends immediate recourse to human efforts for the correction or mitigation of the evil" of a redundant population, he says:

I have never adverted to the check suggested by Condorcet without the most marked disapprobation. Indeed I should always particularly reprobate any artificial and unnatural modes of checking population, both on account of their immorality and their tendency to remove a necessary stimulus to industry. If it were possible for each married couple to limit by a wish the number of their children, there is certainly reason to fear that the indolence of the human race would be very greatly increased, and that neither the population of individual countries, nor of the whole world, would ever reach its natural and proper extent[2].

Whatever may be thought of parts of the above passage, it should be sufficient to absolve Malthus of advocating checks which are widely in use to-day, and which rightly or wrongly have brought his name into such discredit.

He has been attacked for a measure he never advocated, and has been deprived of the merit of pointing out the check which is in almost universal operation to-day among most classes of society. The age of marriage among all classes probably, certainly among all but those engaged in the least skilled branches of manual labour, was lower in Malthus's day than it is now; Malthus recommended that the age of marriage should be raised, and he advocated nothing more. Even such a writer as Mr Harold Cox, who is careful to be fair to Malthus, appears to fall into the common error. He states clearly in one place that Malthus assumed "that the only practicable way of limiting the birth rate was postponement of marriage"; but elsewhere he talks about passages from Malthus "in which he lays stress on the necessity for birth control." The term "birth control"

---

[1] *Edinburgh Review*, 1833, XXXVIII. p. 125.
[2] Malthus, *Essay*, 1817 ed. Appendix, p. 393, or p. 512 in the (7th) 1872 ed.

has come to have a meaning so entirely different from anything
that he advocated that it is very misleading to use the term at all
in connection with Malthus. Except in so far as the postponement of marriage is birth control, Malthus did not advocate it,
and nowadays, nine times out of ten, birth control means
something very different from postponement of marriage[1].

The checks which Malthus repudiated were urged in his
lifetime by others. Francis Place was prepared to stand the
criticism and abuse which a discussion of the subject created,
and he suffered considerable social ostracism for his advocacy
of this growing neo-Malthusianism[2]. A Malthusian by con-
viction, he had been saved from a disreputable youth by his
own early marriage, and had been reduced to great difficulties by
a large family. These influences prompted him to modify the
position of Malthus; he was unwilling to advocate any postponement of marriage, though in this he was arguing from the
particular to the general. To secure his object, therefore, he
was compelled to advocate some other check, which he does
with his wonted directness. In less obvious ways also he was
active; he was a great letter writer, and it is very possible that
he was responsible for a pamphlet which his opponents called
"The Diabolical Handbill." In 1826 he thought that his check
was gaining ground in Lancashire[3]. In 1822 he published a
book, *Illustrations of the Principle of Population*, in which he
directly urged other methods of checking the growth of population. He recognised that in doing so he was advocating measures
of which Malthus would not approve, not so much, Place felt,
from any abhorrence of the practice, though he was scarcely
justified in making that assumption, "as from the possible fear
of encountering the prejudices of others."[4] Place was quite
ready to encounter the prejudices of others and seems to have
borne the brunt of the scandal for a measure which was supported
by the general opinion of the inner circle of the Benthamite
group[5]. He argued that "if it were once clearly understood,

[1] Cox, *The Problem of Population*, pp. 114 and 163.
[2] G. Wallas, *Life of Francis Place*, 1918 ed. p. 169.
[3] Field, "English Propagandist Movement," *Am. Econ. Rev.* 1911.
[4] Place, *Principles of Population*, p. 173.
[5] G. Wallas, *op. cit.* p. 169.

that it was not disreputable for married persons to avail themselves of such precautions as would, without being injurious
to health or destructive of female delicacy, prevent conception,
a sufficient check might at once be given to the increase of
population beyond the means of subsistence."[1] Cobbett, who
in this matter used Malthus as a whipping boy, seems to have
had some such check in his mind in spite of all his fulminations,
for he said that if a labouring man "have more than four children
some of them ought to be doing something." It is argued that
Malthus never carried his anxiety as to children further than
the marriage contract, but that Cobbett "seems to go a good way
beyond this degree of providence and moral restraint, otherwise
how is a labouring man to comply with the rule of having only
four young children at once?"[2]

Presumably there is one other check, beyond a postponement
of marriage and beyond the various artificial measures which
were then and subsequently recommended, to which exception
cannot be taken, and which must be perfectly "moral." This,
however, is not a discussion of the ethics of birth control; the
matter is one for the individual much more than for theorists.
The interesting point in the early nineteenth-century discussion
of the matter is this: Malthus regards the postponement of
marriage as the desirable check, but holds that subsequently
the arrival of children must be allowed to take its chance. Place
and the others, who do not lay stress on the postponement of
marriage, consider that even after marriage there must be some
check or checks which, with sufficient accuracy, can be termed
mechanical. Both parties contemplate the arrival of children
up to the physiological limit unless one or both of these measures
are adopted.

We have seen previously, however, that the fertility of
marriage, as shown in Table VI, exhibited considerable variations between 1780 and 1830, and it is therefore difficult to
believe that the fertility of marriage can be regarded as anything
like a constant factor apart from the use of modern contraceptives. But even if we distrust the earlier figures and consider

[1] Place, *op. cit.* pp. 165, 176.
[2] *Edin. Review*, xxxviii. p. 125, Review of Cobbett's *Cottage Economy*.

that in pre-Malthusian times in England—we may leave out of account primitive peoples among whom other practices were known to exist—marriage did mean children up to the physiological limit, we are confronted by the facts that Malthus turned his attention to the subject at a time when the marriage rate and the birth rate were high and that during the time that the later editions of his work were appearing these rates fell. As a matter of fact, as we have seen, the birth rate rose steadily from 1710 to 1790 by some 16 per cent. At the time that Malthus first wrote, the fertility of marriage was astonishingly low, it then rose for some time until 1815 and from then fell steadily until 1830. An explanation of this on Malthusian lines would be that his warning did immediately check the marriage rate and the birth rate, which would be all that he desired; and that when Place and others in the course of time began to advocate more direct methods the fertility of marriage also fell. Another explanation, which is encouraged by the fact that the fall in the marriage rate and the birth rate can be detected slightly before the first edition of the *Essay* made its appearance, would be that Malthus was foretelling an inevitable state of affairs; namely, that as the demand for population was supplied chiefly by a rapidly falling death rate—which was a much more startling movement than anything which happened to the birth rate—the rate of increase would automatically stop of itself in some way, in this case by a fall in the marriage rate and the birth rate, followed at an interval by a fall in the fertility of marriage.

The actual figures are an interesting commentary on these views and on the effect which these theories and propositions may have had on practice. But a comparison of them with the much more startling fall in the death rate turns one's attention to the most important cause in the growth of the population and suggests that Malthus had been emphasising the wrong side of the question.

The Malthusian controversy and the neo-Malthusianism which arose out of it have laid the emphasis on the marriage and the birth rates, and it is this emphasis which has given the tone to the discussions of population ever since. In endeavouring to account for the increase of the population the chief attention has been paid to the rise in the birth and marriage rates, and any desire or effort to check the increase has instinctively turned to these two, on the assumption that it is their level that is chiefly responsible for the increase and that to lower their level will check the rate of increase—which of course is bound to be perfectly true, though it does not follow that it is the crux of the problem. The check that Malthus advocated, and still more the check that Place advocated, show how true it is that their attention was directed mainly to problems of the birth and the marriage rate; their effort being to ensure that the rate of increase should be checked by fewer children being born.

To be fair to Malthus it is necessary to say, that, although he did strongly emphasise the birth and marriage side of the population problem, he was conscious that there was another and important side to it. He did acknowledge the importance of a declining death rate. After discussing "a very marked improvement in the condition of the lower classes of people in France," he goes on to say that "it is next to a physical impossibility that such a relief from the pressure of distress should take place without a diminution in the rate of mortality; and if the diminution in the rate of mortality has not been accompanied by a rapid increase of population, it must necessarily have been accompanied by a smaller proportion of births."[1] From this it is clear that he recognised the decline of the death rate as an important if not a predominant factor in the increase of the population. Elsewhere he says that he hopes he has made it clear that the principal argument of his book is that more children ought not to be born than the country can support, so that the greatest number of those that are born may survive, from which he goes on, logically enough, to say that "in every point of view a decrease of mortality at all ages is what we ought to aim at."[2] This involves him definitely in the acceptance of the promotion of the movement which more than all others was responsible for the increase of the population. His answer would be that he did not object to the population increasing so long as it was a healthy increase; that whereas an increase by a rise in the birth rate might not be a healthy increase and would be

[1] *Essay*, 1817 ed. II. p. 39. [2] *Essay*, 7th ed. p. 472; see also p. 488.

followed by a high rate of mortality, an increase as a result of a declining death rate would be a healthy increase. Elsewhere he says that "the present diminution in the proportion of marriages is partly a cause and partly a consequence of the diminished mortality observed of late years."[1] In so far as this is true Malthus had succeeded in turning an unhealthy increase into a healthy increase, according to his ideas, and had again emphasised the importance in the problem of a declining death rate. The context of the last quotation makes it clear that Malthus, who knew from the Census that the population of England was increasing, recognised that the increase was largely due to a decline in the rate of mortality[2].

Although in such ways Malthus did lay stress on the importance of the decline in the death rate, it is still true to say that in general estimation his contribution has laid the emphasis on the side of births and marriages more than on the side of deaths and has tended since his time to obscure the importance of the death rate. Had he realised to the full the importance of the death rate and the part it was playing, he would either have realised that there was not nearly the same necessity or justification for the *Essay*, or if he had still felt that it was his mission to advocate a check in the rate of increase, he might have been tempted to advocate measures which, instead of checking the birth and marriage rates, should check the decline in the death rate. The obvious impossibility of advocating such measures is probably one reason why it was not done. In any case, however, it is a matter of degree, for even if the chief part in an increase is being played by a declining death rate, the final increase can be checked and swamped if the decline in the birth rate is carried far enough.

One reason possibly why Malthus and others at that time laid so much stress on the birth rate is that, in the absence of full

---

[1] *Ibid.* p. 195.

[2] *Ibid.* p. 195: "In the earlier part of the last century, Dr Short estimated this proportion at about 1 to 115 (the marriage rate). It is probable that this calculation was then correct; and the present diminution in the proportion of marriages, notwithstanding an increase of population more rapid than formerly, owing to a more rapid progress of commerce and agriculture, is partly a cause and partly a consequence of the diminished mortality observed of late years."

statistical information, one result of a declining death rate may appear to observers to be due to a rising birth rate. If in the early nineteenth century there suddenly appeared to be a great many more children playing about the streets and the fields, it may have been due to two causes, a rising birth rate or a declining juvenile rate of mortality. Either of these causes would lead to more children being seen about, and although the same number of children may have been born in earlier times, many more of them would have to be sought for in poor churchyards and would not contribute to the number of those seen like their more fortunate successors.

This discussion of the theories in relation to the figures seems to show three things:

First, that Malthus is open to the charge of having emphasised the wrong side of the problem.

Secondly, on the side he did emphasise, that the fall in the marriage and birth rates after the time at which he began to write may have been partially due to his views, though the fact that the drop is visible slightly before he published his first edition may incline one to the belief that he was merely giving forcible expression to an inevitable movement.

Thirdly, that the drop in fertility after 1815 may reflect the results of Place's extension of orthodox Malthusian principles and the introduction of more direct checks than Malthus himself had contemplated.

CHAPTER V

Factors affecting the Birth and Marriage Rates: Conditions of Employment

THE general use of child labour in this period has been quoted as a great cause of the increase in the population. The fact that the birth rate was steadily rising until such time as the additional supply would be forthcoming as a result of a falling death rate, increases the possible importance of this question which must be examined.

The theory is that the early employment that could be secured for children, and the large part they played in the new industrial scheme, rendered them a profitable investment to the adult workers even if they were not an absolute necessity. The 1821 Census accepted the theory that marriage was encouraged by the early age at which children could be employed in factories and the consequently small cost they entailed on their parents[1].

This tendency to an increasing population is illustrated from the history of the mining industry. The condition of the mines did not attract the same attention as that of the factories. It was not until 1842 that an extensive inquiry was made into the condition of juvenile labour in the mines, and then the story was worse than any that had been told about the factories. The fact that the mines had been outside the restricting regulations that had followed the inquiries into the factory conditions meant that in many cases children, when they were debarred from working in the factories, were sent to work in the mines, and until inquiries were instituted the mines were sinning unseen[2].

[1] Prelim. Obs. 1821, p. xxx.
[2] *Reports*, 1840, XXIV. p. 686. In the case of children excluded from factories, "their parents first endeavour to get employment for them in other factories, or in collieries." *Ibid.* p. 687: "While in the north of England, I took some pains to inquire into the fact which I had heard asserted in several quarters, that one effect of the factory regulation bill had been to send many of the children formerly employed in factories to work in coal pits. I found the statement correct, but to what extent I have of course no means of judging."

The 1842 Report reveals a state of things in which the children were sent to work earlier than in the factories. Except in North Staffordshire, where the potteries gave employment to many of the children, and in Warwickshire, where the coal was very hard and came out in masses which they were unable to handle, the ages at which the children began to work in the pits are given pretty generally at five, six and seven[1].

If the theory be true that it was the profit which could be derived from the employment of children in industry that was responsible for a large part of the increase, then this must have been particularly operative in the mining population; for if in this part of the population the children were employed earlier and with less regulation than in other sections of the industrial population, the profit to be derived from children would appear as a more immediate prospect than in industries where there was more regulation. The Report bears witness to the fact that in certain cases at any rate it was the action of the parents which thrust the children into the mines at very early ages; if this was general, it may strengthen the view that it was the economic value of children which caused a part of the increase in the population. The blame may not have rested with the parents; it may have been their economic necessities which made the earnings of the children essential to them; the important fact, however, is that, if for any reason they had realised the economic value of the children and were prepared to act upon it, this would have a great influence in the increase of the population. After stating that one of the reasons why the children are employed so young is that the parents say that they themselves were employed at an equally early age, the Report goes on to say that in some districts it was the practice at that time to take children into the coal mines at earlier ages than at any former period[2]. It is by no means clear that the wages which the miners earned rendered them so dependent on the earnings of their children as workers in other less remunerative industries.

---

[1] *Reports*, 1842, xv. p. 48, N. Staffs, p. 55, Warwickshire, p. 46, S. Staffs, common at seven; p. 49, Salop, as early as six; p. 59, Derbyshire, at five and between five and six; p. 63, West Riding, not uncommon at five and very common at six; p. 85, Durham, sometimes at five and by no means uncommon at six.   [2] *Reports*, 1842, xv. p. 118.

This subject of the economic gain to be derived from children is of wider application than if it applied merely to the mining industry. The early age at which children could be of use to the family by their earnings, and the necessity of those wages to the family, may have meant that on that ground there was some conscious effort and intention on the part of the parents to see that they had children to fulfil that function. It would be very difficult to prove this, as the matter resolves itself into a question of motive which would have been very hard to gauge satisfactorily even at the time. The feeling that in this there was conscious intention may be strengthened by the evidence that it was the parents, as much as, if not more than, the manufacturers, who were responsible for the early age at which the children were set to work. In the 1816 Report on children in factories, statements to this effect are made from many parts of the country, from Glasgow, Lancashire, Cheshire, Yorkshire, Somerset and Warwickshire[1]. In 1833 the same story is told. It was stated that the certificates of the ages of the children were forged in order that they could be employed earlier than was legal[2].

Ure, writing in 1833, emphasises the value of children's labour to the family, for in the manufacturing districts, he says, the demand for juvenile labour is so great as to render a large family not a burden but a source of comfort and independence to poor people[3]. It is also said that to exclude from factories everybody under twelve would inflict great hardships as it would compel the mother to work as well as the husband[4]. It is arguable, even rejecting the theory that the economic value of children was largely responsible for the increase in the population—a theory which is scarcely tenable—that this measure, instead of causing the mother to work harder, might have caused a fall in the birth rate.

[1] *Reports*, 1816, III. pp. 5, 53, 75, 76, 80. P. 119, Skipton; if there was a restriction on the employment of children before they were ten "the parent would be injured thereby because many children under ten years aid the sustaining of the family by their wages." Also pp. 123, 257.
[2] *Reports*, 1833, XX. pp. 69, 761, 815, 863, 874, 884.
[3] Ure, *Philosophy of Manufactures*, p. 357.
[4] *Reports*, 1833, XX. p. 783.

It has sometimes been assumed that this economic advantage of children was one of the chief stimuli to the growth of the population, for instance in the *Town Labourer* we find:

> But a more powerful and a more general stimulus to population (than the Poor Laws) was provided by the new industrial system, for that system made a money wage earned by women and children the basis of the workman's economic life. In respect of its enduring consequences this was the most important fact about the new civilisation[1].

We have seen that there is a good deal of evidence to the effect that it was to the parents' interest to send the children into the factories early, and that they depended to a considerable degree on the children's earnings; this may create a presumption that such a state of affairs would act as a direct stimulus to population, but it does not amount to a proof. The work mentioned above goes on to quote a speech of Sir Robert Peel, the elder, in 1806, to the effect that the new cotton industry had promoted comfort and therefore early marriages and a rising birth rate, and then replies that, as our fuller knowledge tells us, it is a decline in the standard of life that has the effect of increasing the population. It should be remembered that at this time the birth rate was falling, and before implying that an increase in the population is a sign of a declining standard of life, it should be remembered that the increase which was taking place at that time was due to the decline of the death rate more than to the rise of the birth rate, and that at the time when Sir Robert Peel made the statement referred to, the death rate was in the middle of its remarkable fall.

Although the figures of the birth rate in the first thirty years of the nineteenth century, particularly in the new manufacturing towns and districts, are liable to be defective, a rate, based on the baptism figures corrected by the addition of 15 per cent. as the figures for the whole country were corrected, has been worked out in four counties, Lancashire, the West Riding, Durham and Monmouth, counties which figure very high in the rate of increase in the first decades of the century. On these

---

[1] Hammond, *Town Labourer*, p. 13.

figures it is by no means clear that the birth rate in the four counties that have been taken was very markedly higher than in the country at large or that these counties show any very clear rise in the birth rate during this period[1]. These figures are, however, less likely to be accurate than the general averages for the whole country, owing to the defectiveness of the registers; some part of the increase which appears as the result of immigration should actually be put down to a rising birth rate.

The feeling that the new industries would provide employment for the children at an early age and enable them possibly to help the family exchequer would tend, undoubtedly, to make parents contemplate a large family with equanimity and may have acted as a sort of encouragement to population without the more definite incentive implied in the theory that it was the value of the children's work which led to the increase of the population. The same result—large families—is to be attained no less by a fall in the death rate, which at this time was taking place, than by a rise in the birth rate, which was not taking place in the country as a whole nor appreciably in these industrial counties.

There are also other reasons to account for this increase in the manufacturing populations without relying on the theory of the economic gain of children. There were various reasons making for the lowering of the age of marriage, and in 1833 in the manufacturing districts this is shown to be very low indeed. In a general statement in the Factory Report of that year it is said that the operatives marry "generally early, earlier than other classes," and the proposal to exclude from factories all under eighteen was objected to as "many of the operatives are married before they are eighteen years of age "[2]; whereas the 1841 Census Report stated that the age of marriage had again risen[3].

[1] County birth rates per 1000 of the population (five-year averages):

	1801	1811	1821	1831
Lancashire	38·5	35·7	34·6	32·7
West Riding	34·6	31·5	35·2	35·7
Durham	33·3	34·8	36·2	34·7
Monmouth	24·3	24·0	23·4	19·2
England and Wales	32·1	33·7	33·6	32·3

[2] *Reports*, 1833, xx. pp. 799, 857.
[3] Preface to 1841 Census, p. 13.

This habit of early marriage, combined also with the fact that increased medical skill had reduced infantile mortality to a considerable degree, is sufficient to account for the increase of the population without our having to fall back on the theory of the direct stimulus given by the economic value of children. There is, however, evidence that the parents derived advantage from the earnings of the children when they were quite young, and also evidence that somehow money for the children had in many cases to be raised. Under the old Poor Law the children are represented as being allowed to run wild, the allowance providing the family with a certain amount of money in respect of the children[1]; when this was stopped under the new Poor Law the suggestion is made that the children had now to work harder, and make a contribution to the family exchequer as there was no longer the allowance to assist, but this is primarily a country phenomenon[2].

The comparison of the natural with the actual increase of the population of the various counties shows that there were many primarily agricultural counties which were not able to support their natural increase; even if inclosure was increasing the amount of employment and tending to increase the population, there were other causes at work which were increasing the population of those counties beyond the limit of safety. One of these causes was the change that had been introduced into the social organisation of the agricultural population by the inclosure movement and the growth of larger farms and estates. The inclosure movement in agriculture, like the contemporaneous movements in industry, served to break down the restrictions on early marriage which had existed. When agriculture was mainly concerned with supplying the wants of an immediate neighbourhood, chiefly agricultural or at any rate not subject to the increasing and fluctuating demand of growing industrial

---

[1] *Reports*, 1834, XXVII. p. 96.

[2] Hasbach, p. 225. *Reports*, 1843, XII. p. 219: "Their children were not then obliged as now to work for their subsistence. Their time was at their own disposal." *Ibid.* p. 217: "The present state of the labour market, combined with the effect of the new Poor Law, in throwing the labouring classes mainly on their own resources, almost compels the parents to take their children from school as soon as they can earn anything in the fields."

areas in the neighbourhood and not enabled by improved transport to move its produce any great distance, so long there was little incentive for the population to increase and little chance of more than the comparatively fixed number of inhabitants finding work. In such a community there was no call for building, the village did not increase in size, each man would hope to live where his father had lived and to cultivate the lands which his father had held, and the less subdivision there was the better for him. All through the period with which we are dealing there runs the cry that the lack of cottages was one of the things which checked marriages. Arthur Young, writing in 1771, says that the efforts of landowners and tenants to keep the poor rates low had given rise to an "open war against cottages."[1] In 1804 the lack of cottages was said to be checking the population[2]. At the time that the agitation to promote emigration was on foot it was stated that it was no use advocating any such measure unless it were accompanied by a destruction of cottages, for so long as the cottages were there the people would not be long in following[3]. With the perversion of the Poor Law, cottages became a profitable speculation in those parishes in which rent was paid out of the poor rates, but Malthus considered that the only reason why the country had endured the Poor Laws so long as it had was that the difficulty of getting cottages had prevented the increase which he was convinced the Poor Laws tended to cause[4]. Even in the 1834 Poor Law Report we find the confession that "marriages are regulated more by cottage room than by any administration of the Poor Laws."[5] Thus it is obvious that it was felt that throughout the period cottage room was a very important consideration in the increase of the population.

In the old days land had been cultivated by the family or, where that had not been the case, the necessary labourers had lived in the farmhouses almost as members of the family. Under the agricultural changes of the period this system decayed and the labourers ceased to live in the farmhouse; they were put

---

[1] Young, *Farmers' Letters*, p. 302.　　[2] *Annals*, 1804, XLI. p. 227.
[3] *Reports*, 1826–7, V. p. 234.　　[4] *Reports*, 1826–7, V. Q. 3361.
[5] *Reports*, 1834, XXIX. Appendix A, Part II. p. 329.

in cottages and the modern agricultural labourer developed. To the labourer living in a cottage marriage became natural, if not almost a necessity, and as an agricultural labourer could earn as good wages when he was young as when he was a good deal older there was no obstacle to his marriage.

The farmers were becoming bigger men, they farmed more land and wanted more labourers. We are told in 1785 that "there is a very great share of indolence and luxury of late introduced among the farmers' wives and daughters."[1] They were getting grand, and would not care for the old plan whereby they were responsible for the board and lodging of the labourers on the farm, and in 1833 this is given as the reason why farmers of a certain rank had got rid of as many of their indoor servants as they could and had recourse to labourers[2]. The consolidation of farms not only made the farmers bigger men and their wives less inclined to look after the indoor labourers, but provided for the accommodation of outdoor labourers[3]. Little farms were purchased by opulent farmers, who took the land into their own occupation, and converted the houses into cottages. Where farms were increased in size or waste lands taken in, with the result that extra cultivation was required, we find recommendations that cottages should be built "so that the number of married labourers should be increased rather than that of household servants"—the whole plan being directed to secure an increasing population[4].

That this system of outdoor labourers was increasing there is abundant evidence. There are certain general references to what is happening. The 1821 Census Report, in a discussion of the causes of the increase of the population, said that the

---

[1] *Political Enquiry*, 1785, p. 75,

[2] *Reports*, 1833, v. Q. 6984 et seq.

[3] *Annals*, vol. XXXVI. 1801, p. 114: "In the parish where I am resident three small farmhouses have been each divided into three tenements. If every family be multiplied by five, forty-five souls will now be found to occupy the dwellings which were before inhabited by fifteen. Here is an increase of thirty, which will proportionately increase the number of births in the register." See also Davies, *Case of the Labourers*, p. 35: "For the engrossing farmer, occupying sometimes half a dozen farms, converts the farmhouses into dwellings for the poor."

[4] Plymley's *Shropshire*, 1803, p. 121.

system of farmhouse labourers had decayed, with the result that "the dismissed labourer could not but become a cottager, and in his new situation could scarcely fail to become a married man."[1]

Throughout the Reports about this time there are various statements to the same effect, and for different parts of the country. In Suffolk in the 1824 Report on the Poor Laws the "system of not retaining servants in farmers' houses, which throws young men out of a comfortable home," is made to share with the allowance system the blame for early marriages, for the men "are induced to marry; whereas on the old system of retaining them in the farmers' houses, they did not marry until they were perhaps near thirty years of age, and until they had got a little money and a few goods about them."[2] In the same Report one of the reasons given for the increase of rents in Surrey was "fewer servants being kept in the farmhouses."[3] The third Report on Emigration emphasised the inducement to early marriages created by the change in the system[4]. The element of improvidence in these marriages formed a subject of comment in the Lords Report on the Poor Laws in 1831[5]. Again in 1834 this system was made to share with the allowance system the blame for early marriages; and this is remarkable testimony, for the writers of the 1834 Report were not inclined to let any other factor than the administration of the Poor Laws

---

[1] Prelim. Obs. 1821, p. xxv.

[2] *Reports*, 1824, VI. p. 460. [3] *Ibid.* p. 447.

[4] *Reports*, 1826–7, V. Q. 3882: "There is another change that has taken place, and that has affected very much the character of our labouring population; the labourers no longer live in farmhouses, as they used to do, when they were better fed and had more comforts than they get now in a cottage, in consequence there was not the same inducement to early marriages; because if a man up to the age of twenty-five or thirty had been accustomed to live in a better way of life, he would consider twice before he married and went to live in a wretched cottage upon potatoes and tea."

[5] *Reports*, 1831, VIII. p. 76: "Upon the subject of improvident marriages, I would venture to state that probably much of the evil would be remedied if the farmers would return to the method that prevailed some years ago, of keeping their unmarried servants as servants in the house, boarding them and lodging them and giving them pecuniary wages." *Ibid.* p. 206: "I think that system which prevailed in former times is greatly conducive to the comfort of the labourers, and tends to prevent early and improvident marriages."

be blamed for the evils of which they complained[1]. In 1831 we are told that the practice of having house servants in Derbyshire to work the farms was more general than in other parts of the country[2], and that in Sussex the practice of having the labourers in the farmhouses had actually increased in the previous ten or twelve years[3]. In 1833 in Cumberland and Westmorland the system appeared to be comparatively prevalent though it was decaying even there, for it was now the custom for "farmers of a certain rank to get rid of as many of their domestic servants as they can and have recourse to labourers."[4] The system is thus obviously connected with the consolidation of farms, the growth of bigger men in the farming world and the larger ideas which these men held of their own importance and position; for forty years earlier we are told that "there were probably few counties, in which property in land was divided into such small parcels as in Cumberland, and those properties so universally occupied by the owners."[5] On the other hand, at that earlier date in another northern county the system was already in decay. It was said of Northumberland in 1794 that generally throughout the county and especially on the large farms very few servants were kept in the house and that "ploughmen, carters, barnmen and shepherds each had a house of their own and were generally married."[6] In Shropshire "waggoners and ploughmen and cowmen or whatever they may be" are still kept in the farmhouse, and the system is "much about the same" as it was twenty years earlier[7]. In Somerset, on the other hand, the practice had "diminished within these twenty years."[8] In Wiltshire the system of having labourers living in

---

[1] *Reports*, 1834, XXVIII. Appendix A, Part I. 24: "'I married to increase my income' was the general answer which I everywhere received. But I will not attribute the increase of early marriages to this alone. The system, which except in the remote parts of the kingdom has fallen into disuse, of lodging and boarding the labourers by the farmer, must bear its share in the promotion of early marriages. None but a day labourer can appreciate the comfort of having his food prepared for him and his cottage cheered by a companion after a hard day's work."

[2] *Reports*, 1831, VIII. p. 206.   [3] *Ibid.* p. 38.

[4] *Reports*, 1833, v. Q. 6984.

[5] Bailey and Culley, *Cumberland*, 1794, p. 11.

[6] Bailey and Culley, *Agriculture of Northumberland*, 1794, p. 53.

[7] *Reports*, 1833, v. Qs. 397, 580.   [8] *Ibid.* Q. 9437.

the farmhouses "has gone very much out of practice,"[1] though it is said that the system "has not ceased altogether," and carters and shepherds were mentioned as still being kept in the houses. Two years later we are told that in the East Riding the class of farmers that used to keep their farm servants in their own houses was nearly extinct. The young men went to the manufacturing districts or to America and the married men were chiefly employed as day labourers[2]. No provision appears to have been made for the young agricultural labourer who was not married, and the young man who went to the manufacturing town was likely to marry there. In Lincolnshire there were not many instances where the labourers lived in the farmhouses, at any rate it was not a general rule[3].

It is evident that the decay of the system of keeping farm hands in the farmhouses was looked upon as a general agricultural phenomenon and was felt to lead to early marriage. As the farms grew larger more labourers would be required, and to keep them in the farmhouse would be a much more serious undertaking, whilst the farmers were becoming people of greater consequence and less inclined to be troubled with such arrangements; the movement to do away with this system was further encouraged by the circumstance that in many cases the very consolidation of farms secured suitable accommodation for the labourers in the farmhouses which were no longer used by the farmers themselves. The labourer, when he was deprived of the additional comfort and convenience of being looked after in the farmhouse, had a strong inducement to marry, and it may well be that the change in the social organisation of the country population which was caused by the decay of this old system was one of the chief factors which made for an increase of the population among the inhabitants of the rural parts of the country. If this was the case it must have been very intimately bound up with the growth of a definitely wage-earning class, whose greatest earning age came fairly soon after the period of earning was reached, and in which there was no great motive to delay marriage.

[1] *Reports*, 1833, v. Q. 1244.   [2] *Reports*, 1836, VIII. Q. 5434.
[3] *Ibid.* Q. 5855.

In industry the question of the increased prevalence of marriage is bound up with changes in the conditions of industry which broke down certain restrictions on marriage which had existed in the old organisation of industry, and with the rise of new industries which in their nature did not admit of or did not require those restrictions. The important question which requires examination in this connection is that of apprenticeship.

Apprenticeship in its fully grown Elizabethan form required that those learning any trade then practised in England should serve an apprenticeship for seven years or until he was twenty-four years of age, with the possible exception of agriculture in which it was sufficient that he should attain the age of twenty-one if the parties had been unable to agree on twenty-four. It is clear that these provisions were looked upon quite as much as a check on the exuberance of youth as essential for the technical education of the country[1]. In London this was clearly the case about the time of the Elizabethan statute, and until the end of the apprenticeship regulations the same feeling continues as is shown by the form of indenture which was used in later times, and which was procurable at stationers and ready for the names to be filled in, of which the following is an example:

During all which term the said apprentice his said Master well and faithfully shall serve...fornication and adultery shall not commit....At dice, cards, tables or bowls or other unlawful games he shall not play....Taverns or Alehouses shall not haunt or frequent. ...Matrimony with any woman within the said term he shall not contract[2].

The original intentions of the Elizabethan Act were soon whittled down in certain cases. Unskilled trades were held by the Courts not to require apprenticeship, and we find that upholsterers were looked upon as unskilled[3]; if the line drawn was as difficult to justify as in their case many other trades may have been exempted. On the other hand, an amendment was moved to a bill in 1785 dealing with hawkers and pedlars "for

[1] E. Arber, *Transcript of the Stationers Company's Papers*, XLI. 1556. Cunningham, II. p. 30.
[2] This particular extract is from the apprentice indenture of William Hey, the surgeon, in 1751, and was for seven years, which as a matter of fact made him twenty-one when it ended.
[3] *Engl. Econ. Hist. Select Documents*, Bland and Tawney, p. 356.

enabling Hawkers and Pedlars to set up trades in Cities and Corporate towns without having served an apprenticeship," and this amendment was lost[1]—the line distinguishing skilled from unskilled trades seems to have been arbitrary. The Courts similarly restricted apprenticeship to trades which were in existence when the statute was passed, which for our purpose is an important reservation. The results were somewhat ridiculous at times; Eden quotes a case of the wheelwrights and coach-makers[2], in which coach-making was looked upon as a trade which was newer than the Act and therefore not subject either to its limitations or to its protection, whereas the craft of a wheelwright was an ancient calling and protected by the Act, with the result that a coach-maker could not make his wheels, whereas a wheelwright might with impunity try his luck at making a coach. In the Apprenticeship Report in 1812 coach-making is among the trades which are declared to be outside the protection of the Act for this reason, and in which apprenticeship will not be enforced[3]. Other trades came in the same category, among them such comparatively unimportant callings as those of "Morocco and Spanish leather finisher," "journeyman paper-stainer," "journeyman tobacco pipe maker."[4] Makers of patent locks were exempt from the operation of the Act "as there were no patents in the reign of Elizabeth,"[5] and so also for the same reason were engineer smiths[6]. In another case some men were accused and convicted of not having served seven years, but they were principally employed "in turning materials for the making of chairs," and it was held that this was part of the business of a chair-maker and therefore not within the purview of the statute of Elizabeth. An attorney who had had considerable experience of the working of the statute said that such great difficulties were thrown in the way of solicitors in prosecuting upon that statute that he was strongly of opinion that no further actions would be brought[7].

[1] J.H.C. 1785, XL. p. 1139.
[2] Eden, I. p. 433.
[3] Reports, 1812–13, IV. p. 51.
[4] Ibid. pp. 19, 22, 43.
[5] Ibid. p. 51.
[6] Ibid. p. 52.
[7] Ibid. p. 52.

In ways like these the fully developed system of apprentice-ship as contemplated by the statute of Elizabeth was reduced by the action of the Courts.

Legal apprenticeship was, moreover, being modified in the period by legislative interference and by the natural pro-cesses of decay. In 1767 Jonas Hanway, whose concern for the welfare of the young people of London is in no doubt, con-demned a system whereby people were "compelled to drag on a servitude till 24, in a business wherein they were adepts at 17; preventing marriage, discouraging industry and laying the foundation of perpetual discord between master and 'prentice."[1]

The attitude was changing; in the same year in which Han-way wrote, a Parliamentary Committee reported in very much the same strain; they were afraid of depopulation and they desired marriage, therefore they attacked the apprenticeship regulations, and in 1778 an Act was passed terminating the apprenticeship of parish children at the age of twenty-one[2].

The pamphlet *Britannia Languens* of 1680 speaks as though the apprenticeship regulations were in fairly full force, and objects to them on the grounds that in most trades it is un-necessary to subject people to such a long period of drudgery before they can reap any benefit from their labour and that parents are putting children "to other more easy and ready employments."[3] Tucker, writing in 1757, also speaks as if the apprenticeship system were in full force, though he is con-cerned to prove that it is prejudicial to trade and manufacture[4].

From quite early in the eighteenth century it was necessary in the case of textile trades to affirm the apprentice regulations, but the effect of this steadily diminished as the century went on. In 1705 Salisbury issued a very comprehensive attempt to enforce the seven years' apprenticeship in all branches of trade and industry within the town[5].

[1] Hanway's *Letters* (1767), I. p. 132.
[2] 18 Geo. III, c. 47.   [3] *Brit. Languens*, p. 154.
[4] Tucker, 1757, *Instructions to travellers*, p. 51.
[5] *Hist. MSS. Com.* Cd. 3218, p. 252, Town Council of Salisbury, 1705–6: "For remedy thereof it is ordained that no person whatsoever not being free of the said city having served as an apprentice within the said city by the space of seven years" shall exercise or "use any art, trade or mystery what-soever" within the said city.

In the very early years of the eighteenth century there are complaints from various parts of England that the trade is being damaged by the fact that regular apprenticeships are not being served[1]. Towards the end of the century the decay in the apprenticeship system was hastened; we are told that from 1700 to 1750 efforts were made to keep the system going in Leeds, but that after 1750 the attempt was given up[2]. Towards the end of the century the Cloth Halls made a modification in the custom by reducing the length of the apprenticeship to five years[3]. At the end of the century the Reports give the impression that the system was in a very decayed condition. In the Report of 1802 there is evidence of decay from the west of England; from Gloucestershire come the statements that "a very great proportion of the weavers at present employed have not been apprenticed," and one weaver states that he "never recollects the statute relative to apprentices being enforced."[4] From Wiltshire the statement comes that the clothiers "never heard of the statute relating to apprentices being enforced in Gloucestershire until lately," and from Chippenham that two-thirds of the weavers were unapprenticed, that dyers and cloth workers were unapprenticed, and that the speaker had "never heard when the statute respecting apprentices was enforced."[5] From Somerset there comes the statement that it is only "within these few months" that the law relating to apprentices has been enforced[6]. A man who had been employed in the trade in Bradford for thirty years said that he had never served an apprenticeship himself and that very few of the master manufacturers in general had been legally apprenticed[7]. In Halifax at the same time the apprentice statute was considered to be obsolete, and a seven years' apprenticeship to be quite unnecessary—"a youth from sixteen to eighteen years would learn the art of weaving in twelve months"—not one in ten of the

---

[1] *J.H.C.* 1700, XIII. p. 376, Crediton; 1702, XIV. p. 67, Taunton; 1740, XXV. p. 664, Stroudwater, and places adjacent in the county of Gloucester; p. 665, Wootton Underedge; p. 686, Burford, Witney and other places adjacent in the county of Oxford.

[2] Heaton, *Yorks woollen and worsted industries*, pp. 309–310.

[3] *Reports*, 1806, III. p. 13.   [4] *Reports*, 1802–3, V. p. 245.

[5] *Reports*, 1802–3, V. p. 249.   [6] *Ibid.* p. 249.

[7] *Ibid.* p. 306.

workmen employed in the woollen manufacture had served a regular apprenticeship, many had not been apprenticed at all, and others only for three, four and five years[1]. The Report of 1806 tells the same story; apprenticeships were not so common as they used to be, and nineteen out of twenty people had not served regular apprenticeship as there was no difficulty in teaching them the business, and the apprenticeship regulations had never even been heard of. It should, however, be remembered that when the regulations came to be repealed there was a great deal of petitioning in favour of the old system[2].

In these trades then it is pretty clear that the apprentice system was in an advanced state of decay by the last quarter of the eighteenth century. The introduction of machinery had something to do with it, for with machinery there was not the need for technical education that had existed before. The growth of a more capitalist organisation was probably the greatest cause of the decay; as in the case of the farmers, the manufacturers became bigger men and were less likely to take apprentices into their houses[3]. The Committee of 1806 stated that apprenticeship was obviously more suited to the domestic than to the factory system and they were therefore not surprised to find that it had maintained its ground more generally in the north than in the west of England; while the domestic clothiers in the north frankly allowed that they wished to retain the law because it embarrassed the carrying on of the factory system and might thereby counteract its growth and even in the north apprenticeship had very largely decayed[4]. Not only did the factory organisation make for the decay of the apprentice system, but the actual power of capital on which the factory system was based tended in the same direction. It was said in 1804 that the penalties imposed to enforce the statute were so very small that they could not be felt by the wealthy manufacturers should they

---

[1] *Reports*, 1802–3, V. p. 305.
[2] *Reports*, 1806, III. pp. 71, 184, 197.
[3] *J.H.C.* 1803, LIII. p. 334. Leave to bring in a bill to repeal App. regs. Petitioners against, pp. 351, 354, 382, 452, 549, but p. 368, petition from Yorks in favour as the system "hath become obsolete, and is inapplicable to the present state of the manufacture."
[4] *Reports*, 1806, III. p. 13.

be inclined to transgress the law[1]. The growth of the worsted trade in Yorkshire tended to destroy the system, partly because it was organised on capitalist lines from its earliest days, but also because it was always run on specialised lines and the amount of training required to attain proficiency in one branch was very little, which facts probably account for the small part played in the cotton trade by the apprentice system. In other trades the system seems to have been maintained more successfully[2]—among the bakers and butchers, for instance, in the last quarter of the eighteenth century. In the early part of the nineteenth century apprenticeship seems to have been most successfully upheld in occupations which required special skill; it was general, for instance, in the potteries, where we are told in 1816 that children are usually taken at thirteen or fourteen, though even in these cases the apprenticeship ends at about twenty-one[3]. In 1804 the same was the case among the calico printers[4], and in 1817 the watchmakers in London seemed to adhere to the system in its original form; theirs was a highly skilled trade which the early mechanical inventions would not be very likely to affect or make easier to learn, but even in this case an apprenticeship from fourteen to twenty-one is recommended, which, however, was after the Apprenticeship Act had been repealed[5].

The question whether the apprentice lived with his master or elsewhere is important for our purpose as our chief concern is with the system as a means of discipline. Apprenticeship might go on under the old statute, but the portion of the contract about living with the master and refraining from matrimony and so on might be neglected. It is probable that this part of the system decayed earlier than the training part. In 1806 it was said by a witness, speaking of town conditions of trade in the West Riding, that he did not consider that apprenticeship

[1] Reports, 1804, v. p. 325.
[2] J.H.C. 1779, xxxvii. pp. 187, 214, 258, 320, 346. P. 286, petition from Bristol against the proposal to allow bakers and butchers to dispense with apprenticeship, "An innovation of the established law of the land, as in few or any cases whatever, trades are suffered to be carried on without the trader having first served a regular apprenticeship."
[3] Reports, 1816, iii. p. 61 (Evidence of Josiah Wedgwood).
[4] Reports, 1804, v. p. 889.   [5] Reports, 1817, vi. pp. 11 and 52.

had any very favourable effects on morals, as the apprentices were not usually kept in the domestic clothiers' houses as in the villages[1]. In 1816 the state of the young workpeople in Birmingham was said to be bad, and this is attributed to there being "so many out-door apprentices; they are thus out of doors late at night and a great deal of mischief I conceive arises from this circumstance."[2] They were getting out of hand if nothing more. The Coventry watchmakers put down most of their distress to the system of outdoor apprenticeship, and it is in this Report that we get the most definite statement in favour of the indoor system and against the outdoor system. It is stated that it was a "very injurious system to have apprentices boarded out of doors; that they ought to be in the master's house for their morals to be watched over."[3] But the difficulty is further complicated by the fact that one man who stated that he had served an outdoor apprenticeship produced his apprentice indenture which contained the clause forbidding marriage in the same way as the indentures of the indoor apprentices used to do, so that it is not perfectly clear that even an outdoor apprentice was at liberty to marry, though presumably there would be less check on him if he desired so to do than there would be on an indoor apprentice[4]. The moral advantages of the apprentice system are urged in the case of agriculture in Reports in the early forties, though a good deal is urged on the other side as well[5].

On the whole, it is probably a fair summary to say that by the latter part of the eighteenth century the system of apprenticeship in most of the old-established industries was rapidly decaying, that the length of service had been shortened, the age of ending reduced and the disciplinary side of the system even further destroyed by the decay of the indoor apprentice system. Thus in these trades the legal restrictions on marriage were removed. There is evidence that this did lead to earlier marriages in the industrial districts. At any rate there is one piece of

---

[1] *Reports*, 1806, III. p. 172 (Cookson).
[2] *Reports*, 1816, III. p. 124.
[3] *Reports*, 1817, VI. p. 52; see also p. 91.
[4] *Ibid.* p. 78.
[5] *Reports*, 1843, XII. pp. 43, 46, 51, 54, 103, 110.

evidence that the end of the period of apprenticeship meant marriage, and it is probably typical of a good many others,

> But when my seven long years are out.
> Oh, then I'll marry Sally[1].

A pamphlet published at Darlington, quoted in the Extracts from the Poor Law Commission Report published in 1833, says that "the well behaved apprentice has a light heart and many sources of enjoyment; and if he be not so unwise as to marry immediately he is out of his time, these sources of enjoyment are greatly increased by more freedom and more money."[2] From this we may not unreasonably infer that wisdom was not always displayed and that marriage was apt to follow very rapidly on the end of the period of apprenticeship. In the same year there is some evidence from the habits of the parish apprentices in cotton mills, who, it is stated, were usually apprenticed from about ten to twenty-one years of age, and it must be remembered that in their case the age of ending had been cut down to twenty-one by legislation in 1778. When they pass away from the age of pupilage we are told that they almost always married, very often among themselves, and remained attached to the same factory as operatives[3].

There are two pieces of evidence from the Handloom Weavers Commission of 1840 which are worth quoting at length. The first is from the Report of H. S. Chapman on the West Riding:

The young weaver just out of his apprenticeship, is perhaps as well able to earn as he will be at any future period. Setting aside the domestic comforts incidental to the married state, his pecuniary condition is in the first instance improved by uniting himself with a woman capable of earning perhaps nearly as much as himself, and performing for him various offices involving an actual pecuniary saving. A married man with an income, the result of the earnings of himself and wife, of 20s., will enjoy more substantial comfort in every way than he alone would enjoy with an income of 15s. a week. This is alone an inducement to early marriage, an inducement which we shall hereafter see increased.

---

[1] *Sally in our Alley*, Henry Carey, d. 1743.
[2] *Extracts*, 1833, p. 171.
[3] *Reports*, 1833, VI. p. 680.

In obedience to this primary inducement, the weaver almost invariably marries soon after he is out of his apprenticeship[1].

If this evidence, which is from 1840, can be assumed to have represented a state of affairs that had been developing or that had been in operation for some time, it is of even greater value. The second piece of evidence is from the statement of the Mayor of Coventry, reviewing conditions forty years earlier:

The journeyman...did not generally marry very young, for he remembers there were many single journeymen, the young men did not think much of sotting themselves in a public house, but took much active exercise at bowls, skittles, etc....The young men of those days with their habits of activity did not make sexual attachments so early as they do now. The instances of a youth marrying before his time was out were very rare, and they seldom were out of their time until 21, sometimes not till later. There were no such things as children's marriages. The only one of his father's apprentices he remembers to have been married before he was out of his time was at the age of 23. The age of marriage has become much earlier with the increase of indoor habits[2].

Discounting the element of painting a rosy past, we gather from this that by about 1800 people were not ending their apprenticeships before the age of twenty-one, that there were only few instances of their marrying before they were out of their time, but that by 1840 the habit of early marriage had increased.

While the apprenticeship regulations were decaying and being swept away, and the habit of early marriage was growing in those trades in which apprenticeship had been a living force, new trades were growing up which, both because they were new and consequently were not included in the statute of Elizabeth, and because of the nature of the work, did not require apprenticeship. These trades sprang into existence in the same condition in which the older trades were when the apprenticeship regulations were decaying and the factory system was being established—the full earning power was reached by a man very shortly after he took up the trade.

Among these must be classed the heavy iron trades and mining.

---

[1] *Reports*, 1840, XXIII. p. 540.
[2] *Reports*, 1840, XXIV. p. 299.

The rapid development of the iron trade is the more remarkable from the precarious condition it occupied early in the century. Cunningham says that the history of the trade is almost entirely concerned with the struggle to overcome the difficulty that arose from the increasing scarcity of fuel[1]. Scrivenor, in his *History of the Iron Trade*, speaking of the early part of the eighteenth century, says that the iron trade seemed to be dwindling into insignificance and contempt owing to the destruction of tracts of woodland which had until then been dedicated to the supply of the blast furnaces[2]. There are numerous complaints in the Journals of the House of Commons that the condition of the trade is very serious. This decay is put down to various causes. In 1709 it is said that the encouragement to the exportation of unwrought steel and iron to the Plantations is damaging the trade[3]. In 1717 it is complained that the war in the Baltic has made direct importation of iron from Sweden impossible, that it has been necessary to secure it second-hand at great loss and it is suggested that the establishment of iron works should be encouraged in the Plantations[4]. This suggestion is attacked on the ground that, as most iron of English manufacture goes to the Plantations, it will do more harm than good to encourage the Plantations to produce their own[5]. In 1737 the subject is resumed. A petition of the manufacturers of iron at Birmingham and the neighbourhood states "that till of late their trade hath gradually increased and flourished in proportion to the American colonies; but is now in a declining condition," and that the continuance of the industry in this country was dependent on its suppression in the colonies[6]. Another petition of the same year says, "the quantity of British iron is already greatly decreased, and will soon come to nothing, unless something be speedily done in their favour."[7] A Committee was appointed and presented a considerable report in which it was agreed that the production of bar iron in Great Britain had decreased, and suggested the restriction of the works in the Plantations. A bill on these lines was ordered but was not brought in[8].

[1] Cunningham, II. p. 523.   [2] Scrivenor, p. 56.
[3] *J.H.C.* 1709, XVI. p. 179.   [4] *J.H.C.* 1717, XVIII. p. 691.
[5] *Ibid.* p. 733.   [6] *J.H.C.* 1737, XXIII. p. 15.
[7] *Ibid.* p. 21.   [8] *Ibid.* pp. 109, 157, 172.

The year 1760 is marked by Cunningham as the turning point[1]. In that year Roebuck founded the Carron works, and with the assistance of Smeaton erected furnaces to use coal[2]. Shortly after that Watt took out his patents, and first of all was in partnership with Roebuck and later (in 1774) with Matthew Bolton at Soho. In 1783 further advances were made by Gort of Gosport, and by the end of the century the rate of increase in the industry was becoming remarkable[3]. The production of pig iron increased at an immense rate, and at the beginning of the nineteenth century Scrivenor says it was computed that some half-million people were engaged in its manufacture[4]. The revival of the iron trade in Monmouthshire was dated from the introduction of coal smelting about 1760. In 1801 it was stated that 600 tons of pig iron were being produced weekly in that county whereas fifteen years before only 60 tons had been produced, and 300 tons of bar iron whereas previously there had been none[5]. Another means of gauging this increase is provided by a table of the amount of iron carried on the canals of Monmouthshire[6]. These trades were of a kind that did not require careful or prolonged training; their chief demand was for bodily strength and they created many side employments around the works that were entirely unskilled. The full earning power would be achieved very soon after manhood was reached, there was no inducement to celibacy and the trade was one that would be likely to lead to early marriages.

In connection with the growth of the iron trade which resulted from the discovery and use of coal in the working of iron,

---

[1] Cunningham, II. p. 524.   [2] Smiles, *Lives of Engineers*, II. p. 61.
[3] Scrivenor, p. 136. Amount of pig iron made in England, Wales and Scotland:

1740	17,350 tons	1825	581,367 tons
1788	68,300 ,,	1830	678,417 ,,
1796	125,179 ,,	1839	1,248,781 ,,
1806	258,206 ,,		

[4] Scrivenor, p. 104.
[5] Coxe, *Historical Tour in Monmouthshire*, 1801, p. 229.
[6] Scrivenor, p. 124: Iron carried on the Monmouthshire canals:

1802	1,901 tons	1820	45,462 tons
1805	22,431 ,,	1825	78,800 ,,
1810	34,070 ,,	1830	112,647 ,,
1815	46,207 ,,		

there was also a growth of the mining industries. Cunningham says that the degradation of the mining population was not in any way due to the introduction of machinery and therefore it was only indirectly due to the Industrial Revolution[1]; it was owing to the demand for the increased output of coal, combined with the fact that the mining industry was not controlled until later than the other industries, that the evils continued and grew.

The history of the mining industry illustrates two tendencies in the industrial conditions of the time that were making for the increase of the population.

The mining industry, for reasons which we have just noticed in connection with the iron trades, was one in which there was no great inducement to refrain from marriage, apart from any other causes that might exist to encourage marriage. In 1840 it is stated that the average wages of the miners were 24s. a week, garden-ground, cottage-rent and coal free[2]. It is emphasised elsewhere that these conditions of the industry were making for early marriages. Labourers engaged in the mining industries of the Tyne and the Wear earned from the age of eighteen between 20s. and 30s. a week as hewers, with the consequence that they became independent of their natural guardians at an early age and "assumed the most important office of manhood at the earliest age which nature or passion prompted."[3] The same Report lays down the theory that the trades in which the full earning power is soon gained have this effect, and illustrates it from the mining population, stating that a period of prosperity led to a rush of early marriages more than to the accumulation of funds for a rainy day[4]. It appears also that a considerable element of gambling came into the bargains by which the terms of employment were arranged. The earnings were subject to very violent fluctuations, the miner spent his money as he liked and relied on credit or possibly on the Poor Laws in the bad seasons and this doubtless encouraged improvident marriages[5].

The conditions of work put the opportunities of marriage

---

[1] Cunningham, III. p. 803.   [2] *Reports*, 1840, XXIV. p. 688.
[3] *Reports*, 1834, XXVIII. p. 130.   [4] *Reports*, 1834, XXXVII. p. 125.
[5] Cunningham, III. p. 803, quoting *Georgical Essays*, by A. Hunter, 1803, II. p. 49, "On the situation of the mining poor," by Rev. T. Gisborne.

very closely within the reach of these people, and in 1798 it was said that at most of the mines there were a number of women who had been employed in various odd jobs since childhood, "a young mining labourer takes a hasty liking to one of these young women, and marries her without thinking about consequences."[1] The conditions under which the women worked in the mines may have had worse consequences than those indicated above. In the Mines Report of 1842, women and young girls are described as working underground in certain parts of the coal fields. In this respect Yorkshire and Lancashire appear to have been the worst offenders[2]. The definite accusations of immorality in this Report and in these localities are much more substantial than the very vague and general charges that are brought against the factory population. The condition of the underground work in the isolated galleries, where a man had a girl "hurrying" for him, afforded opportunities and temptations to immorality that are mentioned on many occasions in the Report. Much of the evidence is quite revolting and is perfectly accessible in the Report to which references are given[3]; clearly there is no doubt that much immorality went on and that illegitimacy was the result. It was the Poor Law policy in certain parts of the country to compel marriages when there were illegitimate children. This practice of compelling marriages, which might be commended on moral grounds, is protested against as a source of increase of the population, for it is said that it probably leads to the parish having to support not only one illegitimate child but sundry legitimate ones[4]; if this policy was adopted in the case of the

---

[1] *Reports* of S.B.C.P. I. p. 372.

[2] *Reports*, 1842, XV. p. 119: "In England...it is only in some of the colliery districts of Yorks and Lancs that female children of tender age and young and adult women are allowed to descend into the coal mines." *Ibid.* p. 148, S. Staffs, no female underground, same in N. Staffs, Salop, Warwick, Leicester, Derby, Oldham, Cumberland (all but one colliery), Durham, Northumberland, N. Wales, Forest of Dean (rare), S. Glos, N. Som.

[3] *Reports*, 1842, XV. Appendix, Part I. pp. 246, 251, 254, 261, 284.

[4] *Reports*, 1824, VI. pp. 434, 447; 1831, VIII. p. 63; 1834, XXVII. pp. 92–99, esp. p. 97: "The effect of the law as it now stands will be to oblige him to marry her. The consequence is that the parish, instead of keeping one bastard child, has to keep half a dozen legitimate children the result of the marriage."

mining population it would tend to the increase of early marriage
in that case also, though it must be remembered that the Poor
Law was chiefly a rural problem and therefore not likely to apply
to the mining population to the same extent.

The question which arises as to the effect of this state of
affairs on the growth of the population is almost purely a medical
and technical one. It was the aim, in times rather earlier than
those we are now discussing, to make an effort to promote
morality rather than immorality as the surer help to a growth of
the population. Are we then to look upon this evidence of
immorality as a check to the increase of a population in which
conditions, apart from immorality, favoured early marriages and
a rapid increase? Again, are we to suppose that, had the increase
been unaffected by conditions leading to immorality, it would
have been a greater increase still, and, to touch upon the
qualitative question, to consider that it would have been a more
healthy population? It becomes a question whether the number
of children born as a result of these conditions was sufficient
to outweigh the damage that was done to the health of the
population and to the normal marriage arrangements. It is also
a question whether the immorality did lead to such an increase
in the number of children as one might at first anticipate.
It might well be that it would happen that the immorality in
such communities might lead to measures of birth control before
they were thought of elsewhere. The mining villages and districts in many cases grew up in places which, until their development, were very rural, and rural tradition and perhaps the last
remnants of witchcraft may have handed down some methods
of checking the population; for it is very possible that if there
had been any such measures in the old days in this country, it
is here that they might have lingered. In that case it may be
that the immorality did more indirectly to make the rate of
increase slower than it did to hasten it, and that in these populations the methods of birth control that later were adopted in
other walks of life were first practised. For the year 1830 we
have the proportion of illegitimate to legitimate births for the
counties of England, and for the whole country. The average
for the whole country was 1 in 20 births. Durham approached

nearest to the average, Lancashire and Salop were the worst counties, followed pretty closely by the North Riding, Monmouth and Northumberland, the East Riding, Stafford and the West Riding. There is no very definite conclusion to be reached from these figures, they only apply to one year and may therefore give a very wrong impression of the average state of affairs, but with the exception of Warwickshire most of the industrial counties are worse than the average[1].

Conditions similar to those which grew up in the iron and coal industries grew up in many other of the unskilled trades which were connected with the Industrial Revolution. In connection with the improvement of transport there was a demand for heavy unskilled work in which the earning power would soon be at its highest, and there would be no inducements to refrain from marriage except those arising from the migratory habits to which these people had to get used in the development of canals and railways. It is probable that in the early nineteenth century, when such occupations were comparatively new, the migrations involved would be much more than go on now in the same kind of work, because now such work is always going on all over the country and there are sufficient men to do it without migration to secure the necessary supply. These "inland navigators" were just the sort of people to marry young, if their migratory habits did not prevent it. The 1846 Report on the Railway Labourers says that, in certain parts at any rate, the amount of migration is decreasing, as in the case of the Chester and Holyhead Railways[2]. Moreover, there are many instances quoted in which the men have their wives and families with them[3]; in one case they have, as a clergyman said, "what they call their wives with them,"[4] in another case we are told that one of the great difficulties of doing anything with them is that numbers of them had families with them and that they

---

[1] 1830. Illegitimate children, in so many born: Hereford, Lancs, Salop, 1 in 13; Cumberland, North Riding, 1 in 14; Cheshire, Monmouth, Northumberland, 1 in 15; Stafford, East Riding, 1 in 17; Derby, West Riding, 1 in 18; Lincoln, Norfolk, Westmorland, Worcester, 1 in 19.

[2] *Reports*, 1846, XIII. Q. 1794.

[3] *Ibid.* Qs. 61, 949, 2236, 2431. Usually have not, Qs. 184, 296, 678, 755.

[4] *Ibid.* Q. 678.

brought women that were not their wives[1]. The extent of the migration involved is not very clearly indicated. We are told that on the Chester and Holyhead Line there is not so much migration as formerly, that many local men are employed, that in Devonshire many of the men come from Dorset, Somerset, Wiltshire and Devon, and that very few are north countrymen, though many have followed down the line of the Great Western[2].

As the habits of the railway labourers became less migratory, or as they got into the habit of taking their families about with them, they approximated to the condition of the iron and mining families in so far as their contribution to the increase of the population was concerned. While they were so migratory one is apt to wonder if they were like the proverbial sailor with a wife in every port; one wonders how much of the illegitimate birth rate was due to these labourers with their homeless wandering life. The statement, also, that venereal disease was prevalent among them opens up the qualitative question with which we have dealt slightly before[3].

The importance of the railway works on the growth of the population may possibly be increased by the fact that the great extension of the railways was beginning about the time that the new Poor Law rendered necessary the absorption of many people into labour of some kind or other, and whatever view be taken of the effects of the old Poor Law on the growth of the population, the substitution of work for its allowances must have given a sense of security that was all for the good. The Poor Law Commissioners' Reports in the years after the passing of the new Poor Law, mention the absorption of labourers by the railways[4].

On the whole, then, it may be said that during this period in the organisation of industry there were certain influences making for an increase of the population, apart from the fact that the expansion of the industries provided that wealth and subsistence without which no increase of the population can be safe or of long duration. The decay and final abolition of legal

---

[1] *Reports*, 1846, XIII. Q. 2236.   [2] *Ibid*. Q. 184.
[3] *Ibid*. Q. 1138.
[4] Fay, p. 105. *Reports*, 1837, V. Qs. 509, 4041.

apprenticeship removed obstacles to marriage; the growth of new trades outside the old apprenticeship regulations and of new trades which from their nature did not require apprenticeship was a further incentive to early marriage. The nature of many of the new trades, and the effect of the use of machinery in the old trades, caused the full earning time to come comparatively soon after a man took up the trade, which meant that he was in as good a position to marry young as later on. A certain amount of the increase was due to immigration, which probably owed its origin in this period chiefly to the Irish. The amount of migration within the country would have no effect upon the growth of the population beyond contributing people to the towns where they might become part of a society that tended to have a higher birth rate than the rural parts.

It must still be remembered, however, that the fall in the death rate is a much more striking movement during this period than the rise in the birth rate.

CHAPTER VI

Factors affecting the Birth and Marriage Rates: The Poor Laws

I

DURING the period of the Industrial Revolution the Poor Laws are connected with the growth of the population in two distinct ways; at first they are said to have checked the increase, and latterly there is raised a great cry that they form one of the chief incentives to the rapid growth in the population which took place in the nineteenth century.

Whitbread, speaking in the House in 1796 on his bill to regulate the wages of labourers in husbandry, said that the pressure of the times discouraged marriage, that among the labouring classes the birth of a child, instead of being hailed as a blessing, was regarded as a curse, and that he hoped by his bill to remedy that evil[1]. Arthur Young, writing rather earlier, said that in whatever light the Laws of Settlement were considered they "were framed in the very spirit of depopulation" and had "for nearly two centuries proved a bar to the kingdom becoming as populous as it otherwise would have done,"[2] and this opinion was not merely a fad of Arthur Young's, though he repeats it with the persistence of one proclaiming a favourite and individual point of view[3].

With this view of affairs the opinion prevalent in the latter part of the period is in strong contrast. The Reports are full of statements that the Poor Laws are increasing marriages, and particularly early marriages, that these early marriages are favoured, not only by the direct operation of the allowance system but also by the indirect consequences of the method of Poor Law administration, and that they are responsible for the

---

[1] *Parl. Hist.* XXXII. p. 704.
[2] *Farmers' Letters*, p. 303; *Tour in Ireland*, 2nd ed. 1780, II. p. 195.
[3] See Graves, H. of C. 28th April, 1773. Quoted in McCulloch's evidence, *Reports*, 1830, VII. State of the Poor in Ireland.

great increase of population. An article on the Poor Laws in the *Quarterly Review* for 1818 expressed the view that marriage had become "the well calculated method of extorting relief from the parish"[1] and that the birth of each child simply strengthened the claim. The Report of 1824 on Labourers' Wages, which is full of information about the Poor Laws, says that the excess of population in many parts of the country "is in great part to be attributed to the Poor Laws during the latter years of the late war."[2] The Committee on Emigration, which reported in 1826 and had largely been created because of the widespread fear of over-population, traced the root of all the evil to the allowance system which had been introduced after Speenhamland[3].

The extracts which have been given are sufficient to show that the problem is different in the earlier and the later parts of the period respectively. A series of laws which had throughout the period the same object—the relief of poverty—were stated to be responsible for diametrically opposite results on the growth of the population.

The historical background of the Poor Laws in the eighteenth century is tolerably clear. The Act of 1722 which introduced some kind of workhouse test was in the spirit of the Elizabethan Code, whether this was realised at the time or not. Gilbert's Act of 1784, which improved the machinery of parochial administration, is, with the discontinuance of the workhouse test, usually cited as the beginning of the end. It is very doubtful if in this there was any intention of serious modification. It must also be remembered that Gilbert's Act was only permissive and that a comparatively small number of parishes availed themselves of the power of incorporation[4]. The change from the orthodox course, laid down by the legislation of Elizabeth, was completed by two further enactments in the early years of the long wars with France.

[1] *Quarterly Review*, 1818, XVIII. p. 295.   [2] *Reports*, 1824, VI. p. 405.
[3] *Reports*, 1826, IV. Q. 1962 (L. T. Hodges, Kent).
[4] Fay, p. 90: "The importance of this Act has been exaggerated. For it applied only to those parishes which chose to incorporate themselves into Unions under the Act, and in 1834 only 924 out of the 20,000 parishes in England and Wales were so incorporated."

In 1795 a great modification was introduced in the Settlement Code, which made it illegal to remove persons until they had become actually chargeable on the parish in which they were residing, which, Eden hoped, would remove the "vexatious consequences" of the laws[1].

The second change is more famous. In May, 1795, the Berkshire county magistrates met at the Pelican Inn (now destroyed) at Speenhamland, a suburb of Newbury, and decided that it was inexpedient for the magistrates to revert to the Elizabethan practice of regulating wages in accordance with the price of wheat, but that to meet the existing conditions of distress they would aid the wages of the labourers on a scale which they drew up, which granted aid varying in amount in proportion to three factors—the rate of wages, the price of the quartern loaf, and the number of the family. This became famous as the "Berkshire Bread Scale" and the "Speenhamland Act of Parliament." It was not original; traces of a similar custom are to be found before, but it was proclaimed with a great flourish of trumpets. The trumpeting has been kept up to the present day, and the "Speenhamland Act of Parliament" is much more famous than 36 Geo. III, c. 23—the wreck of Pitt's Poor Law Bill, which he had been compelled to withdraw in deference to the objections of "those whose opinions he was bound to respect"[2]—and this for all practical purposes is Speenhamland sanctioned by another Parliament.

II

In the period before these changes it is the Settlement Code which is attacked as the check to the growth of population. The necessity for the Settlement Code arose from the fact that each parish was responsible for the maintenance of its own poor, and consequently some protection against its having to maintain all and sundry who cared to come was only right and fair. A national rate and administration would have been one way of avoiding that particular difficulty, and, in point of

[1] Eden, I. p. 333.
[2] Bonar, *Parson Malthus*, p. 44. Malthus and Bentham are referred to. See also Bentham, *Observations on the Poor Law Bill of 1796*.

fact, we do find recommendations that the evil would be lessened by an increase in the size of the administrative unit[1]. The Settlement Code, with its ultimate principle of "adscripti glebae," was a relic of the feudal conception of life regulated by status and not by contract, which provided food and habitation for the labourers, though the price of this was a modified slavery. This modified slavery involved a comparatively stationary population. The strict application of this Code was bound up with the maintenance of a state of subsistence, agriculture and industry of an almost similar kind; indeed it might almost be said that the Code had been invented to perpetuate their maintenance. With the decay of agriculture with the village as the chief consumer, and with the growth of wider markets, with, in short, the Industrial Revolution, there was bound to be an outcry against the Laws of Settlement. Under the conditions which then arose, it is obvious that anything like a strictly enforced and widely applied Law of Settlement would severely hinder the free movement of labour and in that way tend to prevent the development of those new industries which would create the demand for more and more workers, and with the demand before long there would come the supply.

There is no scarcity of evidence on the subject of Settlement in contemporary writings and in the Parliamentary Reports, but it is very difficult to find any statistical evidence in support of the opinions expressed. The evidence of contemporary literature is very contradictory.

Eden, on the whole, tends to the view that the evil effects of Settlement on the mobility of labour have been exaggerated, but he goes on to say that the Code has acted as a deterrent to marriage, and has resulted in an increase of the number of illegitimate children[2]. The Poor Law Report of 1834 says that the Law of Settlement seems to have rendered the transference of labour from parish to parish a "matter of considerable difficulty."[3] A hundred years earlier something of the same kind is said by Hay in his *Remarks on the Poor Laws*, in which he

---

[1] *Reports*, 1774–1802, IX. Committee to consider several laws which concern the relief and settlement of the Poor, Ap. 1775, p. 241.

[2] Eden, I. p. 182.   [3] *Reports*, 1834, XXVII. p. 132.

declares that the Law of Settlement leaves a man's residence in a parish to the "humour or caprice" of the parish officers[1]. A few years later another writer said that the "forced and expensive way of relieving the poor" made parishes contrive means of lessening their number by preventing them from acquiring a settlement and by discouraging or hindering marriage when there was a chance of their becoming chargeable[2].

Then we come to Arthur Young who is untiring in his condemnation of the Law of Settlement. We have already noticed his general disapproval; this he expanded by at least two important observations. First, in 1771, he said that single labourers were preferred to married ones as they were "not in danger of becoming chargeable,"[3] which is of particular interest as a contrast with the subsequent state of affairs which was also caused by the working of the Poor Laws. Secondly, in 1774, he said that "wanton restrictions" were thrown in the way of the increase of the population and that the law gave a "strong and effective motive to very many people to do everything in their power against population by raising an open war against cottages."[4]

Adam Smith, of course, was thoroughly opposed to the Law of Settlement, partly because it did not exist in Scotland, but chiefly, as is to be expected, from his general principles of *laissez-faire*. Such an "evident violation of natural liberty and justice"[5] could hardly be acceptable to him. He does not, however, appear to have condemned the Code with any particular eye to the effect it was having on population.

About the time that the law was modified in 1795 there is considerable evidence. The Act which forbids the removal of people until they are actually chargeable implied that many people who were confined to one parish by the action of the laws could in many other parishes maintain themselves and their families without being a burden[6]. Pitt, speaking on his

[1] Quoted, Eden, I. p. 297.
[2] Alcock, *Obs. on the Poor Laws*, 1753, p. 19. Quoted by McCulloch, *Reports*, 1830, VII.
[3] Young, *Farmers' Letters*, 1771, p. 300. Quoted by McCulloch, *Reports*, 1830, VII.   [4] Young, *Political Arithmetic*, 1774, p. 93.
[5] Adam Smith, *Wealth of Nations*, I. p. 128.   [6] 35 Geo. III, c. 101.

Poor Law Bill, took up much the same position. He declared that the laws "prevented the workman from going to the market where he could dispose of his industry to the greatest advantage," and he thought that the modifications had not gone far enough, that an industrious workman might still "from the pressure of a temporary distress, be transported from the place where his exertions would be useful to a quarter where he would become a burden."[1]

These views did not go unanswered. Howlett, criticising Pitt's speech, considered that with regard to the manufacturing towns the general effect of the laws had been "very trifling indeed," and instanced in support of this view the growth of such towns as Sheffield, Birmingham and Manchester[2]. It is obvious that the Code would be likely to fail first of all in large and growing towns. The Code came into being under conditions very different from those that prevailed in the towns created by the Industrial Revolution. It was created "against the principle of free labour,"[3] and as such had no place in the growing towns of that period, which fell between the old municipal regulations and the creation of the nineteenth-century Factory Code. The immobility of labour, and the dislike of the migration of labourers which the Poor Law Report of 1834 still considers a factor to be reckoned with, was a principle which would have been fatal to the existence, or, at any rate, to the rapid progress of the towns. The towns appear to have taken steps to counteract the natural tendency of the Laws of Settlement. From time to time the original law of 1662 was modified, with the idea of rendering its provisions less irksome, though the alterations had not always that effect. In 1697 it was made possible for two justices of the peace to grant certificates which accepted responsibility for persons intending to leave their legal settlements, and made it impossible for them to be removed from the parishes in which they settled until they became actually chargeable. Later explanations of this regulation made it clear that these certificates did not confer a new settlement

[1] Nicholls, *Hist. of the English Poor Laws*, p. 125.
[2] Howlett, *Examination of Mr Pitt's speech.* Quoted, Eden, I. p. 297.
[3] *Parish Settlements and Pauperism*, 1828, p. 23.

unless the person rented a ten pound tenement in the new parish
to which he had gone. It is clear, however, that this regulation
was in some cases avoided, and that as regulations were made to
modify the laws, greater efforts were made to avoid their consequences, and the overseers of the poor became in effect officers
for the prevention of the acquisition of settlements[1]. On the
other hand, the towns were a source of attraction in the times
when trade was good, and a plentiful supply of labour was
essential to them. They were thus ready to accept inhabitants
under the certificate system, but were less ready to accept the
responsibility of certificating their own labourers, and probably
reluctant, in a period of temporary trade depression, to dispense
with workpeople who might again be necessary to them at no
distant period. In Eden's *State of the Poor*, 181 places are dealt
with; in 126 of these there is no mention of certificates or
removals; in seventeen of the remaining fifty-five it is stated
that certificates are never or very rarely granted. These seventeen
places contain some growing towns and manufacturing neighbourhoods. In Sheffield "certificates are very seldom granted."
In Leeds and Skipton "certificates are never granted." As it
is stated that in Leeds "removals frequently occur," it appears
that the town was not contented to be burdened without limit
by the settlers from other places, though it was evidently not
prepared to risk parting with those who had established their
legal settlement within the city. In Settle "certificates are
seldom granted." In Halifax "certificates are not granted at
present, only three in the last 18 years." Similar evidence
comes from Cumberland and Chesterfield. It is noticeable that
these examples are nearly all from the manufacturing districts
of the north, though not entirely, as in Winchelsea "certificates
are seldom granted." It appears that these places were availing
themselves of the modifications in the Law of Settlement to
secure the additional workpeople who were attracted to them
and whom they required, but were not prepared to allow that
modification to deprive them of workpeople who had either
changed their minds as to town life, or who, though not im-

---

[1] Burn, *Hist. of the Poor Laws*, 1764. Quoted in McCulloch's evidence,
Reports, 1830, VII.

mediately useful or profitable to them, might soon again be necessary. This tendency was not everywhere operative; from Wrexham there comes the information that in consequence of disputes in the iron and lead works, many of the workmen had migrated to distant parts of the country[1]. In the towns there would be greater temptation to evade the Law of Settlement and greater reward for so doing. The evidence seems to show that the towns were keen to overcome its restrictions, and the increase of population in those places shows that the regulations failed to draw a very definite line at which to check the population.

Speaking of the agricultural labourers, Howlett says, "they range from parish to parish and county to county unthinking of and unrestrained by the Laws of Settlement."[2] Sanders, a magistrate in Kent, writing in 1799, said that he did not allow removals before the people had become actually chargeable[3]. This is answered generally by the statement that Settlement has made families "of necessity stationary, and obliged them to rest satisfied with those wages they can obtain where their legal settlement happens to be."[4]

There is thus, of its kind, a considerable body of evidence in support of the contention that the Poor Laws, of which the Laws of Settlement were "an integral part,"[5] were a check to population before the period of the great wars, although this evidence does not go uncontradicted. The evidence before the beginning of the nineteenth century may possibly be suspect as being under the influence of the depopulation theory. On *a priori* grounds the Settlement Code is obviously a possible check to population, and under the influence of a movement which declared that the country was being depopulated, such a code would be blamed for some of that depopulation. After all, the problem is to explain what did happen, not to forecast what, under certain conditions, might happen, which decreases

---

[1] Eden, III. p. 893.
[2] Howlett's *Examination of Pitt's speech.* Quoted, Eden, I. p. 297.
[3] Mackay, *English Poor Law*, p. 348.
[4] *Annals*, XIV. p. 205. Brown's *Agricultural Survey of the West Riding*, 1799. Quoted, *Reports*, 1830, VII.
[5] Mackay, p. 341.

the importance of this particular point. Moreover, Arthur Young, who was writing under the influence of the depopulation theory, expressly states that, although he considered that the Settlement Code was a check on the population, he recognised that other causes were at play which more than counteracted its influence[1]. Eden, who said that the effects of the Code had been exaggerated, was writing at the time that the most obvious and unjustifiable results of the laws had been prevented, and at the time which is generally accepted as being the period of change in the administration of the Poor Laws. Any evidence, therefore, which Eden gives to the effect that the laws did not check the freedom of the labourers, and consequently did not check population, may be somewhat suspect.

In the Report on the State of the Poor in Ireland, McCulloch has collected some interesting statements to the effect that the laws did check increase in England until the time of Malthus. He declared that there is no evidence to show that before 1795 the Poor Laws were a stimulus to the growth of the population, and stated the reverse as his own opinion and as a contemporary opinion generally held[2]. He was writing at the time of the great outcry against the Poor Laws in England as a pernicious stimulus to population. He was dealing specifically with the great increase of population in Ireland, where there were no Poor Laws. He was writing, and this is more important, under the influence of the theory, which was emphatically that accepted by the Commissioners of 1834, that a great change had been made in the Poor Law administration about the time of the Speenhamland Act, and that what up to that time had been a salutary check, became, under the operation of those modifications, a pernicious stimulus.

There were striking contrasts in the Poor Laws before and after the period of the wars. Before the wars there had been in England some kind of opposition to the building of cottages; after the wars the tendency was more for landlords to look upon cottages as a gilt-edged security with the whole resources

[1] Young, *Political Arithmetic,* 1774, p. 93.
[2] *Reports,* 1830, VII. Q. 6455.

of the parish as a guarantee for their rents[1]. Before the wars the fear of the Laws of Settlement causing a parish to have many people requiring relief, led to a preference for single labourers[2]. The manner of administration after the wars had reversed that, and in some places men were almost compelled to marry in order to derive support either from their work or from the parish rate.

There are two further points that are worth mentioning.

First, the Laws of Settlement may have acted in the following indirect manner as a check on the growth of population. The class of labourers who had the greatest incentive to improve or at least to maintain their position were those who were living in a parish in which they had not their legal settlement; on such people the fear of removal would act as an inducement to providence which would not be so operative in the case of those who were habitually living where they could get all the relief they could ever hope for. In 1834 settlement by residence was reported against owing to its probable demoralising effects on unsettled labourers who at that time were "confessedly superior, both in morals and in industry" to those who were settled in the parishes in which they resided[3]. If there is any truth in the theory that improved social status and the desire of bettering the standard of life act as checks on the size of the family, as indeed appears to be the case, then it is arguable that the fear of removal had some such effect, and gave the labourers a sort of goal at which to aim, or, at any rate, something to avoid.

Secondly, certain effects of the Laws of Bastardy should be considered. Marriage was one of the qualifications by which a woman gained a settlement. Leaving the moral question apart, it is obvious that if an illegitimate child arrived and the putative father belonged to a parish other than the legal settlement of the mother, it was to the interest of the parish authorities to

---

[1] *Letter to the Magistrates*, 1828, p. 23: "Another imprudent abuse...is the payment of rent or rates of cottages out of the poor rates"...(this system) "actually offers a bonus for the erection of cottages within their limits as fast as paupers can be multiplied to occupy them...as soon as the parish offers to pay rent for all the poor...it becomes the most secure of all possible speculations to build rows of cottages."

[2] Young, *Farmers' Letters*, 1771, p. 300.

[3] *Reports*, 1834, XXVII. pp. 192–3. See also *Reports*, 1817, VI. p. 83.

insist on them marrying, thereby transferring the responsibility for the mother and the child, with of course the probable result that, instead of one illegitimate child, there would in due course be many legitimate ones[1]. Again the evidence is contradictory. In one report it is stated that this practice of forcing marriage very much increased "the number of early improvident marriages."[2] On the other hand, this tendency is denied in evidence in the same report; it is said that the Bastardy Laws do not lead to many marriages. This, however, is not necessarily to say that, in the circumstances detailed above, the parish authorities do not attempt to promote marriages[3]. In this particular case the Laws of Settlement may possibly have tended to increase the population, but the activity of this factor can only have been very limited.

It must be remembered that in this period the Poor Laws are represented as a check on a population which in spite of all checks was increasing; it is at best a negative factor, but negative factors may be very important. It is, however, more important to remember that the Poor Laws had been in operation for a long period before the great increase in population began, and in particular that the Law of Settlement, which is the part of the law specially attacked, had been in operation since 1662. For some time after that, the population had not increased to any considerable extent. If it is contended that the stationary position of the population for some time after 1662 was due to the Law of Settlement, then it must be allowed that after about the middle of the eighteenth century it ceased to be any more than a minor check. If it is contended that the population did not increase in the earlier period for reasons other than the Law of Settlement, then it must be allowed that it may have increased afterwards for reasons other than modifications in the Law of Settlement, and for reasons which the Law of Settlement was comparatively powerless to restrain. It may be urged that as time went on the Law of Settlement was found to be too severe and was modified to allow greater freedom. From time to time new qualifications were added. For instance an Act of

---

[1] *Reports*, 1834, XXVII. p. 97.   [2] *Reports*, 1831, VIII. p. 63.
[3] *Ibid.* pp. 74, 202. *Reports*, 1834, XXIX. Appendix A, Part II. p. 62.

William and Mary added settlement by paying taxes, serving
a parish office, and being hired for a year; another modification
was the granting of certificates, and in 1793, two years before
the general modification, no members of Friendly Societies
were to be removed until they were actually chargeable[1]. These
modifications all tended in the direction of making mere residence
a qualification for settlement. It is not at all clear, however,
that these modifications had the effect expected and intended
by the legislature; as the law was modified to render it less
severe, so were the efforts of those concerned redoubled to
prevent those modifications from taking effect; the hiring
qualification had the effect of decreasing the custom of hiring
by the year[2]. That this was the tendency and that the fear of
mere residence as a qualification persisted is seen from the
statements in the reports with regard to cottages; it is represented that any attempts further to modify the existing law in
the direction of giving a residential qualification for settlement
would lead to the destruction of cottages[3]. The most striking
example of this occurs in the 1834 Poor Law Report. The
Commissioners obviously wanted to treat the laws radically,
and to reduce them to "Settlement by residence...the most
natural and the most obvious" qualification. This had been the
tendency of legislation for some time, but its effect had been
to urge people to greater feats of ingenuity to evade the intentions of the laws. The Commissioners, and it must have been
pain and grief to them, were compelled to reverse the drafting
of the law to attain the same desired effect. They recognised
that to make the obtaining of a settlement legally easier would
not do so actually, and therefore they reverted to the stricter
form and recommended that the settlement of children should
follow that of the parents or surviving parent, and that after
sixteen years of age it should be their place of birth. In this
way the parishes would have security that they would not be
held responsible for persons who did not belong to them, and
would thus be less hostile to their making their home in the
parish. This plan was recommended expressly to maintain the

[1] *Reports*, 1825, IV. p. 5.
[2] Adam Smith, I. p. 125. [3] *Reports*, 1817, VI. p. 88.

position of the unsettled labourer and to prevent the demolition of cottages[1].

After the end of the wars the cry that the Laws of Settlement were checking the growth of the population was swamped by the cry that the allowance system was increasing it; the former cry was prevalent at a time when there was a formidable body of opinion that the population was decreasing, the latter cry began when the Censuses had proved that the population was rapidly increasing. After the wars there were not the same legal restrictions involved in the Settlement Code as there were before the Act of 1795, and the war against cottages was modified in respect of the profit to be derived from pauper cottages; at the same time the Laws of Settlement continued to operate, and from the prevalence of the allowance system they would derive a new source of power, for, from a short-sighted view, it was the labourer's interest to stay in his own parish at all hazards, for there alone could he get the parish allowance, and the Laws of Settlement encouraged him to do this. In this latter part of the period the Laws of Settlement are more a problem of industry than a Poor Law problem, and there is evidence that there was a considerable migration in spite of the laws and also that there was not as much migration as was wanted. It is broadly a question of tendency; figures are difficult to obtain. On abstract grounds there may be some reason to suspect that the laws would tend to check population, but during the period under discussion population had begun to increase at a rate which compared favourably with the more striking increase in the nineteenth century, and this after the laws had been in operation for many years. Thus, at the most, the laws can only be regarded as an imperfect check to the increase, and on the evidence the most that can be said, in all probability, is that the case against the Laws of Settlement is non-proven.

III

With the end of the period of wars there began the outcry against the Poor Laws; during the wars the effects had been

---

[1] *Reports*, 1834, XXVII. p. 192.

disguised by the general plenty of employment. The Committee of 1817 was the first of a series that reported almost continuously until the great Poor Law Commission of 1833–4. In these days we probably have more to think about than our ancestors of a hundred years ago, and it is certain that there is no domestic subject that occupies the same amount of thought as the Poor Laws did in those days; the persistence of the outcry is remarkable for the length of time it continued, and for the multiplicity of places in which it is found.

The actual nature of the complaints varies, but there is general agreement that it was the system of parish allowances in aid of wages that was responsible for the evils. This system was enunciated by the Berkshire magistrates in 1795, and received legislative sanction in the following year. During the next few years it was widely adopted, particularly in the agricultural counties of the south and west[1], though in some counties it does not appear to have come into practice until after the war[2].

The allowance system is attacked from three points of view which have a bearing on the problem of the population.

First, the result of the system was that the net income of a labouring family was made up of two items—wages and allowances. The same net income might be composed in varying degrees of these two elements, and the result so far as purchasing power was concerned would be equal; but the effect on the feelings and the outlook of the family receiving most of its income in the form of allowance would be very different from those of the family receiving all its money in wages. Apart from the feeling of reluctance to apply for parish relief which a continued reliance on it was calculated to remove, the man who received his money chiefly in parish rate was dealing in

---

[1] *Annals*, 1801, XXXVII. On the wages of labourers in husbandry, Extract from the letter of a country clergyman. *Reports*, 1818, v. p. 99. Villiers, "Report on Warwick, Worcester, Gloucester and North Devon," *Reports*, 1834, XXIX. p. 14. In Warwick 1797 mentioned as the date of its commencement. In Devon it "has been in full operation since the year 1801": and in the other counties "previously to the year 1800." *Reports*, 1826, IV. Q. 1961.

[2] *Reports*, 1818, v. p. 161, Hunts and Beds: "in the last two or three years." *Reports*, 1824, VI. pp. 429, 432, 433, 442, 444, 448. *Reports*, 1828, IV. p. 142.

certainties more than the man who was entirely dependent on wages[1]. The parish rate had at least the credit of the whole parish behind it, wages had only the credit of the particular farmer and the condition of the market. This receipt of parish rates in aid of wages was calculated to destroy the feeling of independence of the labourers, to make him feel that whatever happened he would always have that relief and to destroy any feeling for the necessity of exercising prudence and restraint. In so far as a feeling that there is nothing to care for, no improvement to be made by individual care and prudence and no reason to save against a rainy day, everything tends to a reckless increase of the population, and this system might reasonably be expected to promote that increase. The system also was coupled with additional ramifications which make that result even more likely[2].

Secondly, in certain parts of the country the allowance was given in the form of rent of the cottages occupied by the family requiring relief[3]. Malthus maintained that one of the reasons why the country had been able for so long to continue a system of Poor Laws which promised the impossible was that, in consequence of the parish responsibility for paupers, landowners "were more inclined to pull down than to build cottages."[4] This was still a check during the war period, landlords were not building extensively and this was probably natural. In 1804

---

[1] There is some evidence, even when the system was very widely spread, that reluctance to apply was still shown. It is noticeable, however, that these instances do not come from the agricultural counties which are mentioned as being badly affected by the allowance system, but from counties in the north of England which are examples of counties not badly affected by the system. *Reports*, 1826–7, v. p. 5, Emigration, 2nd Report (Lancs Hand Loom Weavers). *Reports*, 1831, VIII. p. 136, Northumberland. *Reports*, 1833, v. Q. 6692, Cumberland.

[2] *Reports*, 1817, VI. pp. 42, 58; Appendix H, Letter of the Suffolk J.P.'s: "It tends to debase the industrious labourer to the class of the pauper. It habituates him to the reception of parish relief, it teaches him to look to the rate for his usual maintenance, instead of applying to it reluctantly in sickness and old age; and it saps the vital principle of industry, and obliterates the little remaining honest pride of independence." *Reports*, 1818, v. p. 101. *Reports*, 1834, XXVII. pp. 52–54, Cowell's evidence. An elaborate picture of the moral degradation resulting from the Poor Laws.

[3] *Reports*, 1834, XXVII. pp. 10, 11, Habit of paying rent out of rates common in Anglesea, Suffolk, Surrey and Sussex.

[4] Malthus, 1817 ed. II. p. 344.

a writer in the *Annals* said that house and family were synonymous terms, that he did not know a parish in which more cottages could not be built and let at any reasonable rent and that when marriages did not take place it was "for want of more habitations."[1] This question was next raised in the Emigration Reports of 1826 and 1827. Throughout the Reports there runs the fear that emigration will really be useless because of the natural tendency of the "vacuum" created to fill up and it was obvious that steps would have to be taken at the same time to see that the gap was not immediately filled up. There were two main ways suggested for securing this; it was generally agreed that if emigration was to take place from England it must simultaneously take place from Ireland, and it was often suggested that some means must be adopted to prevent the further increase of habitations and to secure the destruction of some of those evacuated by the emigrants[2].

At the same time there were the Poor Laws working in the opposite direction. These laws exalted cottage property into a profitable form of investment and thus the possibility of adopting some measure of emigration combined with a diminution of cottage property was hindered by their operation[3]. The interaction of the fear of the vacuum filling up and the interest of cottage holders is evident in many places; in Sussex, for instance, "the ratepayers were very anxious that a system of destruction of cottages should follow the removal of paupers."[4] But as a counteraction to this we find it stated as very unlikely that a landlord, if he were a select vestryman, would consent to the demolition of his cottage property[5]. From Kent there comes the same feeling that the provision of cottages was increasing the

[1] *Annals*, 1804, XLI. p. 227.

[2] *Reports*, 1826–7, V. Q. 3395. *Reports*, 1826, IV. Q. 1401. A landowner in Kent had been induced to "concur with other cottage proprietors, who are going to take down from twenty-six to thirty cottages as soon as the persons are out of them, if they emigrate, as we think they will do; for if we leave the buildings standing young people of seventeen and eighteen years of age and even still younger would immediately marry and thus the evil would continue."

[3] *Reports*, 1826, IV. Qs. 1394, 1961: "It is notorious that almost numberless cottages have of late years been built by persons speculating in the parish rates for their rent."

[4] *Ibid.* Q. 607.   [5] *Ibid.* Q. 500.

population and should in some way be checked, and a considerable tax on cottages was suggested "as the best means of preventing early marriages."[1] The county magistrate whom we have met before was alive to the evils of the system, and condemned the payment of cottages from the poor rate. He said that "the only direct artificial check" to the increase of the population was the destruction of cottages as soon as their inhabitants die, whereas the existing system offered a direct bonus, and it became "the most secure of all possible speculations to build a row of cottages."[2]

The system was looked upon as illegal by Beecher, the organiser of the Southwell experiment. There were suggestions that the burden of the rates of the cottages should be transferred to the landowners and thus make their cottage property a less attractive investment[3].

Evidently the system of paying the rents of cottages out of the poor rate was tending to promote early marriages, and was acting as an incentive to landlords to invest in cottage property, which in its turn was erecting an obstacle to any reduction in the number of cottages which was generally looked upon as the only safe way of reducing the large increase that was going on in the population. It was said that "marriages are regulated more by cottage room than by any administration of the Poor Laws."[4]

This system of paying the rents of cottages out of the poor rates merges in the third and greatest objection to the allowance system—that it promoted early and improvident marriages and, by the allowance for children, was conducive to large families. This had a more direct application to population than the other objections to the system with which we have hitherto dealt. We saw that in the period before the war the preference had been for unmarried labourers; the result of the allowance system was that married labourers were preferred to unmarried labourers, and that in some cases it was almost impossible for unmarried labourers to get employment. The allowance system

---

[1] *Ibid.* Q. 3875.   [2] *Letters to the Magistrates*, 1828, p. 23.
[3] *Reports*, 1826–7, v. Qs. 2133, 2308, 4135.
[4] *Reports*, 1834, XXIX. p. 329; XXVIII. p. 541.

was an assistance to the farmers, who were thereby enabled to get their labourers cheap; their wages were depressed and the balance was made up out of the poor rates. An incidental evil of this system was that the burden of the wages of labour fell on the wrong people, the farmers being able to shift the burden on to those inhabitants of the parish who did not employ so many labourers as they did themselves[1]. Labourers' families were liable to require relief in any case. The system led the farmers to prefer labourers who were receiving relief and therefore they preferred to employ married labourers. Unmarried labourers were less likely to require relief and therefore it was an economy to employ married labourers and supplement the wages by the relief, for in so doing the farmers shifted some of the burden on to others. In times of a scarcity of work, when relief would be required on a more extensive scale, the temptation to employ all the married labourers first would be even greater[2]. That was bad enough but it was not all. Not only were the farmers reluctant to employ single men, but when they did they were in the habit of giving less wages than to the married men and the effect of this was to encourage them to marry. The feeling of despair also engendered by this system was said to encourage marriage; a Sussex witness thought that early marriages were promoted because there was no inducement for the labourer to refrain from marriage, and they had no hope of raising themselves from the caste in which they were born[3].

The evidence with respect to the promotion of improvident marriages by the Poor Laws is so voluminous and miscellaneous that it is relegated to an appendix[4]. Throughout the evidence there runs the double feeling, that by marriage only would labourers

---

[1] *Reports*, 1817, VI. p. 167, From the Suffolk Magistrates: "...it becomes an assessment, not so much for the relief of the poor as of their employers.... If indeed poor rates were levied solely upon those who employed labourers the evil, though great, would be less oppressive....The professional man, the annuitant, the shopkeeper, the artisans, all are taxed for the payment of labour, from which they derive no immediate benefit." See also *Reports*, 1824, VI. p. 444; *Extracts*, 1833, p. 173; *Parish Settlements and Pauperism*, p. 31; *Letter to the Magistrates*, p. 5.

[2] *Reports*, 1824, VI. p. 448. *Reports*, 1834, XXXVII. p. 125, Sussex: "the farmers have acted upon a very absurd and stupid plan. They will not employ single men; the consequence is that a man immediately marries."

[3] *Reports*, 1831, VIII. p. 190.　　　　　　[4] Appendix II, p. 262.

obtain employment, and that the allowances held out considerable attractions[1].

There is one clear enunciation of the evil that is worth inserting here. In the report of Villiers on Warwickshire, Worcester, Gloucester and North Devon, it is stated:

> I was informed that the consequences of the system were not wholly unforeseen at the time (of its introduction before 1800) as affording a probable inducement to early marriage and large families; but at this period there was little apprehension on that ground.... The unfortunate circumstance, however, which is to be traced in connection with the system, is the total change of feeling among the labourers upon the subject of parish relief...by making their marriage and the number of their children the great condition of relief[2].

Towards the end of the time the allowance system was creeping into the towns. There, however, the earnings of children took the place to some degree of the rural allowance made in respect of them, and by 1824 the system does not seem to have gained any considerable hold. When Lord John Russell moved for a Committee to inquire into the payment of labourers' wages out of the poor rates, he had drawn his motion wide enough to include the town districts, but Peel objected that the terms of reference were needlessly wide and consequently the towns were left out[3]. In 1834 the allowance system, though formidable in the towns, was less serious than in the country districts, possibly owing to the fact that the manufacturers had not the same influence in the town vestries as the farmers in the country vestries[4]. This system was evident in the case of decaying trades, as in the woollen industries at Bocking and Braintree, and as the silk trade also in these particular places was in a bad way, the distress was still further increased in these parishes and we are told that "the wages of both manufacturers and agriculturists are made up out of the poor rates."[5] Towns in Kent and Sussex, in both of which counties the allowance system among agricultural

---

[1] See Appendix II, at end.
[2] *Reports*, 1834, xxix, p. 14.
[3] Thorold Rogers, *Six Centuries*, ii. p. 495.
[4] *Reports*, 1834, xxvii. p. 35.
[5] *Reports*, 1834, xxviii. Appendix A, Part i. p. 229.

labourers was prevalent, were "comparatively free from it."[1] In the case of the linen weavers in Darlington the system seems to have been fully developed[2]; it appears to have gained some ground in the textile districts of Lancashire, while in Oldham it was certainly in operation to some extent, though it was not regarded as a general practice[3]. In Wigan it is stated that weavers and spinners were the only people who received relief, but it does not state, as in the case of Oldham, whether this was done on the principle of allowance in aid of wages, or merely in the event of unemployment[4]. In the general Report on the Lancashire district Henderson says that the depression of wages due to power loom weaving and the difficulty of finding employment, especially among the older weavers whose habits were fixed, had led to the introduction of the allowance system among those of them who had more than two children[5], and in Cheshire there is evidence in the Emigration Report of the existence of the same system[6]. A modification mentioned in Henderson's evidence by which the relief is reckoned on what might be reasonably supposed to be earned by an industrious weaver is a mitigation of the worst evils of the system. It must also be remembered that in Lancashire and Cheshire there still lingered a considerable body of weavers in the country districts who were as much agriculturists as they were weavers, and as such they may have tended to come under the allowance system in their capacity of farmers as well as in that of weavers. On the other hand, of all the counties of England Lancashire had the lowest poor rates per head of population.

In Nottingham, for instance, the question of the connection of industry and agriculture is expressly raised. It is stated that the manufacturers double the rôle of farmer and stocking maker. It is further stated that they recognised that the interpretation of the law in force at Southwell was the correct one, but that "the practice of granting relief to persons partially employed has so long prevailed, that they found it difficult to discontinue

[1] *Reports*, 1834, XXVIII. p. 892.
[2] *Extracts*, 1833, pp. 170–1.
[3] *Ibid.* p. 357.   [4] *Ibid.* p. 366.
[5] *Ibid.* p. 340.
[6] *Reports*, 1826–7, v. Q. 424.

what they could not altogether approve."[1] A system very like this was in force at Barnard Castle[2].

In the iron districts, also, the system in some variety seems to have existed. In Birmingham and Coventry the vestrymen, who were chiefly tradesmen, were threatened with loss of their custom if they attempted to curtail relief, and in this case it looks as if it were the allowance system to which reference is being made. Its close connection with agriculture is seen from the remark that "in its first stage it recommends itself to farmers and manufacturers, as increasing profits by lowering wages."[3] It is also stated that the stoppage of Crowley, Millington and Co.'s ironworks at Winlaton in 1815, "introduced the allowance system from which the township has never since been able to redeem itself," though it is by no means evident that this was the allowance system in the sense in which that term is usually employed, namely as an allowance in aid of inadequate wages[4].

It is safe to say that, at any rate sporadically, the allowance system was gradually being introduced into the towns, though it appears to have been confined to trades which were decaying, like that of the hand loom weavers in Lancashire or Cheshire, or, in cases like that reported from Winlaton, when there had been some definite failure to account for the distress. It is true also that the two periods of greatest increase of population in the towns were, for the larger towns 1821–1831, and for the smaller towns 1811–1821. These two periods cover the time in which the poor rates were the most burdensome. In the big towns, however, in which the increase was greatest at the time when the allowance system was threatening them, there was usually some more obvious cause to be found in the industrial development; while in the smaller towns, in which probably the system was a greater danger, as being more likely to be affected by the allowance system in the agricultural districts from which in many cases they cannot have differed much, the great increase of population was over before it is suggested that the allowance system was becoming a serious menace in

[1] *Reports*, 1834, XXIX. p. 113. *Reports*, 1834, XXVII. p. 44.
[2] *Extracts*, 1833, p. 173.   [3] *Reports*, 1834, XXVIII. p. 640.
[4] *Reports*, 1834, XXVIII. p. 137.

the towns, though on the evidence it seems a very possible result to have followed[1]. There were not wanting, however, those who hesitated to believe that the Poor Laws did act in the way which the Poor Law Commissioners, in common with a great part of the country, thought that they did. Malthus, who was no lover of the Poor Laws, and from whose principles the radical Poor Law Commissioners had largely learned their views on those laws, seems to have been more ready than the Commissioners to admit that the Poor Laws may not have done what they were expected to do. He maintains that the general tendency was obvious, but is inclined to admit "that under all the circumstances with which they have been accompanied they do not much encourage marriage."[2] Much the same view is taken in the Preliminary Observations on the Census of 1821 by Rickman, who mentions the persistent accusations made against the Poor Laws and admits that a stimulus to population might seem "very naturally to follow from the compulsory nature of the relief afforded to the poor in England." He is, however, sceptical and says that there is "reason to suspect" that the Poor Laws have been much less conducive to an increase of population than is usually asserted[3].

The Report on Labourers' Wages classifies certain of the counties into those that are adversely affected by the existence of the system of paying relief in aid of wages, and those in which the system is not prevalent:

We are happy to be able to say that the evil of which we complain is partial, and that many counties in England are nearly, if not totally, exempt from the grievance. In Northumberland, wages are twelve shillings a week, and labourers having families do not usually receive assistance from the poor rate. In Cumberland, wages vary from twelve shillings to fifteen shillings a week and the report is equally satisfactory. In Lincolnshire, the wages are generally twelve shillings per week and the labourers live in comfort and independence. ...In Suffolk, Sussex, Beds, Bucks, Dorsetshire and Wiltshire the plan of paying wages out of the poor rate has been carried to the greatest extent[4].

---

[1] *Reports*, 1824, VI. p. 404.   [2] Malthus, 1817 ed. II. p. 373.
[3] Census, 1821, Prelim. Obs. p. xxv.
[4] *Reports*, 1824, VI. p. 405.

To this, one county must be added for special mention. The Report says elsewhere: "Sussex still remains as the county in which the expenditure upon the poor bears the highest proportion to the number of the people, and Lancashire continues at the other end of the scale."[1] As the problem to be examined is chiefly an agricultural one it is not right to admit Lancashire, though it would strengthen the argument if it were admitted. In the 1831 Census there are only two "hundreds" in Lancashire in which the families put down as engaged in trade and manufacture are not very greatly in excess of all the other families put down as engaged in agriculture and in other occupations not included under the two former heads; these two "hundreds" are Lonsdale North, and Lonsdale South of the Sands[2]. Moreover, the increase in population in the rural districts of Lancashire in the three decades from 1801 to 1831 ranges distinctly higher than that in the rural districts of the other counties to be examined; and the issue would be further complicated, more than in other counties, by the existence of the system of combining agriculture and industry.

This classification of the counties is confirmed by the 1828 Report on the Poor Laws, in which the passage quoted above from the 1824 Report is given, with the comment by the writers that they do not believe any material improvement to have taken place in the counties alluded to in that Report[3].

Thus we have two groups of counties, one in which the allowance system was rife, and one in which its burden was slight[4].

To show that there was a consistent policy over a period of years, and to show that, during that period, in the counties which were most affected by the allowance system the burden of the Poor Law expenses was more serious than in the counties which were not so much affected, the expenses per head of the population on the actual maintenance of the poor have been

[1] *Reports*, 1824, VI. Committee on the Poor Rate Returns, p. 374.
[2] *Statistical Journal*, XLIII. Price Williams.
[3] *Reports*, 1828, IV. p. 142.
[4] Counties seriously affected: Bedford, Bucks, Dorset, Suffolk, Sussex, Wilts. Counties little affected: Cumberland, Lincoln, Northumberland.

given. The Census figures nearest to the date at which the expenses were incurred have been used, and the figures for the expenses are those which are given in the returns as actually devoted to the maintenance of the poor. The years taken were selected from various stages in the period, with reference to whether the Poor Law expenses of the country at large were rising or falling. The first year taken, which is 1803, is in the middle of a period of generally rising expenses. The year 1813 is at the top of one peak in the country's Poor Law expenses, while 1818, in which year six out of the nine counties under consideration reached their highest figure in the period, is at the top of the biggest peak recorded. The years 1823 and 1824 are the two lowest years between the peaks of 1818 and the next and last peak in the period of the old Poor Law, namely that in 1832, which is the last year taken, while 1829 is half-way up the ascent from the low expenses of 1823–4 to the peak of 1832. In all those years the average expenses in the one group are always double or more than double the average expenses in the other group (Table X)[1].

This is confirmed by a slightly different grouping of counties which is given in Strickland's *Discourse on the Poor Laws*. The Poor Law expenses in 1826 were taken in conjunction with the 1821 Census. Two groups of counties were selected, one southern and the other northern, with a total population in each case of approximately two millions. In the southern group there were three of the counties previously stated to be badly affected by the allowance system, and in the northern group Cumberland, Northumberland and Lincoln were included. The Poor Law expenditure in the northern group was

---

[1] The information on which this table was constructed was obtained from the following sources.

The population of the counties in all cases from the figures of the Census nearest to the year in question.

Poor Law expenses:
- 1803. *Reports*, 1804, Supp. III, p. 714.
- 1813. *Reports*, 1824, VI. p. 381.
- 1818. *Reports*, 1830–31, XI. pp. 208–9.
- 1823. *Reports*, 1824, VI. p. 381.
- 1824 and 1829. Strickland, *Dissertation on the Poor Laws and Reports*, 1830–31, XI. pp. 208–9.
- 1832. Accounts and Papers, 1833, XXXII. p. 349.

Table X. EXPENSES PER HEAD ON THE RELIEF OF THE POOR IN VARIOUS ENGLISH COUNTIES

	(1) 1801 Census 1803 Expenses			(2) 1811 Census 1813 Expenses			(3) 1821 Census 1818 Expenses			(4) 1821 Census 1823 Expenses			(5) 1821 Census 1824 Expenses			(6) 1831 Census 1829 Expenses			(7) 1831 Census 1832 Expenses		
	£	s.	d.	£	s.	d.	£	s.	d.	£	s.	d.	£	s.	d.	£	s.	d.	£	s.	d.
Bedford		12	0		17	0		17	8		15	0		15	0		16	2		16	0
Buckingham		16	6	1	2	0	1	2	0		15	0		15	0		17	0		19	6
Dorset		11	6		17	0		16	4		11	0		11	0		10	3		11	6
Suffolk		11	9		19	0	1	1	6		17	0		18	0		16	3		18	6
Sussex	1	3	3	1	12	0	1	8	0	1	1	0	1	0	0		17	3	1	0	9
Wiltshire		14	0	1	3	0	1	1	0		12	0		13	0		14	10		16	6
Average		14	10	1	1	6	1	1	1		16	2		16	4		15	10		17	1
Cumberland		5	0		7	0		7	3		6	0		5	0		5	0		5	6
Northumberland		6	10		8	0		9	5		7	0		7	0		6	6		7	0
Lincoln		9	6		11	0		11	9		11	0		11	0		10	9		11	1
Average		7	1		8	6		9	6		8	0		7	8		7	5		7	10
Lancashire		4	10		7	0		7	0		4	0		4	0		4	0		4	6

less than half that in the southern group[1]. In the decade 1821–1831 the average increase in the population in the northern group was 16·64 per cent. and in the southern group 17·92 per cent.—a difference of 1·28 per cent.

It is true that these groups do divide themselves into north and south and therefore some of the difference in the expense may be due to differing costs in the two parts of the kingdom, or it may be that the expense of the upkeep of workhouses was greater in the south than in the north. On the other hand, with reference to workhouse expenditure, it must be remembered that the figures given represent the amount actually used in the maintenance of the poor, which would rule out some of the expenses of upkeep, and also, that where the allowance system was in full swing there would probably be less use for the workhouse than in counties where the allowance system was strenuously resisted, and that therefore one would expect to find a greater expenditure on workhouses in the northern group than in the southern. In any case, the margin of difference is so considerable as to leave no doubt, when taken in conjunction with the evidence from the Reports, that the system was much more prevalent in the one group than in the other.

The burden of the allowance system in certain of the counties which were severally affected by it, and in Northumberland which was but slightly affected, can be seen from some returns of the number of poor persons published in 1829. These returns show the population of certain districts in these counties, the total number of persons relieved, and the number of able-bodied men receiving assistance, specifying in what particular way that assistance was given. These are chiefly made up of "allowance for children," "making up wages on account of families," "cottage rent" and a certain amount of parish and

---

[1] Strickland, *Discourse on the Poor Laws,* Sec. XVI. p. 111. 1821 Census. Expenses for the year ending 25th March, 1826:

Southern group: Kent, Sussex, Surrey, Oxford, Wilts, Berks, Norfolk, Dorset.

Population 2,037,665.   Expenses £1,511,697.

Northern group: Yorkshire (three Ridings), Lincoln, Westmorland, Cumberland, Northumberland, Durham.

Population 2,070,366.   Expenses £754,500.

occasional labour. A glance at the table will show the small amount of relief to able-bodied men in Northumberland compared with any of the three counties which were more affected by the allowance system[1].

The next point to determine is how the population increased in those counties during the period. For this purpose the last twenty years of the period, from 1811 to 1831, have been considered separately. These twenty years were the most burdensome in the history of the Poor Laws, and during the greater number of them the compensating tendencies, which had concealed their real effects during the war, no longer continued to operate. Then the whole period, from 1801 to 1831, has been considered. This embraces the whole of that period of the old Poor Law for which there are reliable figures for the county population, with the exception of the years from 1831 to 1834. During the whole of this period the Poor Law expenses were high, and were steadily rising throughout the first decade.

Two tables are given which confirm one another. The problem is a rural one and therefore the town populations have been left out. In the first table (Table XI) the populations are taken from the Census returns of the counties, certain towns which are specified in the note on the construction of the table being left out. The second table (Table XII) is compiled from an article in the *Statistical Journal*. The actual populations of the counties given in this table are smaller than those in the other, nor is it stated how they are obtained; the probability is that greater deductions have been made in respect of urban districts. This makes the percentages derived from the second table range rather lower than those obtained from the first, but the difference between the percentages is not very great and the relative positions of the percentages in the series remain the same in both cases.

[1] *Accounts and Papers*, 1829, XXI. Return of poor persons in certain districts in the following counties:

	Population	Total number relieved	Total able-bodied men relieved
Wiltshire	3139	349	101
Sussex	8658	2954	776
Bucks	3921	596	354
Northumberland	3537	115	9

Table XI. INCREASE OF POPULATION IN COUNTIES
VARIOUSLY AFFECTED BY THE ALLOWANCE SYSTEM

			1811–1831 Total increase	1801–1831 Total increase
Counties least affected:				
Lincoln	1801–1811	13·97 %		
	1811–1821	19·10		
	1821–1831	11·90		
Northumberland	1801–1811	12·57 %	28·82 %	46·04 %
	1811–1821	13·30		
	1821–1831	10·40		
Cumberland	1801–1811	13·31 %		
	1811–1821	15·40		
	1821–1831	7·80		
Counties most affected:				
Bedford	1801–1811	10·37 %		
	1811–1821	19·27		
	1821–1831	13·13		
Buckingham	1801–1811	9·41 %		
	1811–1821	13·47		
	1821–1831	9·28		
Dorset	1801–1811	7·67 %		
	1811–1821	14·20		
	1821–1831	10·38	26·36 %	38·64 %
Suffolk	1801–1811	11·68 %		
	1811–1821	19·28		
	1821–1831	8·60		
Sussex	1801–1811	14·94 %		
	1811–1821	17·36		
	1821–1831	10·66		
Wiltshire	1801–1811	4·49 %		
	1811–1821	14·98		
	1821–1831	7·91		
	Difference		2·46 %	7·40 %

The following towns in the several counties have been omitted from the
population figures used in the construction of this table:

In Lincoln	Lincoln	In Dorset	Weymouth
	Grantham		Poole
	Stamford	In Suffolk	Bury St Edmunds
In Northumberland	Newcastle		Ipswich
	Berwick		Sudbury
In Cumberland	Carlisle	In Sussex	Chichester
	Whitehaven		Lewes
In Bedford	Bedford		Brighton
In Buckingham	Buckingham	In Wiltshire	Salisbury
	Aylesbury		

Table XII. INCREASE OF POPULATION IN COUNTIES
VARIOUSLY AFFECTED BY THE ALLOWANCE SYSTEM

Figures derived from tables given in Price Williams's article on the population of England and Wales in *Stat. Journ.* xliii. The actual county figures
range rather smaller than those on which Table XI is based, probably owing
to rather more being omitted as urban:

		1811–1831 Total increase	1801–1831 Total increase
Counties least affected:			
Lincoln			
	1801–1811	11·79 %	
	1811–1821	13·38	
	1821–1831	10·96	
Northumberland			
	1801–1811	9·02 %	
	1811–1821	10·60	25·55 % 39·55 %
	1821–1831	8·51	
Cumberland			
	1801–1811	12·69 %	
	1811–1821	13·41	
	1821–1831	6·45	
Counties most affected:			
Bedford			
	1801–1811	9·80 %	
	1811–1821	14·57	
	1821–1831	11·20	
Buckingham			
	1801–1811	7·29 %	
	1811–1821	14·83	
	1821–1831	7·57	
Dorset			
	1801–1811	8·03 %	
	1811–1821	14·49	
	1821–1831	8·44	23·89 % 34·60 %
Suffolk			
	1801–1811	8·61 %	
	1811–1821	15·13	
	1821–1831	8·07	
Sussex			
	1801–1811	13·61 %	
	1811–1821	14·70	
	1821–1831	7·13	
Wiltshire			
	1801–1811	4·23 %	
	1811–1821	11·28	
	1821–1831	7·71	
	Difference	1·66 %	4·95 %

Taking the first table and the period 1811–1831, the total increase in the counties most affected by the allowance system was 26·36 per cent. The total increase in the counties least affected was 28·82 per cent. The difference being 2·46 per cent., the counties least affected recording the larger increase. Taking the same table and the whole period, the total increase in the counties most affected amounted to 38·64 per cent.; and in the counties least affected to 46·04 per cent.—the difference being 7·40 per cent., again the counties least affected recording the larger increase.

Taking now the second table and the period 1811–1831, the total increase in the counties most affected was 23·89 per cent. as against 25·55 per cent. in the counties least affected; a difference of 1·66 per cent. In the whole period from 1801 to 1831, the total increase in the counties most affected was 34·60 per cent. and in the counties least affected 39·55 per cent.— the difference being 4·95 per cent., and in both cases the counties least affected recorded the larger increase.

These results are somewhat remarkable; in the period during which the allowance system was most seriously felt, the counties least affected increased either 2·46 per cent. or 1·66 per cent. more than those which were most affected. Taking the whole period, the counties which are least affected by the Poor Laws again increased faster than the counties which were most affected, the difference being 7·40 per cent. or 4·95 per cent. according to the two tables. According to the data on which the second table was compiled, in the decade 1831–1841 the counties which were not affected by the allowance system increased 9·52 per cent. as against 6·81 per cent. in the counties most affected, and this period, though it includes the new Poor Law and the years of low Poor Law expenses which followed it, also includes the last high peak of expenditure under the old Poor Law.

The conclusion that it is legitimate to draw from these figures is that, contrary to general opinion, the allowance system did not greatly tend to the increase of the population. The evidence in the Reports would, by itself, justify the opinion that the allowance system had this effect, but it must be remembered that the people who wrote the Reports were really convinced, probably before they had inquired into the matter, that the Poor Laws did increase the population. The country generally, however, was afraid of its rapidly increasing population and seemed powerless to stop it. Those who held the opinion that the Poor Laws were increasing the population would derive some encouragement from this view; for here they were dealing with a clear body of laws which, if they were not doing what was wanted, were capable of being changed. A check to this supposed increase of population owing to the action of the Poor Law was, in point of fact, one of the aims of the Commissioners of 1834 and was involved in the principle of "less eligibility" with which they prefaced the constructive section of their Report[1]. But the figures for the two groups of counties considered—in one of which the allowance system was stated to be more extensive than elsewhere, while in the other it was not prevalent—seem to justify the view that the effect of the allowance system on the population has been very much exaggerated.

There are two objections that may be offered.

First, Malthus objected to the Poor Laws because he thought that they tended to the production of more children than the country could support and he said that the very reason why "more children ought not to be born than the country can support" was that "the greatest possible number of those that are born may be supported."[2] It is, however, possible that even if this tendency had no appreciable effect, and the Poor Laws did little or nothing to increase the frequency of marriage and the size of the family, and in consequence to increase the population that way, they may have had an effect on the other side and have reduced the death rate by the attention which they directed to people who came directly under their view, and who, without the medical attention of the Poor Laws, would have

---

[1] "The first and most essential of all conditions...is that his (the pauper's) situation on the whole shall not be made really or apparently so eligible as the situation of the independent labourer of the lowest class." "Every penny bestowed, that tends to render the condition of the pauper more eligible than that of the independent labourer, is a bounty on indolence and vice." *Reports*, 1834, XXVII, p. 127.
[2] Malthus, 1872 ed. p. 472.

died. In the case of infant mortality the effect in both cases would be the same, namely, a greater number of children; but this would be secured in the one case by a rise in the birth rate and in the other by a decline in the death rate, and the latter is, generally speaking, more important in this period than the former. Rickman thought that the medical attention in connection with the Poor Laws was one of the causes which had reduced the rate of mortality[1]. The matter is only slightly touched upon in the Reports; the 1834 Report discusses shortly the contract system, and states that on the whole medical attendance seems to be adequately supplied, and there are a few other remarks to the same effect in other parts of the Report[2]. In 1836 a Medical Society published a report on the subject in connection with the new Poor Law; this report is chiefly concerned with a denunciation of the contract system as it existed in the days of the old Poor Law and as it threatened to exist under the new Poor Law, but it also goes to show that there had been some system of medical attention for those people who relied on the Poor Law before the reform[3].

Secondly, the population of the counties especially affected may have in reality increased faster than the returns make out, and the increase in comparison with the other counties may have been equalised by migration within the country. As this migration would naturally, if it took place, be from the south to the industrial north, it must be considered. First, it would be unlikely to take place to any extent to the rural districts of the three counties, which are the parts of those counties that we are considering[4]. Secondly, there is one form of migration which is known to have taken place, that of parish apprentices to the mills in the north; this was chiefly, however, from London to the mills of Lancashire, Cheshire and the West Riding. Thirdly, it is unlikely that any considerable migration of the kind required to vitiate these conclusions would have taken place, under the existing condition of the law, without a great deal more being

[1] *Accounts and Papers*, 1831, XVIII.
[2] *Reports*, 1834, XXVII. p. 25; XXVIII. pp. 6, 12, 23, 536, 662, 728.
[3] *Report of Committee appointed by the Provincial Medical and Surgical Assn. on the New Poor Law*, 1836.
[4] Cumberland, Lincoln, Northumberland.

said about it. The Poor Law Report of 1834 was quite clear that the Law of Settlement still prevented anything like the free movement of labour, and gave a large portion of its space to a consideration of the best way of mitigating this particular evil.

At that time the Poor Law was largely founded upon the maintenance of the Settlement Code, and under existing conditions of transport and communication the temptation to move cannot have been great enough to make a very serious inroad on a law which was accepted, though grudgingly, as part of the order of things. If such a migration had taken place there would hardly have been the outcry about the oppression of the Law of Settlement.

The obvious glee with which the first two annual Reports of the Poor Law Commissioners state the measure of success which had attended their efforts to promote migration from the south to the industrial north, and the requests of the manufacturers in the north, show that before that time the extent of the migration had not been very extensive. To the same conclusion tend the statements that the migration took place with considerable reluctance, and that the supply of labourers that did migrate into these counties did not come from the south but from such neighbouring counties as the rural parts of Yorkshire, Cheshire, Derby and Westmorland[1].

This does not, however, dispose of the question of migration. In the parish register return of the 1831 Census, comparisons are given of the natural increase in the various counties and the actual increase as shown by the Census returns in the same counties. These figures show that between 1801 and 1831 there was a considerable loss by migration in the six counties which were most affected by the allowance system and a considerable gain in the three counties not affected. This, in the thirty years, amounts to a loss in the one case of 37,405 people, and to a gain, in the other, of 40,138. The tendency of all such migrations was from the country districts to the towns, and the problem that we are dealing with is primarily a rural one. On more

---

[1] *Reports*, 1835, xxxv. 1st Annual Report of P.L. Commrs. pp. 21, 216. *Reports*, 1836, xxxiv. State of the Irish Poor in Great Britain, pp. xxvi, xxvii.

perfect data the loss might be shown as larger owing to the greater inaccuracy in the figures for baptisms than in those for burials. In the three counties least affected by the allowance system this migration probably affects the question very little, as the migration would be chiefly to the towns, though in Northumberland the increase of more or less scattered mining villages may have had the effect of drawing migrants to parts of the county which at the beginning of the century were definitely rural. In the other group of counties, as the migration would be chiefly from the rural parts to towns outside those counties, it is more important. As the figures are given for the whole counties, it is impossible to correlate them satisfactorily with the previous population figures given in these counties, because these were for the rural parts only. It may be worth while, for the sake of argument, to assume that the actual increase —that is, the increase which the Census returns show—was a healthy growth of the population, and that the natural increase in excess of the actual increase—the extent of the migration—was an unhealthy growth caused by the Poor Laws. The first objection to this assumption will be that in these counties part of the actual increase, in addition to that arising from migration, may have been due to the Poor Laws and that further migration did not take place because of the action of the Laws of Settlement, which, it will be said, this assumption entirely ignores. This is no doubt in part true, but it is probably counteracted by other factors which come in on the other side.

To maintain this assumption, however, the unhealthy increase of the population due to the Poor Laws in these six counties would in that case amount to 37,405. Now in the year 1821 the population of these six counties was one-eleventh of the whole population of England. If, therefore, we say that, in the thirty years, the increase of population in these counties caused by the Poor Laws was in the same proportion to the total increase in all England caused by the Poor Laws as was the population of these six counties in the middle of the worst part of the period to the population of all England, we shall find that in the thirty years the total increase that can be put down to the Poor Laws was 411,455 persons. This figure is rather more than one-twelfth of the total increase of England in the thirty years, and one-ninth of the natural increase in the same period.

If, however, the objection is maintained that the increase caused by the Poor Laws in those counties was really more than the amount of the migration, then these figures are too small—at least the figures given for the six counties, before these figures were applied to the whole country, are too small.

But, on the other hand, it may be urged that two-thirds of that excess of the natural over the actual increase in the six counties occurred in the first decade of the century, which was a decade almost entirely of war with by no means the least strenuous moment at the time of the second Census[1]. These figures are based on the actual enumeration given in the Census returns which do not include any addition for the men on active service. It is right, therefore, to assume that at any rate a considerable part of this apparent migration is due to service conditions. It should also be remembered that so far from being the worst of the three decades in the Poor Law history this war decade was the best.

Further, to apply these figures to the whole of the country is pretty certainly to be overstating the fact, for these six counties are noted as being the worst in the matter of the prevalence of the allowance system and are not average or representative counties. It is to be presumed that no other counties were so severely affected and we know that some were hardly affected at all. This figure for the whole country is probably much in excess of the truth. Even if some considerable part of the actual increase in these six counties was due to the Poor Laws, it is probable that the figure which has been given as the possible increase in the whole country as due to the Poor Laws, is sufficiently in excess of the truth more than to compensate for this. It is suggested that this figure represents the very outside estimate for the effect of the Poor Laws on the population of the country, and is probably very much too big—and even this amounts to only one-twelfth or one-ninth of the increase in the

---

[1] On the period 1801 to 1831 the six counties lost on their natural increase 37,405. In the decade 1801 to 1811 the same counties lost 22,684.

period, according to whether the total increase or the natural increase is considered.

If, in reckoning the increase in the two groups of counties, the natural increase rather than the actual increase is considered, the results are decidedly different. The group which is said to have been badly affected by the allowance system, which lost a part of its natural increase and will have to be compensated for its loss, would have increased faster than it actually did, and the reverse will be the case in the other group. The possible effect of the Poor Laws may be tested in this way. If the group of counties badly affected is taken and the population of their rural parts in 1801 adopted as the starting point (as in Table XI) and their increase between 1801 and 1831 reckoned on the assumption that they retained their natural increase, their increase is found to be 43·45 per cent. Most of their loss of population would be from their rural districts to towns outside those counties, so it is probably fair to allow for their total loss of population in making this calculation. It must be remembered that if those counties had retained their natural increase their increase would really have been even larger than it appears on these figures, for those people who were retained in the counties would have contributed to the increase by more than their own presence. The group of counties little affected by the allowance system increased by more than their natural increase; in their case the increase has been reckoned also on their natural increase, deducting what they gained over and above it. Their increase works out at 36·25 per cent. Those two results just reverse the position of the two groups in the period 1801–1831 as shown in the figures given in Table XI. In the case of the group which is little affected by the allowance system and which gained population over and above its natural increase, most of the gain was probably absorbed by its urban districts which have been left out of our calculations, so an additional calculation has been made in which from their actual increase not the whole of the number of people they gained beyond their natural increase but 50 per cent. of it has been deducted. In this case the group would have increased by 41·14 per cent. Even these figures reverse the order of the increase as shown in

Table XI, but only make the one group increase by 2·31 per cent. more than the other. There are obviously many sources of fallacy in such a test as this, but it appears to strengthen the conclusion already reached that the effect of the Poor Laws was not very considerable. Even if we take account of the whole of the loss in the one case and the whole of the gain in the other and conclude that the total difference in rates of increase is due to the Poor Laws, it only amounts to 7·20 per cent. in the group of most seriously affected counties. This is slightly smaller than the possible amount arrived at by using these gains and losses in the previous test; and it is pretty safe to say that they represent the very outside possible estimate of the effect of the Poor Laws and probably considerably exaggerate that effect.

The question may be examined with relation to the state of affairs in Scotland. In Scotland, although the framework of the law was very similar to that in England, the unfortunate results of the English law had been avoided. Nevertheless, in 1828 Strickland, writing on the Poor Laws, scouts the idea that they formed a much less serious problem in Scotland than in England, and declares that there was as much need for legislative interference in Scotland as in England, which he appears to attribute to the extent of the Irish immigration into Scotland[1].

The money expended on the relief of the poor in Scotland was derived from a series of odd sources, including such hopeful sources of revenue as voluntary contributions and collections at the kirk door.

It was said that the reason of the small burden of the poor rates was that "even in cases of extreme poverty the relations and neighbours of the paupers have a pride in providing for their necessities in whole or in part." Where legal assessment was introduced it was seen to increase the number of paupers, and there seems to have been sufficient doggedness to put a stop to the system[2]. In the Report on the Scotch Poor Law it is stated that the policy was strenuously to resist the maintenance of able-bodied people and that there was "great repugnance" on the part of the authorities to grant relief for illegitimate children[3].

---

[1] Strickland, *op. cit.* Sec. x.   [2] *Reports*, 1817, VI. p. 145.
[3] *Reports*, 1844, XX. p. 9.

In 1817 in seven counties in Scotland the expenses per head of the population for the relief of the poor amounted on an average to 2s. (Table XIII). Taking the county expenses for the poor in 1843, together with the 1841 Census, the average in those same counties was 1s. 10d. per head, and over the whole of Scotland it was 1s. 6d. The contrast between these expenses and those in England is very striking, and in justification of taking the 1843 expenses in Scotland it must be remembered that the Poor Law was not amended in Scotland until 1845. It is hardly too much to say that in comparison with England the Poor Law in Scotland was negligible.

Table XIII. SCOTLAND. POOR RATE PER HEAD
OF POPULATION IN CERTAIN SCOTTISH COUNTIES

The figures for 1817 are from the *Report on the Poor Laws*, 1817, VI. p. 145. The figures for 1843 are from *Accounts and Papers*, 1843, XLIX. The population figures used in this case are those of the 1841 Census.

Counties	1817 s.	d.	1843 s.	d.
Aberdeen	1	7	1	6
Argyll		7		6
Berwick	5	3	3	6
Sutherland		2½		5
Selkirk	2	2	2	5
Roxburgh	3	0	3	3
Linlithgow	1	3	1	5
Averages	2	0	1	10
Averages over the whole country			1	6

With a Poor Law so little burdensome there was evidently little stimulus to the growth of the population in Scotland from that source, indeed it is sometimes said that the arrangements of the Poor Law, such as they were, actually checked the rapid increase of the population. In any case, there can be little doubt that the Poor Laws did not increase the population of Scotland[1].

In the three decades from 1801 to 1831, the population of Scotland increased 0·5 per cent., 1·5 per cent. and 3 per cent. less than the population of England in the same decades[2]. It

[1] Census Report, 1821, p. xxv.
[2] Enumeration Abstract, 1841, Introd. p. 9:

	1801–11	1811–21	1821–31
England	14·5 %	17·5 %	16·0 %
Scotland	14·0	16·0	13·0

is somewhat astonishing to find that Scotland was increasing so fast in relation to England, for there was not the industrial development to account for it. On the other hand, McCulloch says that in the first half of the nineteenth century the wealth of Scotland had increased faster than that of England, and he puts this down to the consolidation of farms in the lowlands, to the increase of sheep farming in the highlands and to the absence of pauperising and demoralising tendencies in the population, but it should be noted that such sources of wealth are not those which would be expected to lead to a large increase in the population[1].

There has always been a considerable migration of Scots from Scotland to England. Allowing for a certain migration, in this period, the result would be to make the Census returns show a greater divergence between the two countries than is due to their natural increase, for a certain number of Scottish-born people would migrate to England between the Censuses, thereby lowering the figure for Scotland and raising that for England.

It might be assumed for sake of argument that the increase in wealth and skill in the two countries during this period was the same, and that the excess of the English increase over the Scottish was due to the influence of the Poor Laws in England. It might be said, on the other hand, that the increase in the kind of manufacturing skill that tends to the growth of population was so much less in Scotland than in England, that the Scottish increase is really very remarkable and that there must have been other causes at work. But as it is pretty certain that among those causes we cannot include the Poor Laws, this is not very important. The facts with which we are concerned are that in Scotland the population increased at a rate not much slower than in England, that the Poor Laws were not concerned in that increase, that we should expect England to increase at a faster rate and that these facts leave very little room in England for an increase caused directly by the operation of the Poor Laws.

It may also be urged, as already mentioned, that the Poor Laws in Scotland did not merely fail to stimulate the growth

---

[1] McCulloch, *Resources of the British Empire*, p. 429.

of the population but actually checked it, and if this is so it leaves a still smaller margin for any increase in England which can be put down solely to the influence of the Poor Laws. Further, the fact which has been previously mentioned that there was a considerable migration from Scotland to England also tends to lessen the margin for any increase in the latter country caused by the Poor Laws.

Thus we have two countries, the one with a burdensome Poor Law which is said to stimulate and to be responsible for the increase in the population, and the other in which there is a poor rate which is practically negligible. In the first country there are other influences tending to the increase of the population which are not so operative in the second. There is a migration of uncertain amount from the second country to the first, and yet the two countries increase over a period of thirty years with a difference of only from 0·5 per cent. to 3 per cent. Bearing in mind the industrial causes, to mention only one variety of these, which would lead us to expect England to increase faster than Scotland during that period, there is not very much of that general increase in England greater than in Scotland which can be attributed to the action of the Poor Laws.

Table XIV. MARRIAGE RATES IN THE GROUPS OF COUNTIES

Numbers of marriages in the 8th Annual Report of the Registrar General, *Reports*, 1847–8, xxv.

Persons married per thousand of the population

Year	Cumb.	Lincs	Northumb.	Averages
1801	12·5	14·3	11·9	12·9
1811	15·6	17·7	14·7	16·0
1821	13·2	16·7	14·6	14·5
1831	12·8	16·7	15·4	14·9
1841	11·4	13·3	15·9	13·5

General average 14·4

Year	Beds	Bucks	Dorset	Suffolk	Sussex	Wilts	Averages
1801	14·3	14·3	12·0	13·7	14·2	11·8	13·4
1811	19·4	15·9	13·1	16·8	15·9	14·0	15·8
1821	18·3	16·1	14·5	15·5	15·2	15·6	15·8
1831	17·1	15·3	15·5	16·0	16·1	15·6	15·9
1841	16·0	11·6	13·3	15·0	14·0	12·3	13·7

General average 14·9

It is interesting to examine the state of marriages in relation to the Poor Laws in the two groups of counties taken. The marriage rate has been given in the groups at the five Census years, 1801, 1811, 1821, 1831, 1841 (Table XIV). In all the counties the general tendency is for the marriage rate to be higher in the middle three periods than in the years 1801 or 1841. In four of the counties severely affected by the allowance system, that is in Buckingham, Suffolk, Sussex and Wiltshire, the higher rate of marriage in those periods is very clearly marked; in Bedfordshire it is not quite so clearly marked, while in Dorset it is still less so, as the 1841 figure does not fall below the 1811 figure, which it does in all the other five counties in this group. In the expenses for the maintenance of the poor in this group, Dorset has the lowest throughout. In the other group Lincoln is the county in which there is a noticeable increase in the marriage rate in the middle three periods, and this is the county which in its Poor Law expenses in this group most resembles the counties in the other group. In Northumberland the marriage rate, except for a slight check in 1821, goes up steadily throughout the whole period. This may be due to the influence of Newcastle which was by far the biggest town in any county in this group. In Cumberland the marriage rate makes a big jump up in 1811; 1821 and 1831 show no great rise on 1801, while in 1841 the rate falls below any of its previous records.

On these figures it may possibly be a tenable position to adopt that the allowance system accentuated the rise in the marriage rate in the middle three periods. When the average rates in the different groups at the various periods are compared, it will be seen that the group which was most affected had a higher rate than the other in three out of the five periods; it was higher in 1801, it was slightly lower in 1811, and as this is one of the middle three periods it is worthy of mention. In the next two periods, as was to be expected, the rate is higher, and in the last period it falls below the rate in the other group. The difference is, however, never very great; and when a general average in the two groups throughout the whole period is taken the difference is very slight, the rates being 14·4 in one case and 14·9 in the group which was most affected. Thus, on the whole, the average marriage rate in the counties seriously affected by the allowance system was slightly higher than in the other counties.

CHAPTER VII

Factors affecting the Death Rate: Agriculture and Food

THE eighteenth-century inclosure movement and its effect on the population has been dealt with exhaustively by Prof. Gonner in *Common Land and Inclosure*, in which work the conclusions have been supported by an extensive show of figures behind which it would be useless to attempt to go. The problem has also been dealt with by Dr Slater in his book on the English peasantry, and less extensively in his *Making of Modern England*. So far as the general effects are concerned, the conclusions in these works may be accepted. It was only the inclosure of common fields which "decreased the number of inhabitants, while that of commons had the contrary effect," and on the whole it appears that in this century there is no general depopulation to be dealt with as a result of inclosure, as has sometimes been supposed[1].

On the other hand, the increase of the population is sometimes attributed to the inclosures[2]. The chief economic gains of the inclosure movement were increased area under cultivation, improved methods of agriculture and a larger supply of food-stuffs. This increase in the amount of foodstuffs raised came at a time when, with a growing population, it was necessary to increase the amount of home-grown food. The question of the food supply was at the very heart of the population problem. In Ireland it was the easy and plentiful supply of potatoes that

[1] *The advantages and disadvantages of inclosing waste lands and open fields*, 1772, p. 43. *An inquiry into the advantages and disadvantages resulting from Bills of Inclosure*, 1780, p. 12. Gonner, *Common Land and Inclosure*, pp. vi, 411. Slater, *English Peasantry*, pp. 92, 104.

[2] Trevelyan, *British History in the Nineteenth Century*, p. 150: "The rapid increase of the population, so much deplored at this time by the disciples of Malthus, was due very largely, first to the enclosures, and then to Speen-hamland." It was certainly hoped that the inclosure of waste at any rate would have that effect. See *Reports*, 1795, IX. p. 210 (on waste lands): "His mind must indeed be callous, who feels himself uninterested in measures, by which not only the barren waste is made to smile, but of which the object is to fill the desert with a hardy, laborious, and respectable race of inhabitants, the real strength of a country."

rendered possible the growth and temporary maintenance of a large population, and it was the failure of that food supply that brought disaster to the country and started the great rush to emigrate. It is not, of course, at once obvious whether the potato system in Ireland was the cause or the effect of the growth of the population; an increasing population, increasing from other causes, might take to potatoes as its food, or the abundance of potatoes might encourage the population to increase without there being any other and sufficient warrant for that increase. In that case the two facts of increased food supply and increasing population go together. This was the problem at the bottom of all that Malthus had to say on population. Malthus lived in the country and he wrote just at the time that the distress resulting from the wars with France was acute, when the price of wheat was going up and the number of inclosures was becoming greater than ever before, and his argument was that the population would tend to outstrip the capacity of the country to find food for its maintenance, and that it would eventually be kept within the limits which the country could maintain by checks taking in their crude form inadequacy of food and the evils which result therefrom. In so far as the inclosure movement tended to increase the population at this time, it did so by increasing the supply of food which it made available for the people at a time when the nation still had to be more or less self-supporting and by improving its quality in such a way as to reduce the death rate. The inclosure of commons may have increased the amount of work to be done on the land, but this, together with scientific farming, is the improvement in agriculture which corresponds in industry to the labour-saving devices—the spinning and the weaving machines—and to the devices for increasing production—the use of coal for smelting. The ruling motive in all cases was not to employ more men but to produce more goods. The industrial activities, as time went on, employed more men both absolutely and relatively, and under conditions which had certain effects in stimulating the growth of the population; the number of families engaged in agriculture increased until after the 1821 Census, and in the decade following that Census the number of inclosure acts was less than it had been since the middle of the eighteenth century[1]. The point is that, although the agricultural improvements may have provided employment for more people, this was not nearly such a prominent fact as in the parallel movement which was going on in industry, and the real service of the agricultural revolution, if it may be so called, was the more abundant and improved food supply which was rendered possible by it.

The authorities seem to be agreed that the economic gain of inclosure cannot be questioned[2]. Lord Ernle says that by 1790 no voice was raised against the movement on any other grounds than the moral and social evil which it might inflict[3]. The economic gain was admitted. It was the open field system that was primarily attacked by the inclosure movement of the eighteenth century, and it is probable that the bulk of the land inclosed at that time was common field land. With the beginning of the wars with France and with the small signs of their ending for some time, with the rise in the price of wheat and possibly as a result of the first Census, which showed that the population was undoubtedly bigger than many people had imagined, the inclosure movement took a fresh lease of life. In this period it was the common pasture and waste lands that were seriously tackled—the lands that even general opponents of the movement were ready to see inclosed. In some cases the lands merely wanted cultivating, in others they required drainage and preparation; in any case the gain was obvious and the necessity great, and where drainage was required the gain had another side— it was good for the health of the community.

The figures of waste inclosure show that before 1760 it amounted to very little, that it was considerably greater in the last forty years of the century, but that the great period of inclosure of waste was the first forty years of the nineteenth century, and that much the greater part of the amount that took place in that period occurred in the thirteen years from 1802

---

[1] From the Census Reports:
Families chiefly engaged in agriculture
1811   697,353   1821   773,732   1831   761,348
[2] Gonner, pp. vi, 302–5. Slater, *Making of Modern England*, p. 39.
[3] Ernle, *English Farming Past and Present*, p. 302.

to 1815[1]. In the last forty years of the eighteenth century and in the first forty years of the nineteenth century, the total number of inclosure bills was practically the same, but the bills dealing exclusively with common pasture and waste were 521 in the first period as against 808 in the second.

In 1795 a Committee reported that "the present scarcity and high price of provisions" called most forcibly for the inclosure of large tracts of uncultivated land and in this they had the support of practical farmers[2]. It was with such sentiments that the movement to inclose waste lands started, and at the end of the period we find evidence which goes to show that the movement had to some extent achieved its object. In 1833 it was said that the land in Cambridgeshire had been much improved, that there had been a great outlay in draining and that there was a great spirit of improvement abroad[3]. In 1836 it was stated that, in spite of a fear expressed at the time of the Corn Law in 1815 that the country could not produce anything like what it consumed, "the increase of cultivation had far outstripped the consumption."[4]

In the general Report on Commons Inclosure in 1844 the same points are emphasised. Open fields were said to be cultivated with such inconvenience and difficulty that this could not be done to any good purpose. In the first place it was said they were so intermixed that effectual drainage was practically impossible[5], and it was, among other things, the improvement in drainage and the experience in agriculture after that improvement, that had given a stimulus to inclosure[6]. The view is also expressed in this Report that the main object of the inclosures had been successful, namely, the increase of the food supply.

[1] Inclosure of common pasture and waste only.

1727–1760	Acts	56	Acres	74,518
1761–1792	,,	339	,,	478,259
1793–1801	,,	182	,,	273,891
1802–1815	,,	564	,,	739,743
1816–1845	,,	244	,,	199,300

[2] *Reports*, 1795, IX. p. 202. *Annals*, XXXVII. (1801), p. 173.
[3] *Reports*, 1833, V. Agriculture, Q. 2101.
[4] *Reports*, 1836, VIII. Qs. 11, 239.
[5] *Reports*, 1844, V. Commons Inclosure, Q. 3356.   [6] *Ibid.* Q. 255.

The question of drainage is important not only because it was evidently in many instances a necessary preliminary to the successful cultivation of inclosed land, or because it was the stimulus that led to the inclosure of some land, but also because, as was said in 1801, the treatment by drainage of boggy and marshy lands, to take one example, was "of as much consequence to the health of a country as to the agriculture of it."[1]

In the eighteenth century the inclosure of waste lands was not opposed, and it was recognised that such inclosure was at any rate not open to the charge of decreasing the amount of available employment. Similarly in 1844 there was no fear that further inclosure of commons would lead to a decrease of employment; on the contrary inclosure was urged as one means of increasing employment[2]. In cases in which inclosure had taken place it was reported to have had a good effect on employment. In Derbyshire the labourers were said to be provided with better employment as a result of the inclosure and to be quite satisfied[3]. In Lincolnshire the Common Field Inclosure Act was regarded as "one of the greatest boons and public advantages" in an agricultural district, and to the inclosure and employment which resulted is attributed the comfortable state of the agricultural population in Lincolnshire[4].

The agricultural improvements during the period were not confined to those in the cultivation of crops. Cattle farming had been a profitable occupation in the early part of the eighteenth century, but with the improvements introduced by Bakewell[5], and probably with the general improvement of the land, it advanced greatly in the latter half of the century, and this improvement also had an important effect on the food supplies of the country. The contribution of "Turnip" Townsend in the earlier part of the century was directly connected with this improvement in the cattle of the country. As Thorold Rogers pointed out, the general adoption by the farmer of root crops in place of the bare fallows, and the extended cultivation

---

[1] *Annals*, 1801, xxxvi. p. 76. See also *Reports*, 1844, Q. 1520.
[2] *Reports*, 1844, v. Qs. 177–9, 772, 1854, 5328.
[3] *Ibid.* Q. 1854.
[4] *Ibid.* Q. 1385 et seq.
[5] Cunningham, ii. p. 546 (1907 reprint).

of clover, supplied the farmer with winter feed, which was more abundant and better in quality than anything that had been available before. From this increase of winter feed there followed an increase of stock, for a lack of winter feed had been one of the greatest difficulties which the stock farmer had had to face[1]. This increase of stock meant in its turn more fresh animal food, particularly in the winter, and probably also an improvement in the milk supply, both of them important points in the qualitative aspect of the food supply. Further than that, an increased number of beasts meant more manure, and again to quote Thorold Rogers, "the greatly increased produce of the eighteenth century was due entirely to the increased use of natural manures." The Report on Waste Lands of 1795 declared that the difference between the size of cattle and sheep at that time and in the reign of Queen Anne, when half the stock of the kingdom was fed on commons, was hardly to be credited and was to be attributed to the practice of feeding young stock on good inclosed pastures instead of on wastes and commons[2]. Thus the improvement in the cultivation of crops and in the raising of cattle by the use of different kinds of foodstuffs went hand in hand.

It is probably fair, therefore, to summarise thus: throughout the inclosure movement of the eighteenth and early nineteenth century, the quantity and quality of the food, both grain and meat, improved, and the country would thereby be enabled to support a larger population and also probably to preserve a better state of health in that population. Opponents of the inclosure movement in general did not attack the inclosure of wastes, nor did they accuse this of causing depopulation or of decreasing employment, and when in the nineteenth century the relative importance of the waste inclosures increased they were praised as a means of increasing population.

---

[1] Rogers, *Six centuries of work and wages*, II. p. 475. See also *Reports*, 1795, IX. p. 204: "In regard to feeding lambs, colts, or calves, it is apprehended that grounds free from disease, and inclosures properly watered and sheltered can afford grass better and more plentiful and rear them on the whole to better advantage, than wild barren commons, overrun with heath, furze, fern, or brush wood."

[2] *Reports*, 1795, IX. p. 204.

It is not so easy to determine to what extent this increase in the food supply of the nation was a cause stimulating the growth of the population, or whether it was the increase in the population that was taking place for other reasons which made it necessary to increase the food supply and in turn stimulated agriculturists to the required experiment and enterprise. The truth probably lies somewhere between these two extremes. The population could not have been maintained unless the food supply had increased, yet there were other causes at work tending to increase the population, and it is doubtful whether the food supply had so immediate and direct an influence on the growth of the population in this country as it had in Ireland, where there were not the other influences at work to the same extent. On the other hand, the increase of the population is looked upon as the cause of agricultural prosperity[1]. In any case the connection between the inclosure movement and the growth of the population is very close, though it is not easy to decide which was cause and which effect, even if such a clear-cut division actually existed. The connection is easily demonstrated and is interesting.

War, the price of wheat and inclosure were all closely connected. Fear for the food supply during time of war, even without the stimulus of high prices, seems to have led to inclosure. The diagram of inclosure bills and the price of wheat shows that the price of wheat did not begin to rise to any great extent until 1794 (see Diagram IV)[2]. During the American war there was a big rise in the number of inclosure bills and the price of wheat did not rise; the inclosures seem to have done their work, and this, with the feeling of security, is reflected in the small number of inclosures between that time and the beginning of the French wars. After that time the population was growing at its greatest rate, the price of wheat rose to its greatest

---

[1] *Reports*, 1836, VIII. Qs. 15, 965.

[2] Cannan, *Theories of Production and Distribution*, p. 150, gives a similar graph for the years 1793 to 1815. The inclosure figures which he used were got by counting the bills in the statute book, he mentions the three official returns of the bills which have been used in compiling the diagram given here, and points out that they do not agree either with the statute book or with one another.

height and the number of inclosure bills became much greater than before. There are three peaks in the price of wheat and three peaks in the number of inclosure bills and these roughly correspond in time. The beginning of the war seems to have sent up the number of inclosure bills before the price of wheat went up, though the price of wheat followed in 1795 and 1796, but it fell again in 1797 before there was any fall in the number of inclosure bills. The second rise in the price of wheat was from 1798 to 1801, which was the biggest rise recorded; in this case the increase in the number of inclosure bills followed after the rise in the price of wheat, and again fell to 1804 after the price of wheat had fallen; in these two peaks the matter is complicated by a succession of bad harvests. In the third peak, which is the longest in duration, the connection is not so obvious and the number of inclosure bills seems to be ahead of the price of wheat, though even in this peak a drop in the price of wheat on two occasions brings down the number of bills. After 1815 the war motive ceased to operate, and the great drop in the number of bills is also accounted for by the fact that inclosure cannot go on for ever—there is nothing left to inclose. It appears to have been the fear for the food supply that caused the first rise in the number of bills. When the price declined temporarily the inclosure bills fell—people felt they had done their work; then the price rose and this started the inclosures again. The short existence of the peace of Amiens, and the feeling that the second period of the struggle might be long, probably started the third peak. The commercial motive must also be reckoned with; when wheat prices were going up, inclosure to grow wheat would present itself as a profitable speculation. It must be remembered also that an inclosure bill is like a piece of chalk— it may be large or small, inclosing many or few acres—but in spite of these reservations the political inferences from the movement are interesting and reflect the anxiety that was felt about the food supply.

The numbers of inclosure bills and the rate of increase of the population can also be compared, though nothing beyond a fairly rough generalisation can be hazarded from this; the rise of inclosures during the American war destroys a correspondence that might have been more close in that period, but from the decade 1780–1790 the numbers of bills rise, and it is in this decade that the increase of the population becomes really rapid; the two decades which show the greater number of inclosure bills also show the greatest increase in the population.

Gonner publishes some figures showing the amount of inclosure, common field and other, in various decades[1]. Between 1790 and 1820 there are twenty-four counties which show a considerable amount of common inclosure. In the first thirty years of the nineteenth century seventeen of these increased by more than their natural increase, and the remaining seven lost a part of their natural increase. It would look at first sight as though inclosure of waste land in this period definitely acted as a stimulus to population, and even if it did not promote the natural increase it seems to have encouraged migration and may provide a possible explanation of a part of the shifting of the population. If this problem is regarded as an agricultural one, there are some facts that detract from the effect when the counties are examined more in detail. Among the seventeen counties which show an increase greater than their natural increase are Cheshire, Lancashire, Staffordshire and the West Riding, in which the increase must have been due to industry rather than to agriculture, and Essex, Hertfordshire, Middlesex and Surrey, in which the proximity of London may have caused inclosure for residential purposes. In all these cases a certain amount of agricultural inclosure may have taken place as a result of the growing towns and industrial centres which stood on part of the inclosed land. When transport was not so good as it is now and the means of preserving food less efficient, a growing town must have meant, even more surely than it does to-day, such establishments as dairy farms and market gardens in its proximity, and these require inclosed land. Even if in many cases this inclosure of waste was not being turned to the cultivation of crops and the increase of strictly agricultural employment, still the inclosure was necessary to the growth of an industrial population and to the indispensable adjuncts of an industrial area.

[1] Gonner, pp. 279–281.

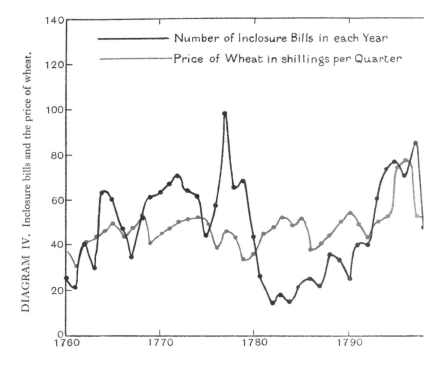

DIAGRAM IV. Inclosure bills and the price of wheat.

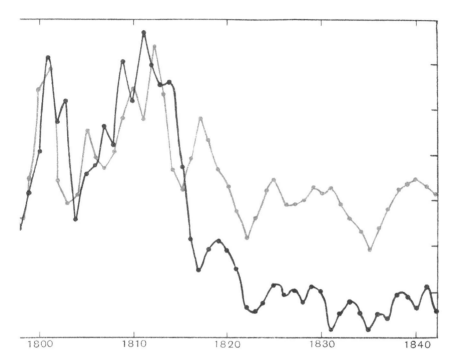

NOTE ON THE CONSTRUCTION OF DIAGRAM IV

The yearly prices of wheat are taken from Prothero's *Pioneers and Progress of English Farming*, Appendix 1.

The three official sources for the number of inclosure bills are:

Reports, 1819, III. Lords Report on the expediency of resuming cash payments. Appendix G 6, pp. 430 and 431.

Reports, 1836, VIII. Part II. p. 501. Third Report from the Commons' Committee on Agriculture.

Accounts and Papers, 1843, XLVIII. 23. Waste Lands (Inclosure Acts).

From these sources the diagram is compiled as follows:

1760–1787	*Reports*, 1836.
1788–1818	*Reports*, 1819.
	(With the 1843 figure for 1808 and 1810)
1818 onwards	*Accounts and Papers*, 1843.

CHAPTER VIII

Factors affecting the Death Rate:
Health of Towns and Factories

IN a period when the trend of the population was towards
the towns and when the organisation that was coming into
prominence was that of the factory, the health both of the towns
and of the factory, and the reduction of mortality in these, are
of great importance in the growth of the population, especially
as the reduction in the death rate during this period of rapidly
increasing population was a more important factor than the rise
in the birth rate.

There are, however, difficulties in dealing with the subject,
for this is not merely a question of quantity, but one of quality
as well. Gaskell, writing in 1833 of the manufacturing population, said that merely because the duration of life was extended,
it by no means followed that the people were a healthier race
than their forefathers[1]. He compares rural life in which "life
is physical enjoyment, and disease hasty death" with the conditions prevailing in the new factory districts, or as existing
in a high as contrasted with a low civilisation, in which life "is
one long disease, and death the result of physical exhaustion."[2]

This consideration may have an effect on the growth of the
population; if it be true that the growth of modern industrial
conditions, although accompanied by a lengthening of life,
lowered the general health level of the community, then in time
that damage to the general health would probably affect the
birth rate.

Apart from this, the information on which one has to rely
for the state of the towns is not of the best for the early part of
the period. It is of a scattered and scrappy kind, and although
there are many statements that the conditions have improved
it is very difficult to get any standard by which to gauge the

---

[1] Gaskell, *Manufacturing Population*, 1833, p. 221.
[2] *Ibid.* p. 226.

improvement. As a test of the conditions in the towns the birth and death rates are very unreliable. Over the whole country the rates before the introduction of civil registration are open enough to the charge of inaccuracy, but it is probable that most of this was concentrated in the towns, and that the town rates are the least reliable. Here the baptism figures are said to be a very inadequate representation of the births, and the burial figures are said to give a false impression in one of two ways; in some cases they give an under-estimate, as many Dissenters were buried in places other than the parish burial grounds, which alone were officially registered; in other cases the towns are said to be burdened with deaths for which they were really not responsible, as for example in the case of people who had failed in the country and had come into the towns as a last hope. On the whole, therefore, the town rates have to be treated with caution[1].

Improvements in London began about 1760; it was stated that since the improvements and rebuilding which had followed the Fire nothing had been done until about that time. In 1762 Westminster set the example of reform and was followed in 1766 by the City. "'Fleet Ditch' was then first covered in....Posts were removed, Signs...were taken down...and cleanliness still further promoted by the more active employment of scavengers"[2] and the increased supply of water. Another account of the improvements at this time gives a list of thirty-five distinct and separate works that were to be undertaken in the City of London[3]. About the same time the newspapers were evidently taking up the song and recommending the removal of the signs which blocked up the streets, on the analogy of the improvement which had resulted in Paris from a similar measure[4]; twenty

---

[1] Gaskell, *Manufacturing Population*, p. 232. *Reports*, 1833, XXI. p. 117.

[2] Bateman, *Reports on the Diseases of London*, 1819, pp. 15 and 19.

[3] Malcolm, *Manners and Customs of London*, 1810, V. p. 383.

[4] *Ibid.* p. 393. Quoting a newspaper of 1764: "In the beginning of the reign of Louis XIV the inhabitants of Paris were ever complaining how sick the city was, and how fast they died; upon which, Louis consulted the medical people what could be the cause of it; and they all agreed that it was owing to the largeness of the signs...which choked up the free circulating air, which ever administers to health (they were then prohibited beyond a certain size). Soon after this edict was published, it was declared by the inhabitants that they found a sensible difference in their health."

years later this is reckoned as one of the notable improvements in the condition of London[1]. In the early part of the nineteenth century it was said again and again that London had improved and particular stress is laid on the period after 1760. The whole of the town was said to be well paved and the streets frequently cleansed, and "what probably most contributes to its salubrity, are the capacious and well arranged subterraneous sewers, which convey from every part to the Thames, there being a natural descent, the filth and ordure of the town."[2] This is probably an unduly rosy account of the state of affairs, as the sewers were found to be in a bad condition when there was an inquiry concerning those of the metropolis in 1834, and in the later town reports much the same was said about the paving and cleansing, though that does not necessarily mean that there may not have been a good deal of truth in these statements when they were made. Heberden, writing in 1807, said that cleanliness and ventilation were the principal causes of the better conditions that existed in London and all big towns at that time compared with the state of the same towns in the seventeenth century[3].

The mortality in London[4] reflected, according to Hawkins also, the general improvement which was recorded: "The annual mortality in the year 1700 was about 1 in 25 (40 per thousand), it seems to have increased from that time to 1720, to have attained its highest point from 1720 to 1750; and from that period to the present to have maintained a constant and gradual decline," and he gives the following rates of mortality: 28·8 per thousand in 1801, 26·3 in 1811 and 25·0 in 1821[5].

Towards the end of the eighteenth century Manchester was said to be healthier than previously. Percival, writing about 1780, said, "there is good reason to believe that Manchester is more healthy now than formerly, the new streets are wide and spacious, the poor have larger and more commodious dwellings, and the increase of trade affords them better clothing and diet than they before enjoyed."[6]

[1] Wales, 1781, p. 18.   [2] *A Picture of the Royal College of Physicians*, 1817.
[3] Heberden, *R.C.P. Med. Trans.* IV. p. 69.
[4] "London" is London within the Bills of Mortality.
[5] Hawkins, *Med. Stats.* (1829), pp. 18, 19.   [6] Percival, III. p. 6.

In Manchester, during this period, the death rate was falling. In 1750, according to Hawkins, it was 40·0 per thousand, and although in 1760, according to Roberton, it was 47·6, it had fallen to 35·7 in 1770, according to Hawkins, and to 33·3 in 1773, according to Roberton, while for 1811 Hawkins and Blane give it as 13·5 per thousand[1]. This last figure is objected to by Roberton, who, writing in 1829, says that "so palpable an error must surely have originated with the printer rather than with the author."[2] The rate certainly is astonishingly low, and it may be that it is an illustration of the difficulty of obtaining safe information from the data that are available, for the death rate for Manchester for the year 1811, worked out on a five-year average of the burials recorded in the Census returns with the Census figure for 1811, is 14·3 per thousand, and this sounds almost impossible.

It was the cholera epidemic of 1831 and 1832 that really turned attention to the state of the towns, and there follows a series of reports each picturing a deplorable condition of things; a condition of things which, if indeed it was the result of a long period of improvement, makes one wonder what the places must have been like before.

In 1833 there was an inquiry into the provision of public walks and places of exercise in the big towns; the provision was found to be inadequate, and to have decreased owing to the enhanced value of property in towns and the tempting opportunities for profitable building which that afforded[3].

In 1837 or 1838 Dr Arnott and Dr Kay made a series of inquiries for the Poor Law Commissioners into the physical causes of fever in London. The mere catalogue, first of recommendations, and then of causes which affected the poor injuriously, some of which originated in their habits and some of which arose independently of these, gives a vivid picture of what the state of the city must have been[4]. The story told by these two

---

[1] Hawkins, p. 19; Roberton, *On Mortality*, p. 19; Blane, *Select Dissertations*, p. 174.

[2] Roberton, p. 19. [3] *Reports*, 1833, XV. pp. 2, 4.

[4] *Reports*, 1837–8, XXVIII. Drs Arnott and Kay. Recommendations:
   (1) Perfect system of drains.
   (2) Plentiful supply of water.
   (3) Effective service of scavengers.
   (4) Free ventilation.

men is confirmed in an independent report at the same time by Dr Southwood Smith, who says that fever was most prevalent in "the immediate neighbourhood of uncovered sewers, stagnant ditches and ponds, gutters always full of putrefying matter." The drainage and sewage system had evidently not made entirely satisfactory progress, the advantage of an improvement in these things was represented as being almost instantaneous in its effects, and the line between districts which were well drained and free from fever and districts which were badly drained and subject to fever was drawn with such certainty that in one part where the improvement had taken place it was said "on the other hand, in the passages, courts, alleys on the very opposite side of the street and from the houses of which there are no drains into the common sewer, fever of a fatal character has been exceedingly prevalent."[1]

The interesting fact in this prevalence of fever and lack of drainage in the thirties is bound up with the conditions under which the towns had been growing. Many of the most recently erected suburbs of the great towns exhibited a spectacle of masses of new dwellings huddled together in confused groups, with narrow streets and inclosed courts, disclosing a complete neglect of the most common and obvious sanitary precautions, owing to the fact that there were no controlling regulations and no town planning authority. The industrial conditions aggravated these evils for they meant that people had to be content with any houses they could get[2].

In his description of Manchester in 1832 Kay Shuttleworth

(5) Keeping separate those processes capable of producing malaria: cattle markets, slaughter houses, cow houses, tripe shops, gas manufactories, burial grounds.
(6) Preventing the great crowding of lodging houses.
Causes arising independently of the habits of the poor:
    (1) Imperfection and want of drains and sewers.
    (2) Uncovered stagnant drains and ditches.
    (3) Open stagnant pools with decomposing matter.
    (4) Undrained marsh land.
    (5) Accumulation of refuse.
    (6) Lodgement of filth in large cesspools.
    (7) Situation of slaughter houses.
    (8) State of some of the public burial grounds.
    (9) Want of ventilation in narrow courts and alleys.
[1] *Reports*, 1837–8, XXVIII. Supp. 2.   [2] *Ibid.* p. 82.

repeats the same theory and states that the evils to which this town is exposed are largely due to its uncontrolled growth[1], and it was said in 1845 that in view of the rapid increase in its population since 1811 "it need excite little surprise if the condition of the town should be in various respects unfavourable to the health of its inhabitants."[2]

In the first report on the health of towns in 1844 the growth is again emphasised as a cause of unhealthiness, and the questions of drainage and water supply are dealt with. Drainage was originally surface drainage only; yet, as the towns grew and sewage rather than surface drainage was required, the old regulations which dealt primarily with surface drainage were maintained, whereas others were needed. The Commissioners state that from an inquiry into the drainage conditions of fifty towns, "in scarcely one place can the drainage or sewerage be pronounced to be complete and good, while in seven it is indifferent, and in forty-two decidedly bad,"[3] and very much the same thing is said about the water supply.

In 1840 there was a report on the sanitary condition of the towns, in which the evil of cellar dwellings, particularly in Manchester and Liverpool, is emphasised. In Liverpool one-fifth of the whole working class of the town lived in cellars and the "great proportion of these inhabited cellars were dark, damp, confined, ill-ventilated and dirty."[4] In Manchester the proportion was not so high. The Committee realised the necessity for some measure which made co-ordinated effort to tackle the problem possible, and recommended a General Sewerage and Drainage Act and a General Building Act[5]. The hand loom weavers' Commission of the same year also harps on the necessity of unified control and the share that Governmental interference should have in this campaign[6].

In 1842, "after a long and patient investigation" the whole

[1] Kay Shuttleworth, *Four Periods of Education*, p. 69. See also *Reports*, 1839, xx. p. 106; *Reports*, 1840, xi. p. 1.

[2] *Reports*, 1845, xviii. Appendix, p. 107.

[3] *Reports*, 1840, xvii. pp. ix, x, xi. (Thirteen towns indifferent, thirty-one bad.)

[4] *Reports*, 1840, xi. p. viii. In Liverpool 7800 inhabited cellars, occupied by upwards of 39,000 people. In Manchester 15,000 people in cellar dwellings.

[5] *Ibid.* p. xv.   [6] *Reports*, 1840, xxiv. p. 680.

system of burials within towns was condemned. The evidence is bulky and unsavoury, but the medical witnesses were perfectly definite as to the evil effects of the practice on health[1].

Table XV. DEATH RATES IN FIVE LARGE TOWNS

The rates for 1801, 1811, 1821 and 1831 are burial rates worked on a five-year average, the years taken in each case being the Census year and the four previous years.
The rate for 1840 is a death rate given in *Reports*, 1844, XVII. p. 13.
For a more modern comparison rates for the decades 1881–1890 and 1891–1900 are taken from the decennial supplements to the Reports of the Registrar General.

Deaths (or burials) per thousand of the population

	1801	1811	1821	1831	1840	1881–1890	1891–1900
Birmingham	14·7	29·7	24·9	14·6	27·2	23·0	24·10
Leeds	26·0	25·5	20·3	20·7	27·2	22·4	21·01
Bristol	19·5	13·8	17·1	16·9	31·0	23·4	20·59
Manchester	24·7	14·3	14·1	30·2	33·8	26·9	26·39
Liverpool	26·5	27·0	24·6	21·0	34·8	33·1	33·20
Average	22·28	22·06	20·20	20·69	30·80	25·8	25·06
Corrected by 10 %	24·50	24·26	22·40	22·75	—	—	—
Corrected by 15 %	25·61	25·36	23·50	23·78	—	—	—

These rates are crude rates, i.e. the rate of mortality calculated from the population and registered deaths without reference to age or sex. No other rates are possible for the early period, and while these rates are useful as a rough measure of the sanitary condition of a given place from time to time, provided no serious disturbance has taken place in the age constitution of its population, they should be used very cautiously in comparing different places. The age-distribution of towns is very different from that of the country: their populations contain very few, relatively, of the aged. When crude death rates are corrected to a standard population they are seen to go down in the case of rural districts and up in the case of urban districts. The following examples will make the point clear.
Supplement to 55th Annual Report of R.G. 1897, p. xxxviii.

Death rates in decade 1881–1890

	Crude	In standard population
Bridge	19·86	16·60
Biggleswade	19·88	17·85
Godstone	19·78	18·03
Uxbridge	19·88	18·55
Norwich	19·83	18·81
Bridgend	19·82	19·70
Chorley	19·82	20·20
Bradford	19·90	20·96
Huddersfield	19·86	21·50
Dewsbury	19·82	21·88

This example is summarised in the Decennial Report of 1907 (Supplement to 65th Annual Report of R.G. p. lxiv) as follows: "As a further illustration

[1] *Reports*, 1842, x. p. iv.

of the varying effects of correction in respect of small areas a table was given showing ten registration districts whose crude death rates were practically identical (ranging only from 19·78 to 19·90 per 1000 persons living) while their corrected rates ranged from 16·60 to 21·88 per 1000." Compare also Supplement to 65th Annual Report of R.G. p. lxv:

Death rates in the decade 1891–1900

	England and Wales	Urban Districts	Rural Districts
Crude death rate	18·19	19·41	16·95
Corrected death rate		20·34	14·88

Death rates for the first four Census years and for 1840 have been secured for five large and representative towns: Birmingham, Bristol, Leeds, Liverpool and Manchester (Table XV). For the first four Census years these have been worked out from the information in the Census returns and the rate for 1840 has been taken from the Towns Report of 1844 and figures for two modern decades added for comparison. The figures are likely to be inaccurate and the great difference seen when civil registration was introduced shows that this was the case. In spite of this the general movement can probably be deduced from the figures, though even this may not be very reliable. Birmingham, after an unaccountably low rate in 1801, improved steadily from 1811 until after 1831; in 1841, even though the rate was higher, it was, on the showing of the death rates, the most healthy of the five towns and in 1840 it had been picked out as a town which "appears to form rather a favourable contrast, in several particulars, with the state of other large towns."[1] Bristol, except in 1811 when the rate was particularly low, improved steadily until 1831. Leeds improved until 1821, and then got worse again, the rate for 1831 being higher than the rate for 1821, and the same to a more marked degree was the case in Manchester. On the showing of these figures Liverpool improved steadily until 1831, but the 1841 figures showed it to have the highest death rate of any of the towns; the number of cellar dwellings was greater than elsewhere and it was said to be the "most densely populated town in England."[2] Two out of the five towns, therefore, had experienced a rise in the death rate between 1821 and 1831, and all of them had done so between 1831 and 1841. This latter rise was no doubt due in part to the

[1] *Reports*, 1840, XI. p. xii.   [2] *Reports*, 1844, XVII. p. 27.

improvement of the information on the introduction of civil registration, but the difference is about 33 per cent., which is more than three times as much as the correction which had to be made in the burial figures all over the country, so it is probable that the 1841 figure really does represent a higher rate than that of 1831, particularly as the general death rate of the country was going up at the latter date[1].

We have seen that at the end of the eighteenth century and the beginning of the nineteenth the towns were considered to be improving. In the thirties and forties of the nineteenth century we have the gruesome stories told in the various town reports, accompanied by statements that it was the rapid increase of population and the unregulated growth of the towns that were causing the bad conditions which were being attacked. These statements are accompanied by others to the effect that it was only lately that the conditions had been recognised as being bad[2]. A possible explanation of the whole movement is that in the earlier part of the period, during which the towns were not increasing as rapidly as they did later on, and during which the movement for town improvement and improvement of health generally was in full operation, the towns really did improve in health. Then when the growth of the towns became more rapid and was not properly watched or regulated, the evils which accompanied this unregulated growth were such as more than to counteract the improvements that had been made earlier and the towns again got more unhealthy. This movement is confirmed in part by the general death rate of the whole country, which as time went on was becoming more and more predominantly urban, and in part by the figures for the five towns which have just been discussed. The complaint, therefore, that

---

[1] The general death rate given for 1831 may have been affected by the cholera epidemic, as the rate is based on a five-year average with 1831 at the centre. The rates given for the individual towns for 1831 are not likely to have been affected as the rates are based on the figures for 1831 and the four previous years, and the epidemic only began at the very end of 1831, and had not spread very far before 1832.

[2] *Reports*, 1844, XVII. p. viii (speaking of Liverpool mortality), "of which the local authorities and the principal inhabitants appear to have been up to a recent period unaware." *Reports*, 1845, XVIII. p. i: "The extensive injury to the Public Health, now proved to arise from causes capable of removal, appears to have escaped general observation."

the towns were suffering from lack of control in their growth and planning is one of the most relevant that was made, and the suggestions leading to a more unified control, or at any rate to a code of regulations laying down the right conditions for the growth of towns, are among the most valuable which were made. The event which turned attention to the condition of the towns was the cholera epidemic of 1831 and 1832. It is interesting to note, therefore, that this came at the end of the decade in which the big towns recorded their largest increase. By 1845 Manchester was said to have improved to an extent which it would hardly have been possible for one unacquainted with the town at the time of the cholera twelve years earlier so much as to imagine[1].

It is therefore suggested that in the history of the towns in this period we have a double movement: first, an improvement in the health of the towns accompanied by a decline in their death rate; secondly, owing to the rapid growth of the population, the lack of proper control and the unregulated growth which was permitted, a loss of some of the improvements which had been made in the earlier period and a rise in the death rate. It is possible that the most unhealthy period in the towns was the decade in which they showed the greatest increase of population, and at the end of which the cholera epidemic occurred, and during the next few years before improvements had begun to tell. The cholera epidemic, which directed attention to the health of the towns just when that question was again becoming really serious, may, therefore, have been a blessing in disguise.

The health of people is affected by the surroundings in which they work, and when large numbers are concerned this must affect the health and life of the nation. During this period the typical organisation of industry changed from a small to a large unit—from the domestic system to the factory system. This change must have had some effect on the general health of the industrial parts of the country.

A great deal has been written about the days of the domestic industry and some very idealised pictures have been drawn. As a broad generalisation, domestic industry is not likely to be the more healthy. For a whole working family to live and work in

_____
[1] *Reports*, 1845, xviii. p. 107.

one place, which has to be both home and workshop, is not a good plan unless the conditions are ideal and unless the alternative to working at home is working in another place which is very much worse than the home. The domestic system was destroyed by the concentration of industry in towns resulting from the greater part played by capital and by the use of steam power, and therefore it was essentially a phenomenon of the industrial organisation of the country before the days of the large manufacturing towns. Any claim that the domestic system can make to be more healthy than the one which superseded it should be based on the fact that it was conducted in small towns, villages, and country places and not in large towns, rather than on the fact that it was conducted at the houses of small masters. An economic organisation which suits one time and one set of conditions may be quite inappropriate at another time, but that is no reason to idealise a previous system or to condemn that which supersedes it. At the time that the population was growing rapidly so also were the towns and the factories; but because it is easy to say many hard things about the factories it does not follow that in the altered circumstances they were not an improvement on what the continuance of the domestic system would have meant.

The health and the moral qualities of the domestic handicraftsmen may have been better than those of the factory workers. Gaskell, who was not unduly opposed to the factories, seems to think that this was the case. From the moral and social point of view work in the home was very likely preferable to that in the factories; "the circumstance of a man's labour being conducted in the midst of his household, exercised a powerful influence upon his social affections, and those of his offspring." He regrets that the new system has had the effect of breaking up families and he also regrets the moral laxity which existed "in the manufacturing population, more especially in the large towns," and he finally declares that "the domestic artisan, as a moral and social being, was infinitely superior to the manufacturer of a later date."[1]

[1] Gaskell, *Manufacturing Population*, p. 19; *Artisans and Machinery*, pp. 22, 111.

It might have been better for the health of the country if it had been possible to maintain the domestic system and to restrict the growth of large towns, though in this case the population would probably not have increased in the way it did. Once, however, the towns began to grow rapidly it is arguable that the days of the domestic industries were over, and that a properly regulated factory system was likely to be more healthy than the decaying domestic system.

The description of the dwellings and workshops in Wolverhampton, where small metal trades were conducted on the domestic system for longer than many other trades, would lead one to the opinion that it would be better to work in almost any kind of factory than to have to live and work in the kind of places which are described[1]. The early factories no doubt were very bad places, they are said to have been hotbeds of fever[2], but the same could be said with equal justice of the dwellings of the workers. Even for some time before the Factory Report of 1833, the conditions of the factories had been vastly improved. Since 1806, said Gaskell, when the steam loom was first brought into operation, many of the first mills had been either much enlarged or in many cases abandoned by the more wealthy manufacturers and supplanted by large and more airy buildings in which the rooms were much more lofty, generally of large proportions and had better windows arranged with a view to good ventilation[3].

In 1833 the health of children in factories was said to compare favourably with that of children employed elsewhere. The "large factories and those recently built have a prodigious advantage over the old and small mills," they were better regulated than formerly and there was much more deformity seen among the factory workpeople thirty years previously than was seen at that time[4].

---

[1] *Reports*, 1843, xv. p. 563.
[2] Gaskell, *Manufacturing Population*, p. 177. Report of the Manchester Board of Health, 1796: "It appears that the children and others who work in the large cotton factories are peculiarly disposed to be affected by the contagion of fever."
[3] *Ibid.* p. 180.
[4] *Reports*, 1833, xx. pp. 16, 804, 861, 873.

As the factories were improving, the conditions of the domestic workers were being realised as the greater evil. In Wolverhampton, in 1843, we are told that "few of the large manufactures are in unhealthy situations, the worst of the localities of workshops will generally be found to be those of the small locksmiths, key makers, and screw makers, who work in little shops and hovels in courts up narrow passages."[1] Where the conditions of the domestic system were still upheld, as in certain midland towns and in the west of England, it was as a country characteristic and as contrasted with the conditions in the towns that this was done[2]. By this time the small and unregulated trades, such as dressmaking and millinery, were beginning to be looked upon as those which required improvement[3].

Manchester was noted for the pallid appearance of its population; its mortality in 1841 was high and it seems to have been defective in the provision of open spaces[4]; the housing conditions were also bad, but if the domestic system had persisted it is probable that the conditions would have been worse still, for by this time the hand loom industry was rightly looked upon as associated with worse conditions than the factory industry[5]. In the west the children were said to be better in factories than at home, and the same was the case in Manchester[6]. The factory conditions were so much improved that a man who had been discharged from the factory and had taken again to hand loom weaving pleaded to be taken back because the conditions of the place in which he had to conduct his hand loom weaving were so unhealthy[7].

The hand loom weavers' Commission of 1840 rebuked a mistake which was said to prevail as to the extent to which factory labour, which was then becoming "the characteristic feature of manufacturing employment," was unfavourable to health, and in this respect considered that the benefits were all on the side of the factory hand rather than on that of the domestic

---

[1] *Reports*, 1843, XV. p. 567.
[2] *Reports*, 1843, XIV. pp. 369, 541.
[3] *Ibid.* p. 557.   *Reports*, 1833, XX. p. 862.
[4] *Reports*, 1840, XI. p. 222.   [5] *Reports*, 1833, XX. p. 953.
[6] *Ibid.* p. 883.   *Reports*, 1840, XXIV. p. 681.
[7] *Reports*, 1833, XX. p. 883.

worker who, "if a steady workman, confines himself to a single room in which he eats, drinks and sleeps, and breathes throughout the day an impure air."[1]

After the initial evils of the factories were got over, there does not seem to have been any reason why the factory occupations should have been more unhealthy than the domestic industries. The industries which might lead to chemical poisoning of one kind and another had not become very important in the period; in one case, that of matches, the question of poisoning did not arise until after 1834 when the old friction match was superseded by the phosphorus match[2]. Scrofula was said to be no more prevalent among factory workers than among others, indeed it is implied that it was actually less prevalent, which may reasonably be accounted for by the better ventilation in the factories[3]. Phthisis, which is promoted by the inhalation of certain kinds of grit and encouraged by lack of ventilation, was said by Gaskell to occur in the steel grinding and polishing trades which were largely carried on in small and badly ventilated workshops, whereas in the cotton industry which was carried on in better ventilated buildings phthisis was not so prevalent, but it must be pointed out that cotton particles are much less injurious[4].

The 1844 Report on the state of large towns discounts the idea that consumption was particularly prevalent among the factory population by pointing out that the death rate from this disease was lower in Leeds and Manchester than in Liverpool where there was "only one solitary mill."[5]

Allied to this there was the effect of smoke, a new and increasing pest of the towns as the use of steam power increased. There were inquiries into this question in 1819 and 1843. The witnesses were in no doubt as to an increase in the amount of smoke in recent years, but the testimony as to its effects on health was by no means uniform. In the 1819 Report statements are

---

[1] *Reports*, 1840, XXIV. p. 681.
[2] Allbutt, II. Part I. p. 998. *Chambers's Encyclopædia*, "Matches."
[3] *Reports*, 1833, XXI. p. 11.
[4] Gaskell, *Manufacturing Population*, p. 247.
[5] *Reports*, 1844, XVII. p. 22.

met with to the effect that in London it is a great nuisance and prejudicial to the health of persons exposed to its influence, and much the same is said about Liverpool[1].

By 1843 people were more cautious in the opinions they expressed about the effect of smoke and they were inclined to regard the dirt which the smoke caused as a greater evil than any tendency it had to promote disease[2]. It was agreed that London was healthier after the more general use of coal, but although the warmth from coal might be beneficial, there were so many other causes at work that it is impossible to distinguish the part played by each[3].

Once the towns began to grow, and with them menaces to public health, the preservation of health became much more a matter of serious calculation and regulation than it had been before, and from that point of view there was a good deal to be said for the factory system. No doubt the early factories were bad, but the condition of the houses of the working classes remained bad for a long time after the factories were put under proper control; it might even be argued that as the factories got better the houses got worse. At the end of the period it was the hand loom weavers and the people employed in small or unregulated trades that were subject to the worst conditions, while the factory hands were more fortunate in the newer and better regulated places of work, even if in certain cases the improvement amounted to little more than a change of surroundings during working hours. So long as bad conditions of housing persisted the change of place for work was a good thing, and in the growing towns the factory possibly provided the best solution of the problem.

Up to this point we have noticed a steady improvement in the condition of the towns during the period under discussion until its last decade or so, and we have examined a possible explanation for the retrograde movement at the end of the period. We have hazarded an opinion that if the large town was to come, the factory system was probably the most hopeful form of organisation and provided the easiest opportunities

---

[1] *Reports*, 1819, VIII. pp. 5, 8.   [2] *Reports*, 1843, VII. Q. 1003.
[3] *Ibid.* Q. 322.

for the inspection which was necessary, and there is ample evidence that during the later part of the period the factories were improving.

As yet, however, the towns and factories have been treated by themselves and considered apart from the rest of the country.

One of the great fears expressed in relation to the towns was that they were diverting population from the country, where the conditions of health were favourable, to districts where the conditions of health were unfavourable, and were thus placing a check on the increase of the population. The most exaggerated form of this is Cobbett's fear of the London "wen"; the same fear is traceable in Malthus, though he confesses in later editions that this possible check appears to have had only a very limited effect[1].

This question is important because of the very striking alteration in the proportion of the inhabitants of this country variously employed during the period under discussion. Prothero quotes 42 per cent. as the proportion of the population engaged in agriculture in 1770, whereas by 1841 the percentage is only 22[2]. Weber has a table which shows that in 1801 only 21·30 per cent. of the population of England and Wales lived in towns of 10,000 inhabitants and over, whereas by 1851 the percentage was 39·45[3]. Between the 1811 Census and the 1821 Census the number of families in England chiefly engaged in manufactures increased by some 194,000, whereas the number chiefly engaged in agriculture only increased by a little more than 76,000. Between the 1821 Census and the 1831 Census, the number of manufacturing families increased by 64,000, whereas the number of agricultural families actually decreased by 12,000.

Bearing in mind the fear that towns were a check on the growth of the population and in view of this very remarkable change in the composition of the population of the country, it is necessary to form some idea of the reality of the fear.

---

[1] Malthus, 1872 ed. p. 215: "What has taken place is a striking illustration of the principle of population, and a proof that in spite of great towns, manufacturing occupations...if the resources of a country will admit of a rapid increase...the population will not fail to keep pace with them."

[2] Prothero, *Pioneers*, p. 111.

[3] Weber, *Growth of Cities*, p. 144.

Again the figures are a barrier in the way of any really satis-factory solution. If the death rate figures for the five large towns which have been considered earlier are taken, and if those of them which occur before 1841 and are based on defective information are corrected by 10 per cent., which is the normal correction that has been applied to burial figures, or by 15 per cent. in view of the fact that in all probability the burial figures were more defective in the towns than over the whole country, it will be seen that with the doubtful exception of 1801 the death rate in those towns was in excess of the general death rate for the country (see Table XV), in spite of the improvements in the conditions of these towns which took place except at the very end of the period. To a certain extent, therefore, other things being equal, this growth of large towns must be con-sidered as a check to the increase of the population, especially as when the crude death rate of towns is corrected to a standard population the rate is usually still higher.

Table XVI. BIRTH RATES IN FIVE LARGE TOWNS

Worked on baptism figures derived from the Census Reports.
Births per thousand of the population

	1801	1811	1821	1831	1841	1881–1890	1891–1900
Birmingham	26·9	28·3	24·6	27·1	26·2	34·64	33·56
Leeds	31·6	32·9	32·0	26·2	42·9	32·98	31·40
Bristol	27·5	24·7	27·9	30·1	16·9	29·98	28·38
Manchester	32·1	33·8	26·5	27·2	42·2	35·95	35·70
Liverpool	32·4	39·4	36·2	63·2	30·4	32·64	33·52
Average	30·1	31·82	29·24	29·36	31·72	33·39	32·51
Corrected by 15 %	34·7	36·6	33·62	33·8	36·5	—	—

But the birth rates in the towns must also be considered before the latter can be definitely classed as checks to the increase. The birth rates in these five towns from the beginning of the Census period have been worked out and corrected by the addition of 15 per cent., the normal correction for the whole country, and, for comparison, figures have been given for two more modern decades (Table XVI). In all probability the correction in these cases should really be more than 15 per cent. as it has been observed that there are likely to be more sources of error in such figures in the towns than in the country. These rates do in all cases turn out to be higher than the general average for the whole country, and therefore this higher level does, to some extent, counteract the higher level of death rate exhibited in these towns compared to the general average of the country. It also discounts in part the theory that the growth of large towns was a check to the increase of the population, although the death rate in these towns is more above the average than the birth rate is higher than its average.

It is certain that the population of this country would not have increased in the way it did had it not been for the growth of the large town, and therefore it is probably quite right to say that the important thing about the towns is that, during the period and taken by themselves, they were improving and being rendered more favourable to healthy conditions of life. If towns were to exist it was all in the right direction that the utmost should be done to make them better and healthier, and any success in that direction was a valuable advance.

With regard, finally, to the theory that the growth of towns was a check to the growth of population, it should be remarked again that the use of crude rates—the only ones available before the middle of the nineteenth century—are not satisfactory for the drawing of safe conclusions. Judging, however, from five big towns, it appears that to a certain extent the death rate in those towns, compared with the general death rate of the country, was tending to make those towns a check on the growth, whereas the birth rate in those towns compared with the general birth rate of the country was tending to hasten the rate of increase. In all probability the most that can be said in condemnation of the towns is that they were not adding to the population in the most economical way possible, but that, considered only from this point of view, they were acting as a slight check to the increase of the population.

CHAPTER IX

Factors affecting the Death Rate: Alcohol

IT is a general statement which is largely true, that throughout the whole period under discussion heavy drinking was very prevalent, and a connection can be traced between this and the death rate.

The first half of the eighteenth century was a period of excessive gin drinking, and an interesting discussion on the subject has recently taken place in an article on the population of London to which reference has previously been made[1]. Legislative attempts were made to stop this outburst of drinking, and in the early stages they were only partially successful. The trade increased to such an extent that in 1729 a charge of £20 was made for the retail licence to sell spirits, but this was repealed four years later owing to the protests of the farmers. In 1736 a new Gin Act was passed which, had it been enforced, would have been prohibitory, as it placed a tax of 20s. a gallon on retailers, and though it did for a few years cause a slight check in the amount of distilled spirits returned officially, even this check did not last for long and was probably more than counter-balanced by the stimulus given to illicit distillation and smuggling. Later on this was recognised; it was said that the object of the bill had been to promote the distillation of spirits as a profitable source of revenue and also to prevent abuses owing to its cheapness, but the heavy expense of the licence, and the duties on spirits gave such a stimulus to illicit distillation and illegal sale as to produce consequences the very opposite of those which were contemplated by the legislature[2].

Evidence of the great extent of the drinking in this period is plentiful. The law of 1736 was condemned as increasing the evil; writers in the fifties complained of the excess of dram drinking[3], and Alcock in his discussion of the Poor Laws was

[1] *Econ. Journal*, Sept. 1922, M. D. George.
[2] *Reports*, 1817, VII. Police of the Metropolis, p. 4.
[3] *Parl. Hist.* X. p. 1215.

very emphatic about the "havoc and destruction" which it had caused, and declared that it "cuts off the bread of life" before people "have lived out half their days."[1]

In 1743 new and sounder principles were introduced; the amount of the revenue duties and the price of the retailers' licences were so lowered as to decrease the temptations to evade the regulations, and for the next few years improvements were added to the law, culminating in an Act in 1751 which finally gave the control of licensing to the magistrates at their Brewster Sessions and did check the amount of spirits consumed[2].

Thereafter the amount of spirits consumed steadily decreased for some time. From the repeal of the first Gin Act in 1733 the amount of spirits consumed had steadily increased until the Act of 1736 was passed. This Act checked the consumption for three years, after which it rose to heights which it had not reached before. From 1751 the consumption dropped from some seven million gallons in that year to the neighbourhood of one million gallons in the early eighties; the initial fall from the first high figure to that of about two million gallons taking place very rapidly in the ten years following the Act of 1751[3].

The consumption of spirits declined, therefore, pretty steadily from about 1750 to 1785 or 1786, and during this period the consumption per head of the population also declined[4]. In 1785 the duty on spirits was decreased and the consumption per head went up until about 1819 when the duty was again increased. About 1785 there began an interesting movement on the part of the magistrates to suppress and to restrict licences. This movement is dealt with fully in the *History of Liquor Licensing*, in which the authors give a long series of cases in which the

[1] Alcock, *Obs. on the Poor Laws*, 1752, p. 48. See also Fielding, *Increase of Robbers*, pp. 27, 29; Tucker, *Advantages and Disadvantages*, pp. 23–24.
[2] *Econ. Journal*, Sept. 1922; Webb, *Hist. of Liquor Licensing in England* (esp. Chap. II).
[3] Consumption of Spirits. See *J.H.C.* XXIV. p. 400. *First Report Inland Revenue Commrs.* 1857, Sess. I. vol. IV. Appendix 19. *Reports*, 1870, XX. Appendix, pp. 4, 5 and 6.
[4] Consumption of spirit per head annually

1760 (3 year average)	·429 galls.	
1770 (5 year average)	·34	,,
1780	,,	·31	,,
1790	,,	·48	,,

magistrates had deprived publicans of licences in consequence of abuses, or refused to issue new licences[1]. This movement does not seem to have had much effect in London[2], and so far as the actual consumption of spirits throughout the country is concerned it is not very evident that the movement for greater strictness achieved anything considerable. It is interesting, however, to note that the great fall in the amount of spirits recorded in the official returns occurs in the decade immediately before that in which the increase in the population in the eighteenth century became rapid; and that the earlier portion of the rise in the consumption per head occurs in the ten years or so from 1790 to 1800, in which there was a check in the falling of the death rate, though the high consumption of spirits persisted while the death rate continued to fall.

The effect of the suppression movement is more noticeable in the figures for the licences granted. The licences of spirit retailers had continued to rise pretty steadily from 1714 to 1780. From then, with certain exceptional years in which they rose, they fell until between 1805 and 1810.

One interesting fact is worthy of mention; while the number of licences was increasing, the amount of spirits passing through the official returns was falling; when, under the influence of the suppression movement, the number of licences was curtailed, the amount of spirits in the returns increased. The probable explanation is that at the same time that the suppression movement began, the duty on spirits was reduced, and this reduction of duty led to an increase in the consumption. It may, of course, have been the case that people were drinking more in spite of the smaller number of houses and in consequence of the reduced tax; or, on the other hand, that the reduction in the tax so far stopped the smuggling, that, although the official returns do show higher figures than before, these higher figures were at the expense of the smuggling trade, and the suppression movement may have reduced the net consumption in spite of the increase shown in the returns. This is a consideration which in some way affects the value of any figures of this kind, and it is a factor which it is not possible to gauge with even approximate

[1] Webb, Chap. III.   [2] Webb, p. 77. *Reports*, 1817, VI. pp. 9, 15–18.

accuracy beyond the fact, which does not get one much further, that smuggling was known to be a considerable business[1].

About the year 1820 discontent with the scale and with the system of taxing became acute with the result that in 1823 the duty was reduced in Scotland and Ireland[2].

Table XVII. SPIRIT AND MALT MANUFACTURED AND CHARGED TO DUTY IN ENGLAND, PER HEAD OF THE POPULATION

Year	Malt (bushels per head)	Spirit (gallons per head)
1710	3·44	·36
1720	4·52	·42
1730	4·28	·61
1740	3·82	1·10
1750	4·33	1·08
1760	4·13	·36
1770	3·58	·34
1780	3·60	·31
1790	3·07	·48
1801	2·58	·44
1811	2·12	·46
1821	2·03	·34
1831	2·14	·54
1841	2·23	·50

The result of this measure in those two countries was so successful that in 1825 the duty on spirits in England was also reduced[3] as was the cost of the retail licence. The effect of these measures is seen in two series of figures given in Table XVII. The official returns of the amount of "British spirits manufactured and charged to duty" at this time show a remarkable and sudden rise. For fourteen out of the previous twenty years the amount had ranged between four and five million gallons, with two figures below the four million and four above the five million. From 3,684,049 in 1825, it jumps in 1826 to 7,407,204; from then until 1840 the production in the year 1827 is the only one which falls below the seven million, and in the last two years of the period it is distinctly over the eight million[4]. Consequently the consumption per head shows a corresponding rise. From being 0·344 gallons in 1821 it rises to 0·543 gallons in 1831 and to 0·500 in 1840.

[1] *Reports*, 1857, Sess. I. IV. p. 8.
[2] *Ibid.* p. 1.
[3] From 11s. 8¼d. to 7s. a gallon.
[4] 1839 and 1840.

The number of spirit licences shows a similar response to the alteration in taxation. From 1820 to 1825, inclusive, some 36,000 licences to sell spirits had been granted in four of these years, 37,000 in another and 38,472 in the remaining year. In 1826, however, the figure was 42,599; and from that date onwards there is a steady rise which amounts to 10,000 in fourteen years, whereas to get a reduction of 10,000 in the number of licences we have to go as far back as the year 1765.

But other things were drunk in England besides spirits.

If the figures of the malt tax can be taken as any guide to the consumption of beer, that also decreased during the period in an even more marked manner. The greatest production of malt in the eighteenth century was in the year 1722, when it was 32,999,688 bushels; this figure was not again reached until the year 1833. A later Report remarks that during the long period of a century, and indeed up to the repeal of the beer duty in 1830, the malt trade showed no expansion, notwithstanding the great increase of population. The Report further observes, adopting a statement made in 1833, that the production of 1722, when beer was the beverage of the people at every meal, gave a barrel of beer per annum per head of the population, but in 1830 the rate of consumption had fallen to half a barrel per head[1]. An examination of the malt figures during this period of rapidly increasing population shows them from 1760 to 1830 fluctuating between twenty and thirty million bushels. There are certain peculiarly low years—1783 and 1799—and in one year before 1830, namely in 1828, the thirty million is touched. But after 1830 the figure never falls below thirty million[2]. The fear that the consumption of beer was being superseded by that of spirits finds expression in the Reports at the time that the removal of the beer duty was under consideration, and this followed by some five years the reduction in the spirit duties.

The consumption of malt per head, therefore, steadily decreased throughout the period with which we have dealt so far, namely from 1760 to the decade 1821–1831[3].

---

[1] *Reports*, 1884–5, XXII. p. 20.
[2] *Reports*, 1870, XX. App. pp. 15–17, for Malt figures.
[3] See Table XVII, p. 201.

The evils of the tied house system, the Tory desire to encourage the growth of hops and barley in order to promote agriculture, and the Radical dislike of restrictions on trade and undemocratic control, led to the relaxation of the reform of the licensing system which the magistrates had instigated in the eighties, and to complaints that in the business of licensing they were exercising functions which were more properly those of a jury[1]. At the same time the reduction in the spirit duty and the retailers' licences soon gave rise to an agitation in the beer trade for some compensating concessions. A Committee to inquire into the sale of beer was appointed in 1830, before which those members of the beer trade who appeared concentrated their attention on securing a reduction in the tax. Following this inquiry the beer tax was removed, and anybody who was rated was permitted to open a beer shop without the formality of securing a licence from the magistrates, but merely on the payment of a small sum to the local excise office, a process as little difficult and as little inquired into as the taking out of a dog licence.

The effect of this measure can be tested by the figures that are available. The production of malt made a sudden upward movement in 1831. From 1760 onwards the annual production had usually been between twenty and thirty million bushels, sometimes falling below the twenty million, and only on one occasion touching the thirty million. From a production of 26,196,470 bushels in 1830 the figure went up to 32,963,470 bushels in 1831, and, throughout the decade that followed, it was only once lower than that and it was generally considerably higher. The production of malt per head of the population had also gone up; in 1821 it was 2·03 bushels, on an average of the five years with 1831 as the centre it was 2·14 bushels, and on an average of five years beginning with 1831 it was 2·43 bushels. In 1841, using the figures of the previous five years, the production per head was 2·23 bushels. This evidence is confirmed by the number of beer and cider retailers' licences granted. From 1810 to 1828 the number of these licences fluctuates

[1] *Reports*, 1830, X. p. 14. For numbers of houses held by brewers. *Ibid.* p. 97. For complaints against the magistrates. Webb, Chap. IV.

between 47,917 and 49,860. In 1828 and 1829 they touch the fifty thousand, and from 1831 to 1840 they rise steadily from 51,000 to 57,000[1].

That the alterations in the spirit taxation in 1825 and the beer taxation in 1830 were causing an increase in the drunkenness of the country is borne witness to by casual writers such as Sydney Smith, by debates in Parliament, by the social literature of the time and by the voluminous evidence in a series of reports which followed in the next few years to deal with the question, and tells the same story of urban and rural districts in widely different parts of the country[2].

The correspondence between the death rate, the fraction per head of the population of a gallon of British spirits produced and charged to duty, based on three- or five-year averages, and the number of bushels of malt charged to duty per head of the population, is remarkable. The correspondence is more remarkable in the case of the malt figures than in that of the spirit figures. There is a very definite general level of malt figures in the eighteenth century up to about 1770, then a very remarkable fall and only a comparatively small rise at the end of the period. The spirit figures are seen to start the eighteenth century at a level which is not high, they then show a formidable peak from 1730 to 1750, followed by a remarkable fall which is in turn followed by a rise towards the end of the period.

On the whole, therefore, in both cases, with the exception of the first two figures for spirit consumption, the early part of the eighteenth century was a period of high spirit and malt consumption—the malt figures marking high points in 1720 and 1750, the spirit figures from 1730 to 1750. Then in both cases there came a remarkable fall during the time that the population was increasing with its greatest rapidity, and, what is more important, during the period when the striking fall in the death rate was taking place. It should further be noted that

[1] *Reports*, 1870, xx. App. pp. 15–17.
[2] Webb, p. 116, quotes Sydney Smith, "the new beer bill has begun its operations. Everybody is drunk. Those who are not singing are sprawling. The sovereign people are in a beastly state." *Hansard*, 24th March, 23rd June, 1831. Gaskell, *Manufacturing Population*, p. 117. *Reports*, 1830, x. p. 100. *Reports*, 1833, xv. *passim*. *Reports*, 1834, viii. (Drunkenness), *passim*.

when, during the general fall, the spirit figures mark a rise from 1780 to 1790, that rise is followed by a rise in the death rate from 1790 to 1795—shown on five-year averages. At the end of the period the death rate and both sets of figures relating to the consumption of alcohol make an upward movement[1].

Too much should not be made of this correspondence between the alcohol figures and the death rate, which is probably more remarkable in a general view than in details. Too great a correspondence should not be looked for, because a sudden check in the consumption of alcohol will not immediately cause a decline in the death rate, any more than a sudden increase in the consumption of alcohol will immediately raise the death rate—these things require time. Again, it is possible that excessive drinking, especially of spirit, was essentially an eighteenth-century phenomenon, as is partially borne out by the comparative lowness of the spirit figures at the very beginning of the century, and should not be regarded as a permanent source of mortality for all time before the period under discussion.

It is true, nevertheless, to say generally that the period of steady or falling consumption of alcohol was coincident with a period of falling death rate, and that the period of increasing consumption and uncontrolled beer houses coincided roughly with a period of rising death rate, though it is only fair to point out that the death rate had begun to rise before the trade was made more free, and had begun to fall again before the trade was once more under proper control.

[1] Some modern figures derived from Denmark during the war are interesting in this connection. In 1917 the Danish food supply became a serious problem and drastic measures had to be adopted to prevent starvation, under this threat the consumption of meat and alcohol was nearly put a stop to. Following these measures the death rate fell in a sensational manner; in the case of men, omitting epidemic diseases, it fell 34 per cent. and in the case of women 17 per cent., the death rate among men came down almost to that among women. Careful examination is said to show that these results were chiefly attained by the practical prohibition of alcohol, and the approximation of the male and the female death rates is said to be a measure of the part played by alcohol in the male death rate in the period before the introduction of these restrictions. See article in *B.M.J.* 12th August, 1922, by Prof. Hindbede of Copenhagen, who was a member of the Committee which recommended the restrictions, also an article in the *Observer*, 10th September, 1922.

Contemporaries were not unwarned. Doctors, since the beginning of the century, had been warning people of the evil effects of the excessive consumption of alcohol, both generally and in connection with particular diseases and men's ability to resist them, though it is scarcely necessary for us to go to contemporary evidence for what is now a well-known fact[1]. The application of this fact to the death figures after the period of free trade began is interesting, though it must not be pressed too far. The death figures for 1831 and 1832 show a very marked rise on the previous figures. Those are the two years following the removal of the beer tax and the great years of beer shop development.

It will, however, at once be said that the excessive number of deaths was caused by the visitation of cholera in those years. No doubt cholera was a most serious danger at the time, but even if the great rise in the deaths in 1832 is to be ascribed principally to the ravages of cholera, it is by no means clear that the rise in 1831 is to be so ascribed more than in a minor degree. Cholera did not reach England until the very end of October or the beginning of November, 1831. The first report of the disease in England occurs in the *Times* of 5th November, 1831, and is from Sunderland; in that neighbourhood it spread pretty rapidly, but it was not reported in any distant part of the country until the beginning of the next year. The Central Committee at Whitehall published on 30th December, 1831, the deaths that had occurred up to that date from the disease; the details of the returns are almost entirely composed of the cases in the immediate neighbourhood of Sunderland, and the total number only amounts to 360. Even if this return leaves out certain places in which the cholera had as a matter of fact caused deaths, the total number of deaths in 1831 from this disease can only amount to a comparatively small proportion of the 24,000 more deaths recorded for 1831 than for 1830[2].

Some weight must also be given to the possibility that the

---

[1] *S.B.C.P.* II., App. p. 29, and v. p. 183, *Reports*, 1834, VIII. p. 523.

[2] *Times*, 5th November, 1831, and 30th December, 1831. For a description of the first arrival of cholera in Manchester in the early months of 1832, see *Life of Sir James Kay Shuttleworth*, by Frank Smith, p. 21.

ravages of the cholera were made worse than they would otherwise have been by the orgy of drinking that was going on at the
time, an orgy to which people had not yet become acclimatised,
if acclimatisation may be supposed to be worth anything in the
face of such a disease. This possibility is strengthened by a
reference to the figures for deaths for the few following years.
The year 1837 was a year of epidemics—various forms of fever
and smallpox. In that year the figures show the most remarkable
rise that had hitherto been recorded, a rise which is far more
striking than that recorded in any previous epidemic years, such
as 1794–5, 1799–1802 or 1817–20. It is possible that the initial
sudden and marked rise as compared with what had happened
at the time of previous epidemics may be ascribed to the fact
that this particular epidemic occurred during a period of heavy
drinking.

CHAPTER X

Factors affecting the Death Rate: Medicine

I

THE most striking series of facts that emerged in the discussion of the population figures was connected with the
death rate. It was seen that there was a fairly well-defined
general level in the eighteenth century, a very remarkable drop
from 1780 to 1820, and a fairly well-defined general nineteenth-
century level, which was considerably lower than that in the
preceding century. During this period also, the birth rate, after
a sustained if not a very great rise during the first half of the
century, fell steadily from 1790.

The two ways in which the natural increase in the population
of a country may be accentuated are by raising the birth rate
and lowering the death rate, and in this period it was the latter
which had the chief share.

Now medical skill may assist both these processes. It may
directly affect the birth rate by checking such things as venereal
disease and lead poisoning which prevent births, and any
general improvements that may be introduced into the practice
of medicine are likely indirectly to have some effect on the birth
rate. But medical skill is more usually seen, as indeed might be
anticipated, in the decline of the death rate. Medical improvements are more likely to affect the health and lengthen the lives
of people who are already in the world than directly to increase
the number of those who are brought into the world, and it is
an object which comes much nearer home to save the lives of
living people than to create a condition of things in which more
people are likely to be born into the world. Of course, every
life saved in circumstances in which with less medical skill it
would have been lost means, in all probability, many more lives
lengthened, and that in turn, while not necessarily raising the
birth rate, will mean more and healthier children born into the
world. In this way a lowering of the death rate will tend further

to an increase of the population by its effect on the absolute numbers of births even if not on the birth rate.

In examining the medical improvements we must bear in mind the remarkable movement of the death rate during the period, as it is on this side of the question that we should expect those improvements to have the greatest effect.

II

The death rate is composed of two elements—infantile mortality and adult mortality.

During the period with which we are dealing it is very difficult to estimate the influence of infantile mortality owing to imperfect data, but it is of very great importance. Dr Mayo in his recent visit to this country said that the decrease in the death rate in the United States arose mainly through lessened infantile mortality, due not only to medical measures but also to improved economic conditions.

Without too clearly defining what infantile mortality is, and is not, the effect of lowering the mortality at various ages may be considered. First, to lower the death rate among comparatively old people will add a certain number to the population for a certain number of years, and will show an improvement in the health of a good many more, but so far as the increase of the population is concerned it may not do much more than add a few units for a few years. Those people, or many of them, whose lives are prolonged by a reduction of this death rate may have already done all they are going to do in assisting to increase the population. These measures will preserve mere numbers for some years, but will not preserve breeding stock. Secondly, to lower the death rate among people from, say, twenty to fifty, is not only to preserve units, but is also to preserve people who may at any time have children and in their case the cumulative effect of the improvement is soon seen. Thirdly, to lower the juvenile death rate is to preserve units and potential parents for the years to come. Measures, therefore, which are particularly calculated to have their chief effect in preserving the lives of the older part of the community will not have the same cumulative effect on the growth of the population as a reduction in the mortality of young people and people in the prime of life. It is this effect on the growth of the population which gives to the whole subject of medical improvement its great importance, for it is the special feature distinguishing these improvements from the other causes tending to the increase of the population that they are, potentially at any rate, exceedingly cumulative in their effects, and they are the bedrock on which other causes of increase are enabled to build. Other causes may exist which tend to an increase of the population and which warrant an increase, but unless there is the requisite medical skill to preserve the increase, it is possible that the country may not be able to maintain the additional number of people which it requires, in consequence of existing evils which medical skill in a greater degree would have checked. Evils, moreover, which in a small population may be comparatively harmless, become in a bigger society intolerable menaces to public health, and therefore an increase of population beyond a certain number without adequate medical skill may defeat its own ends by increasing evils which threaten life. In the period under discussion, for instance, fever, particularly in the crowded parts of the big towns, was one of the most serious menaces to human life that existed, and the serious nature of the menace was very largely due to the fact that the population was increasing and the towns were getting bigger. The medical writings at the time show that the danger was realised, and efforts were made more or less successfully to deal with it. Had the skill not been sufficient to deal with it even to the extent that it was, the fevers would have become more endemic than actually was the case, and the other causes which tended to increase the population would have been thwarted by the fact that the medical skill at the command of the community was insufficient to keep the growing population alive. Again, bad drainage or sump-hole drainage in a country district may have little or no evil effect on health; but this system of drainage, if permitted in areas where the population is growing or in towns, may become perfectly intolerable. As a matter of fact in this period the drainage conditions were very bad, but attention was being directed to them; the medical evils of bad drains were being discovered and there were improvements, largely instigated by doctors like Kay Shuttleworth and Southwood Smith and last, but by no means least, by Edwin Chadwick. Had the skill in medicine been insufficient to detect the evils of bad drains and in some measure to cope with them, the increase of the population might have foundered on sanitary conditions which made its maintenance impossible.

The cumulative effect of the medical improvements is seen more in connection with the mortality of the younger part of the community. A cure for cancer, for instance, would not have the same effect in increasing the population that a cure for some more definitely juvenile complaint would certainly have. In the case of cancer you are saving units, and possibly very little beyond that; on the other hand, improvements which mitigate diseases that particularly threaten the younger portion of the community save not only units but also the potential fathers and mothers of the next generation, and the more of them that are saved the bigger the next generation is likely to be; the healthier they are—and they will be healthier if diseases which have usually destroyed a great many people of their age have been limited and reduced in severity—the healthier the next generation is likely to be.

In the period with which we are dealing, fevers of one kind and another—and they had not been very clearly differentiated —were responsible for a large number of deaths, and in 1816 the diminished mortality among adults was put down largely to the decreased mortality from fevers[1]. These diseases were important because the mortality from them was widely spread over all ages, and also because a reduction in the mortality from fevers generally implied sanitary improvements which were likely to be accompanied by widespread beneficial effects on all sections of the community. Nevertheless a reduction in their mortality might not be so important as in that of a disease which was particularly liable to attack young people. At the beginning of the period smallpox was a most serious

[1] *Reports*, 1816, III. p. 45.

scourge, but it was wonderfully checked by the introduction of vaccination. Smallpox attacked young people, and children under five were particularly subject to it; any mitigation of the disease was therefore likely to have a greater effect on the population than that of a disease which was not so exclusively a juvenile complaint. During the period, also, the practice of midwifery, which throughout the greater part of the eighteenth century appears to have been in a lamentable condition, was greatly improved. It is obvious that any considerable improvement in this branch of medicine shows cumulative effects better than any other, for such improvements will not only preserve the lives of children who are potential parents but will also preserve the lives of mothers who may have more children and who under the old and bad arrangements would have been lost in much greater numbers.

Improvements in the treatment of any disease are indeed likely to have an effect on the growth of the population, for it is very unlikely that the mortality from any one disease will be reduced without a reduction in the mortality from other diseases or without the establishment of improved conditions in other classes than those particularly attacked by the disease. Those diseases, however, which are particularly liable to attack young people and people in their prime, and the treatment of those diseases, should be carefully watched in discussing the growth of the population and the decline in the death rate.

III

In the science and art of medicine during the eighteenth century, "the most important factors of advance were the organisation of medical teaching all over Europe, the rise of morbid anatomy, and the elucidation of a number of special diseases due to these improvements."[1] The impulse to clinical teaching came from Hermann Boerhaave (1668–1738) and in these islands clinical teaching became organised at Edinburgh earlier than anywhere else[2]. In England there was no systematic

---

[1] Allbutt, *System of medicine*, I. p. 32.
[2] *Ibid.* "The example of organised clinical teaching was followed at Edinburgh in 1746."

clinical instruction for a long time after it was organised at
Edinburgh; but the custom of attending hospitals became more
general, and, as these are the great centres of clinical education, it is probable that with the growth of hospitals which was
going on at the time, clinical knowledge and education made
great progress without being highly organised. "Physicians,"
we are told, "during the last forty years of the eighteenth
century attained great celebrity as clinicians."[1] Towards the
end of the eighteenth century careful observation was being
assisted by the careful use of science. An early example is
afforded by the discovery that Devonshire colic was caused by
the presence of lead in the cider. This discovery was made in
1765 by Sir George Baker, who in the chemical part of the
inquiry had the assistance of Dr William Saunders of Guy's[2].
It is difficult to be certain how much or how little this particular
piece of investigation was of practical value, but when we
remember the various manifestations of lead poisoning, and
their relevance to the growth of the population, it assumes an
additional interest[3].

In 1761, Morgagni, the Professor of Anatomy at Padua,
published his "immortal work" *De sedibus et causis morborum
per anatomen indagatis*. Statements are met with to the
effect that until the middle of the eighteenth century there
was no scientific medicine, that Morgagni was its author and
that his book "created an epoch in the history of medicine."[4]
Morbid anatomy up to that time seems to have been largely
ignored. Morgagni's successor in England was Matthew Baillie,
the nephew of the Hunters, who in 1793 published his book,
*The morbid anatomy of some of the most important parts of the
human body*. It was the first book on the subject in English, the
first book which treated morbid anatomy as a subject by itself,
and it excelled in clarity any of the previous Latin works on
the subject[5]. After the publication of this book morbid anatomy

[1] Arnold Chaplin, *Medicine in the reign of George III*, p. 45.
[2] Chaplin, p. 44. *D.N.B.* III. p. 7.
[3] In such things as producing premature senility of the blood vessels at
one end of life and abortion at the other.
[4] J. Lindsay Steven, *Morgagni to Virchow*.
[5] *D.N.B.* Matthew Baillie lived from 1761 to 1823.

was no longer neglected, and "the new science was actively pursued by numerous observers in Britain, Germany, France and Italy, so that at the end of the eighteenth century and the beginning of the next century it was the most important feature in medical progress."[1]

Finally, as a last example, observation assisted by science led in the hands of Jenner, mindful of the advice from Hunter of "Don't think, but try, be patient, be accurate," to the discovery of vaccination. The effect of vaccination will be discussed later, but it should be remembered, that, apart from its immediate and practical utility, this discovery has had a more generally beneficent effect by promoting the hope and the means of securing immunity from specific diseases, by introducing into the body a weakened or altered form of the virus by which they are caused[2].

The elder Hunter, whose fame has been somewhat eclipsed by that of his more famous younger brother, was active in the first twenty years of the period with which we are dealing and has been described as the first great teacher of anatomy in this country[3].

The more famous of the two Hunter brothers was John, who began to assist his elder brother William in his lectures in 1754, having joined him in London about 1748. He was surgeon on the Belleisle expedition in 1761, in which he gained great experience of gunshot wounds. After his return he started practice as a surgeon in London, and in 1763 he began a private class in anatomy and surgery. In 1768 he became surgeon to St George's Hospital, and in 1773 he began to lecture on the theory and practice of surgery. In these lectures Hunter introduced into this country the conception of the principles of repair "including a rational explanation of processes of surgery and a scientific basis for operations." Surgery before Hunter's time was not a prominent branch of medicine in England, and it was not so very long since the surgeons had parted company from the barbers[4]; surgery was chiefly in

[1] Allbutt, 1. p. 33.   [2] *Ibid.* p. 35.
[3] Newton Pitt, *Hunterian Oration*, 1896.
[4] Surgeons remained incorporated with the barbers until 1745. The Royal College of Surgeons was founded in 1770.

French hands, and Paris was the only place where it could be properly studied.

"With the advent of John Hunter surgery ceased to be regarded as a mere technical mode of treatment, and began to take its place as a branch of scientific medicine, firmly grounded in physiology and pathology." Sir James Paget calls Hunter "the founder of scientific surgery."[1]

A pupil of John Hunter's who was active towards the end of the period was John Abernethy, the greatest result of whose life "has been the impetus which he gave to medical teaching at St Bartholomew's and throughout England."[2] In 1791 a lecture theatre was built at Bart.'s and Abernethy began to lecture there, and was full surgeon to the hospital from 1815 to 1827.

In addition to men of this stature there are many others who deserve mention, men who were in many cases associated with the foundation of hospitals or were otherwise associated with the improvements which took place during the period: Lettsom, who was associated with the beginnings of the dispensary movement and founded the London Medical Society in 1773; the two Heberdens; Sir Gilbert Blane, a naval surgeon in his earlier days and later physician to St Thomas's, who was sent in 1809 to report on the state of the troops in the island of Walcheren and who was also a considerable and interesting writer; and in the provinces such men as White and Percival at Manchester, Haygarth at Chester and William Hey, who was instrumental in founding the General Infirmary at Leeds.

When all this has been said the interesting fact comes out that, so far as can be seen, the number of medical men to the population was very much the same then as it is now. There was a medical register published between 1779 and 1783, of which there were three issues. Dr Chaplin in his Fitzpatrick Lectures of 1917–18 has worked out the proportion of doctors per head of the population in 1782 from the register for that year and compared it with the proportion existing in 1911, with the

---

[1] For John Hunter (1728–1793) see *D.N.B.* and Garrison, *History of Medicine*, from which two sources the quotations given above are taken.

[2] *D.N.B.* Moore, *Hist. of St Bart.'s*, II. p. 649.

interesting result that no very marked difference is found[1]. There are more doctors to the population now than in 1782, but that is what one would expect from the number of scientific posts which are filled by medical men who are not normally engaged in active practice. Apart from this it looks as if the number of medical men to the population had remained very steady. May one hazard the suggestion that for some reason the distribution of the country practitioner in relation to the population and the number of people normally attended by the general practitioner in the towns have remained very much the same? It is about these same general practitioners that one would like to know more. Medical skill must start from the teachers and the men at the head of the profession, but it is through the general practitioners that the new methods and the greater skill must have their greatest effect. It is comparatively useless for a few very advanced and skilful men to practise new methods and to save life thereby unless these methods permeate to the more distant parts of the country and to the general practitioners, and the general practitioner is the man about whom it is difficult to find out much.

In the eighteenth century most of the lectures in London on medical subjects were arranged personally by the teachers who delivered them, in many cases at their own homes[2]. The same thing went on in the provinces; in 1800 and in subsequent years William Hey gave public lectures on anatomy in Leeds, and for five years before the School of Medicine was founded in that town one of the doctors held a private school of anatomy[3]. The control exercised by the College of Physicians over those who practised was fairly efficient in London but it does not appear to have amounted to much in the provinces. After the Apothecaries Act of 1815 there was more control over the men

[1] Medical men to the population (Chaplin, p. 134):

	1782	1911
England and Wales	1 in 1752	1 in 1416
London	1 in 840	1 in 705

[2] Chaplin, p. 137. Newton Pitt, *Lancet*, 1896, I. p. 1270: "Until the latter part of the (eighteenth) century there was no education for students in London beyond that given by a few private lecturers, most of those not at the hospitals but at the lecturers' houses."

[3] J. B. Hellier, *On the history of medical education in Leeds* (unpublished).

who were the general practitioners of the day, but it was probably not in the best interests of medical education or medical
efficiency that the control was vested in the Society of Apothecaries and not in the College of Physicians, although the
authority of this body was at the time compromised by an in-
ternal wrangle over the admission to the fellowship and the
position of the licentiates, a wrangle which went on until
legislation was introduced after the report on medical education
in 1834. The Apothecaries Act which led to the general practitioners, especially in the provinces, being better qualified and
which instituted some measure of inspection, possibly also the
"powerful impulse communicated to English medicine when,
after the peace, many British physicians went to study in Paris,"[1]
and possibly the numbers of young men seeking civil occupation
after the wars (though it is unsafe to draw too close a comparison
from our own times), all conspired to give an impetus to medical
education after the period of the wars, and it is in these years
that the great provincial medical schools came into being:
Bristol in 1818, Manchester in 1824, Sheffield in 1828, Leeds in
1831, and Newcastle and Liverpool in 1832.

Although there was still a great deal to be done, there were
certain obvious sources of strength in medical education that
had arisen in the period. There had been some very big individual contributions, there had been some great teachers,
there had been a general quickening in the extension of medical
education, and towards the end of the period this quickening
took a more organised and coherent form in the growth of the
medical societies and provincial medical schools.

IV

At the beginning of the eighteenth century hospitals scarcely
existed in England except in London, and even there the accommodation was very small and inadequate. General hospitals
were represented by the two ancient foundations of St Bartholomew's and St Thomas's, and more specialised hospitals by
Bethlehem and Bridewell. In the provinces there was an ancient

---

[1] Allbutt, I. p. 38.

hospital at Rochester and one at Bath; beyond that, a few wrecks from the medieval system of hospitals, mostly alms-houses[1].

Before 1720 there were in London of general hospitals only the two ancient foundations mentioned above. Between 1720 and 1760 nine hospitals were founded in London; of these three were maternity hospitals and five, which are now famous, were general hospitals. The Westminster Hospital was founded in 1720, Guy's in 1724, St George's in 1733, the London in 1740, and the Middlesex in 1745. Thus, by 1760, seven of the great London general hospitals were in being.

From 1760 to 1800 there was very little hospital building going on in London. In these years a Lying-in Hospital was founded in 1765, a Cancer Charity attached to the Middlesex Hospital in 1792, and a hospital for venereal diseases in 1774. In 1791 a Samaritan Society was founded by some of the Governors of the London hospitals for aiding people after discharge from hospital, and in 1795 the society seems to have been in a flourishing condition[2].

In the first forty years of the nineteenth century fourteen hospitals were founded in London; certain of these, such as Charing Cross Hospital (1818), University College Hospital (1833), and King's College Hospital (1839), were general hospitals, but the significant fact about these early nineteenth-century hospitals is that they were chiefly special hospitals. This fact even without further evidence is a proof that more attention was being paid to the treatment of disease, and the fact that people were beginning to build special hospitals is a sign that at any rate they thought they knew sufficient about the particular diseases for the relief of which they built hospitals

---

[1] These figures and dates of hospitals are, with certain verifications from other sources, obtained from the 1922 or 1923 number of Burdett's *Hospitals and Charities*. This source is of course open to the charge that certain hospitals that existed in the period being dealt with have since ceased to exist. This charge may be true in certain cases, but it is not likely to apply to a hospital of any importance, and if such were the case it would be a sign that the hospital in question was not fulfilling its function.

[2] *S.B.C.P.* II. (1798), p. 93.

to feel that it was worth while doing so and better than relying on the general hospitals[1].

In a pamphlet of 1797 there are figures giving the size of the general hospitals in London at that date. A comparison of these figures with those of to-day shows that in 1797 the hospitals had attained to a considerable part of their present size, and although the growth of hospitals has gone on in London with the growth of the population, the general hospital accommodation in 1797 was nothing to be ashamed of. The number of beds in the seven general hospitals in 1797 amounted to 1970; this figure is probably rather an understatement than an overstatement as Bart.'s was said to have "above four hundred patients" and St Thomas's "upward of four hundred and fifty patients."[2] In 1922 the average number of beds occupied in the same hospitals was 3087 and their total capacity 3621.

In London, then, it is clear that before 1720 there was very little hospital accommodation at all, that there was a considerable increase of hospital accommodation between then and 1760, and that by the end of the century some of the London general hospitals were big even when judged by modern standards.

This growth of hospitals in London before the period with which we are immediately concerned becomes important in that period, because the effect of a hospital is not felt at once and its full effect not for some considerable time after its foundation. The founding of general hospitals in London between 1720 and 1760 would have its effect on the health of the community to a much greater extent after 1760 than before that date. The value of hospitals to the community they serve is not to be reckoned merely by the number of patients who have passed through them and benefited by the treatment;

---

[1] E.g. 1802 London Fever Hospital.
1804 The Royal London Ophthalmic Hospital.
1814 The Royal Chest Hospital.
1816 The Royal Ear Hospital.
1816 Royal Waterloo Hospital for Women and Children.
1816 Royal Westminster Ophthalmic Hospital.
1838 Royal National Orthopœdic Hospital.
[2] T. Champney, *Review of the Healing Art*, 1797, p. 45.

hospitals are the training grounds for those who have to treat diseases, and their value influences a greater part of the community than is ever actually treated in a hospital by securing a generally more intelligent attitude towards hospitals and medical treatment in general on the part of the public who become more used to them and to their work. Between 1840 and the present day something like a hundred hospitals have been founded in London, and, in the light of greater knowledge and more accurate information, there is no doubt that an adequate supply of hospital accommodation is one of the great factors in promoting health and saving life. Since the middle of last century there has been a steady drop in the death rate, which it is reasonable to connect to a considerable degree with the growth of hospital accommodation; to argue backwards from that, it is reasonable to suppose that in the period with which we are dealing the growth of hospitals then will have had the same effect. A warning should be made, however, that it is very unsafe to try to derive much information from the recorded death rates in hospitals. So far from the decline in a hospital death rate meaning that the general death rate of the district it serves is declining, it may mean that the hospital is not fulfilling its function as well as if it showed a considerably higher death rate. A hospital which shows a high death rate may do so because it has secured the confidence of the people it serves and because it attracts all the serious cases. A lower death rate in a hospital which does not enjoy general confidence may even in some degree be the measure of the distrust in which it is held. The class of people, moreover, who are ready to enter a hospital and the general attitude on the part of the community to hospitals vary from time to time and from place to place, the social feeling towards those who avail themselves of hospital treatment varies sometimes in an entirely unaccountable manner, and all these are factors which make any comparisons of hospital death rates untrustworthy for general purposes.

Before 1720 the only hospitals in the provinces seem to have been one at Rochester and a mineral water hospital at Bath; by 1760 there were sixteen hospitals, of which fourteen were general hospitals[1], by 1800 there were thirty-eight, and by 1840 one hundred and fourteen. In the middle of the eighteenth century hospital building was going on steadily throughout the kingdom. Thirty provincial general hospitals appear to have been founded in the eighteenth century, and of these twenty-one were founded between 1735 and 1775[2]. By 1780, when the death rate began to fall, most of the important centres and a good many counties had got general hospitals[3], the three most notable exceptions being Durham, Sheffield and Hull, which did not get general hospitals until later in the century[4].

The movement for the foundation of general hospitals in the provinces followed the eighteenth-century movement in London. The last general hospital founded in London in the eighteenth century was the Middlesex Hospital; this dates from 1746, by which time only nine out of the thirty general hospitals founded

[1] The only two hospitals in the provinces, before 1760, that were not general hospitals, appear to have been two mineral water hospitals at Bath, founded in 1610 and 1737.

[2] Hume, *History of the Newcastle Infirmary*, p. 1, says, "of twenty provincial hospitals founded in the century, fifteen were built in the years from 1735 to 1775." This appears to be an understatement.

[3] 1735 Bristol Royal Infirmary.
1736 Royal Hants County Hospital, Winchester.
1740 Addenbrooke's Hospital, Cambridge.
1740 York County Hospital.
1741 Royal Devon and Exeter Hospital.
1743 Northampton General Hospital.
1745 Liverpool Royal Infirmary.
1746 Royal Salop Infirmary, Shrewsbury.
1746 Worcester General Infirmary.
1751 Newcastle Infirmary.
1752 Manchester Royal Infirmary.
1755 Chester Royal Infirmary.
1755 Gloucestershire Royal Infirmary.
1766 Birmingham General Hospital.
1766 Salisbury General Hospital.
1766 Stafford General Hospital.
1767 Leeds General Infirmary.
1769 Lincoln County Hospital.
1770 Oxford, Radcliffe Infirmary.
1771 Leicester Royal Infirmary.
1771 Norfolk and Norwich Hospital.
1776 Herefordshire General Hospital.

[4] 1782 Hull Royal Infirmary.
1792 Durham County Hospital.
1797 Sheffield Royal Infirmary.

during the century in the provinces had been opened. The only hospitals founded in the eighteenth century in the provinces which were not general hospitals and which appear in present-day lists are the two Bath hospitals, maternity hospitals at Manchester, Liverpool and Newcastle-on-Tyne and a sea-bathing hospital at Margate; as hospitals of this kind are the most likely to have to come to an end or to be merged with other and bigger hospitals there may be some omissions; certainly in 1796 a House of Recovery was opened in Manchester.

These hospitals, valuable as they were, were not all that could be desired. Percival, writing to Aiken in 1772, argued that owing to tainted air, the admission of contagious and infectious cases and the false economy of overcrowding wards, these institutions, as then conducted, could often be ranked among the causes of sickness and mortality[1].

There was a campaign at this time for small wards; the idea underlying this seems to have been sound enough, it was thought to be easier to secure pure air and ventilation in a small ward than in a big one. Thus Percival in 1789, speaking generally of infirmaries, suggests "the propriety of making a division in all the large wards."[2] In 1803, speaking this time more specifically of fever hospitals, he says, "No ward should have more than two beds in it, for the contamination of the air arises chiefly from the crowding of too many sick persons in one chamber.... Small chambers, also, have the advantage of being quickly cleansed and ventilated."[3] In the additions to the Newcastle Infirmary at the end of the eighteenth and the beginning of the nineteenth century small wards were favoured. In so far as this was done to secure ventilation and cleanliness and to avoid overcrowding the root of the matter was touched. Many considerations, however, govern the size of wards, and even to-day authorities are sharply divided on this particular point, so that it is difficult to pronounce a definite opinion on the merits of the methods adopted in this period[4].

The provisions with regard to consumption of alcohol in hospitals are somewhat striking. At Newcastle the common diet

---

[1] Percival, IV. p. 170.   [2] *Ibid.* p. 441, Remarks on Infirmaries.
[3] *S.B.C.P.* III. Appendix, p. 135.   [4] Hume, p. 35.

contained a pint and a half of beer per patient daily, reduced diet contained a pint, and it was only on low diet and milk diet that the patient was cut off his beer[1]. At Nottingham in 1781 there was a daily allowance of two or three pints of beer a day according to the season[2]. In Leeds the money spent on malt, beer, hops and porter at the end of the eighteenth century was about three times as much as it is now, and in those days the number of in-patients treated annually was about a tenth of the present-day figure. In 1920 the average amount of wine and spirit consumed daily by each patient was about one-quarter of a teaspoonful. There is, however, this to be said for the old regulations, that in those days the water supply was generally impure.

Nursing was not up to modern standards. There was room for improvement when the answer could be given to a question as to what happened when a patient wanted anything in the night, "There isn't a deal of 'em wants owt; and if they do they doesn't get it."[3] The women who practised midwifery in London were an unattractive lot; before the founding of lying-in hospitals reliance could only be placed in women who combined nursing with "hawking of fish and vegetables and other less reputable callings."[4] These women were a tyrannous race and fought to maintain their position until well into the nineteenth century[5]. Nor should Mrs Gamp be forgotten.

In spite of all these possible drawbacks, some men at any rate were on the right track. Percival, in spite of his preference for small wards, was right in his aims and he knew what he wanted to remedy. "Ventilation, cleanliness, and the numbers, state and accommodation of the patients are the chief causes which affect the salubrity of the air in hospitals."[6] In 1783 improvements were made at St Thomas's, after which date, as Blane tells us, all the wards were annually whitewashed, and the strictest attention paid to cleanliness. Iron bedsteads had previously supplanted wooden ones as less likely to retain infection[7]. Many of these improvements were empirical, but it may be that such improvements as those indicated above were

[1] Hume, p. 25.   [2] Kirkman Gray, *Hist. of English Philanthropy*, p. 143.
[3] *The General Infirmary at Leeds; its work and progress 1767–1911*.
[4] *Econ. Journal*, Sept. 1922, p. 340.   [5] Chaplin, pp. 54–55.
[6] Percival, IV. p. 437.   [7] Blane, *Select Dissertations*, p. 137.

as important as any that took place; they show that people were adopting the right attitude to health and to the conditions essential to any serious and successful tackling of the problem of lessening the burden of disease and the death rate from diseases affected by these conditions.

v

The development of dispensaries in London was quite as remarkable as that of the hospitals. The object of the General Dispensary was said by Lettsom to be "to administer medicine and advice to the poor, not only at the Dispensary, but also at their own habitations, which latter circumstance is an advantage peculiar to this plan."[1] The very interesting article on the population of London in a recent number of the *Economic Journal*, which has been referred to more than once, deals with the early dispensary movement in London, and points out that medical practice had been chiefly among the rich, and that the dispensaries helped to break this down, to teach the poor the rudiments of hygiene, and the doctors the diseases and conditions of the poor. Lettsom, writing when the General Dispensary had been in existence about five years, claims that it has had a considerable share in decreasing the number of burials recorded, and states, "In the space of a very few years I have observed a total revolution in the conduct of the common people respecting their diseased friends, they have learned that most diseases are mitigated by a free admission of air, by cleanliness and by promoting instead of restraining the indulgence and care of the sick."[2] It is very possible that it was this greater study and this association with the diseases of the poor who were treated at the dispensaries, which led to the greater thought for the treatment of fever which characterised the close of the century, for fever was an affliction which was particularly associated with those conditions which would fall within the experience of the dispensary doctors. The dispensaries would also disseminate medical information in the same way as the hospitals, but would do so over a wider field and with less

[1] Lettsom, *Medical Memoirs*, 1774, p. xix.
[2] *Econ. Journal*, Sept. 1922, pp. 341-343.

paraphernalia than is inevitable with a complicated organisation like a hospital. They were also valuable as a feeding ground for the hospitals, whereby cases which before would have gone from bad to worse without adequate attention were drafted to these institutions. They were valuable as a link in the chain whereby fewer and fewer people who were in need of medical help were left without it.

The first dispensary was opened in 1769 by Dr Armstrong. Between 1769 and 1790 all the thirteen dispensaries founded in London before 1800 were started. By 1840 there were twenty-three dispensaries in London, another ten having been opened after 1800. At present there are sixty-nine dispensaries in London; thus one-third of the present number had been opened by 1840, and of that number one-half had been opened in the first twenty years of the dispensary movement, namely, before 1790. Thus London was more fully provided with dispensaries in 1790 and 1840, in proportion to the number of hospitals then open, than it is now. The period 1769–1790, therefore, showed a remarkable development of dispensaries, all those founded in the eighteenth century being opened in those years and amounting to more than one-sixth of the present number, whereas in the case of hospitals only one-tenth of the present number had been opened by 1800. The slower development of dispensaries in later times is possibly to be explained on the grounds that with more hospital accommodation of a general character and with hospital accommodation for more special purposes, with the greater diffusion of elementary medical knowledge, with the higher standard of the general practitioner and possibly also with the growth of benevolent societies attached to various bodies of organised mankind, the original use of the dispensary has been superseded. If this is so, it enhances the importance that should be attached to its first rapid growth in London at a time when the rudiments of medical knowledge and hygiene were the important things to impress on people, rather than the refinements which might come later; for this work the dispensaries were admirably adapted. Let it be remembered also that it was during this first period of the dispensary movement that the death rate began to fall.

As in the case of the hospitals, the dispensary movement in the provinces came later than in London. Very possibly there was a good deal of imitation in this, for by the end of the century it was recognised that the dispensary movement in London was doing good work and it was being urged that dispensaries, instead of being confined to the metropolis and towns, should be made general throughout the country[1].

Before 1840 eighty dispensaries had been opened in the provinces, whereas before 1800, when the first great burst of dispensary building in London was over, only thirteen had been founded and one of these was an old foundation dating from 1703[2]. Between 1800 and 1840 there were, therefore, sixty-seven dispensaries founded in the provinces. There are now on the register about 107, but as certain of the dispensaries founded in the period under discussion have since become hospitals and are classified as such, this figure is, for purposes of comparison, an understatement; but even allowing for this it is evident that by 1840 the country was well supplied with dispensaries compared with the number in existence to-day, and it is further evident what a large share the first forty years of the nineteenth century had in that development.

The remarks that were made about the utility of dispensaries in London apply if anything with greater force in the country, where hospital accommodation was slower in developing and where medical skill probably lagged behind that of London, at any rate until medical education was systematised and medical schools began to develop in the provinces. Whatever were the motives which led to the growth of dispensaries, there can be no doubt that they were powerful aids to the hospitals in the work of improving the health of the nation, and valuable agents in the education both of the doctors and of the people at large in the treatment of disease, and in directing their energies into the right channels[3].

---

[1] T. Champney, *A Review of the Healing Art*, 1797, p. 100.

[2] Ormskirk Dispensary.

[3] Kirkman Gray, p. 132: Resolution of the College of Physicians, 1687, "That all members of the College, whether fellows, licentiates or candidates, should give their advice gratis to all their sick neighbouring poor, when desired, within the city of London, or seven miles round." This may be the

VI

During this period fevers of all sorts were a very serious evil, and one of the chief sources of adult mortality. In those days, and for some time after, the various kinds of fever were but roughly differentiated, and therefore the matter has to be treated rather generally, particularly by the layman; but as the treatment of fevers in general varies little from fever to fever in main principles and during the rudimentary stages of knowledge, the important thing is to get some idea of the prevalence of fevers in general and of the measures adopted for dealing with them in bulk rather than for the treatment of individual cases. Thus of the continued fevers, it was not until the investigations of Sir William Jenner in 1849–1851 that typhus and typhoid were recognised, in this country at any rate, as different diseases[1]. Typhus, a disease which has from time to time prevailed in all parts of Europe, has had its special haunts in Russia and Great Britain[2], and in the period under discussion it was a disease of which people were very much afraid. The name was first used about 1760, but before that time the disease probably went under a number of other names associating it with particular places—camp, jail, hospital and ship fever—or with particular symptoms—pestilential and putrid fever. Typhus was generally feared when fever was prevalent and things that never ought to have been called typhus were so called[3]—it was

first official and conscious adoption of the practice that has made the modern hospital movement a possibility. The origins may not have been entirely altruistic. The College thought that the Society of Apothecaries were poaching on their domain, and doing more doctoring than they should, and the dispensary movement may have been an attempt on the part of the College to retrieve the lost ground, by doing the doctoring themselves.

[1] Creighton, ii. p.183. But see also Osler and McCrae, *Principles and Practice of Medicine*, Ed. ix. p. 1. The distinction of typhus and typhoid is here attributed to Louis, and the clear definition of the differences to Gerhard of Philadelphia in 1837; and it is stated that the recognition of the differences between the two diseases was slow in Great Britain.

[2] Allbutt, ii. Part i. p. 539.

[3] *Remarks on the prevailing epidemic commonly called Typhus Fever*, 1819, W. O. Porter, Physician to the Bristol Dispensary, p. 3: "I am anxious to relieve your mind from all exaggerated apprehension. I would strip the prevalent fever of the terrible name 'Typhus' to which it has no claim. Typhus is the designation of a malignant fever rarely seen in late years."

certainly confused with relapsing fever. Typhus had a higher mortality than relapsing fever, and in the epidemic of fever in Ireland in 1817–1819 relapsing fever was most prevalent at the beginning, and the higher mortality at the close betokens more typhus[1].

The mortality from fevers within the Bills of Mortality can be seen in the table which is given[2]. During the first half of the eighteenth century the mortality increased until in 1750 it amounted to one-fifth of the total mortality of London. From that time onwards, with the exception of certain periods of epidemic, the mortality decreased in a remarkable manner. The years 1803–1816 were particularly free of fever in this country[3], and, in view of the movement of the death rate this is a very interesting and important fact. In 1817 and in the two following years fevers again became serious, the number of deaths began to rise and the death rate followed in the same decade. Two interesting reports of 1801 and 1818 which discuss the figures attribute the decline of fever to the "improvements in the edifices of the metropolis and the attention to domestic and personal cleanliness," and in the case of the latter report more specifically to the "beneficial effects of the House of Recovery which have surpassed all expectation" and the indirect results which followed from that, for we read that "the early removal of fever patients from their own habitations, and the consequent prevention of infection, the improved methods of treating typhus fever, and the cleansing, purifying and white-

[1] Murchison, *Treatise on the continued fevers of Great Britain*, p. 313.

[2] Fever mortality within the Bills of Mortality.

1701–1710	3230	yearly average	1801	2908
1711–1720	3656	,,	1802	2201
1721–1730	4037	,,	1803	2326
1731–1740	3432	,,	1804	1702
1741–1750	4351	,,	1805	1307
1750	4294	one year	1806	1352
1751–1760	2564	yearly average	1807	1033
1761–1770	3521	,,	1808	1168
1771–1780	2589	,,	1809	1066
1781–1790	2459	,,	1810	1139
1791–1800	2988	,,	1811	906
1800	2712	one year		

The figures for the eighteenth century, *S.B.C.P.* III. p. 286. For the nineteenth century, *Reports*, 1818, VII. p. 18.

[3] Creighton, II. p. 162.

washing the habitations of the poor in those parts of the metropolis where infection peculiarly prevailed have nearly annihilated
this disease in London and Westminster."[1]

These accounts are agreed in general as to the measures
which should be taken to check the infection, but it is interesting
to note how closely the mortality from fevers as shown by the
London figures throughout the eighteenth century corresponds
to the general mortality for the whole country, and in this connection it must be remembered that the decline in the mortality
is more striking than the bare figures would make it appear,
for as the numbers of deaths decline, the population is increasing.
The fever figures rise to their highest point in the period from
1720 to 1750, in which the death rate is the highest and which
was also the gin-drinking period. Some years later Percival was
quite aware of the effect of this when he said, "there is no
assurance of a speedy cure in the case of confirmed dram drinkers,
for with them, contagious fever generally terminates fatally."[2]
There was then a decline in the number of deaths from fever in
the decade 1750–1760 as there also was in the general mortality,
followed in both cases by a rise before the general decline began
about 1780.

In this period the subject of fevers was attracting a good deal
of attention, and the causes were being investigated. We know
now that the organism of typhus, the exact nature of which is
not yet known, and which has not yet been isolated, is conveyed
by body lice, which are associated with filth; the filth without
the lice may be very unpleasant but it will not cause typhus, nor
will the lice unless they carry the organism, but with the filth
the lice are likely to be present and then typhus may follow,
and with imperfect knowledge the filth, which is a comparatively
easy thing to demonstrate, will be put down as the cause. In
this period people were groping as to the cause of these diseases
—fevers in general. Very soon they associated fevers with
conditions of dirt, and hence it followed that the measures they
adopted and recommended were well conceived and likely to
do good, even though they did not know the scientific reasons

[1] *Reports*, 1818, VII. p. 18.
[2] *S.B.C.P.* 1807, v. p. 183.

which, with fuller understanding and consequently for rather
different reasons, would cause such measures as these to be
adopted. They were on the right track, and they were attacking
the right enemy in attacking filthy conditions and insanitary
arrangements, and from this they passed to a clearer realisation
of the work to be done in the towns, which by their very growth
were making the problem a more serious one. In this branch
of the subject nothing very systematic or extensive was done
until the cholera epidemic of 1831 and 1832 had compelled
them to pay serious attention to the condition of the towns.

Once they had realised that this class of disease is associated
with filth, even if they did not know the real reason, they had
the knowledge necessary to suggest the right measures to
counteract them.

Take a description from a modern text-book of the kind of
locality in which typhus is likely to be prevalent, and compare
it with almost any description in the reports of the thirties and
forties of the courts and alleys which were both the dwelling-
places and the workshops of many people in the growing manufacturing towns, and no surprise will be felt at the prevalence of
fevers[1].

In 1782 Milman wrote a treatise on fevers and, while con-
fessing the general ignorance that prevailed as to their remote
causes, stated that experience had already shown that persons
in some situations were more subject to them than others,
especially "people who inhabit damp houses or who live in
modes of uncleanliness," and in view of this knowledge declared
that their virulence should be disarmed by every attention to
cleanliness "in hospital and in jails, on board ship, and in every
situation where a number of people are crowded into a small
space."[2]

In 1788 an anonymous *Treatise on fevers* was published. The
author stated that his remarks on fevers were mostly written
in 1769 and 1770, and appears to have got nearer the truth than
some of his contemporaries when he states that they are caused

---

[1] McVail, *The prevention of infectious diseases*, 1907, p. 34. *Reports*, 1843,
xv. p. 563.

[2] Milman, *An enquiry into Scurvy and Putrid Fevers*, 1782, pp. 114, 116.

not by "a matter putrid in itself, but from invisible insects that, floating in the air at times, are lodged in the skin in innumerable quantities." He also had sound views as to the right remedies and lays particular stress on the necessity of drainage in the flat districts and in the neighbourhood of towns[1].

A good deal has been said to show that the importance of cleanliness and fresh air was being recognised in the treatment of fevers, and throughout the whole period the same principles are being proclaimed. A certificate of several physicians of hospitals and dispensaries in London states that infectious fever "derives its origin principally from the neglect of cleanliness and ventilation; and that its communication from the persons first attacked to the other members of a family, is an almost necessary consequence of the crowded state of the dwellings of the poor."[2]

Practical application was given to these principles in the organisation of the London House of Recovery, a certain portion of the funds of which was spent in "cleansing the apartments of the Poor who are assailed by fever." This, which was claimed as a new movement on the part of a charity, was done by whitewashing. The institution had also acquired its own means of transport, thus "preventing the use of coaches and sedan chairs, one of the means by which contagion is circulated."[3]

A certain amount is said about improved treatment of fevers, but it is pretty certain that any definite alterations in the treatment were very empirical, apart from the general conditions favourable to health which were necessary to any satisfactory solution of the question. It is therefore probable that it was this general realisation of the advantages and necessity of ventilation,

[1] *A Treatise on Fevers*, 1788, pp. 23, 68, 75.
[2] *S.B.C.P.* vol. III. Appendix, p. 55.
[3] *Reports*, 1818, VII. p. 4. John Roberton, *On Mortality*, 1827, p. 47: Diminution of mortality due to "improved habits of living, and cleanliness among the lower orders." Hawkins, *Medical Statistics*, 1829, p. 189, "the counteraction of typhus by means of cleanliness." Heberden, *Increase and decrease of different diseases*, p. 34, speaking particularly of dysentery and kindred diseases, the improvement not confined to the metropolis: "I have no hesitation in attributing it to the improvements which have gradually taken place, not only in London, but in all great towns, and in the manner of living throughout the country, particularly with respect to cleanliness and ventilation."

cleanliness, disinfecting and fresh air that is the most important contribution of this period to the diminution of mortality from this species of disease as well as from others, rather than any specific alteration in the technical methods of dealing with them. Whereas technical methods of dealing with specific diseases touch few people beyond the comparatively small number who are treated, this general improvement in cleanliness and in the rudimentary principles of hygiene is not only the necessary foundation of any more technical improvements that may take place, but affects the health and well-being of many people who may never require medical attention, and thereby improves the general health of the nation[1].

Fever was prevalent in London in 1773, and the eighties of the eighteenth century were years in which fevers took an epidemic form in certain parts of the country. There was also a remarkable outburst of fever in 1794 and 1795, and another at the very end of the century, though the records do not make the 1794–5 epidemic appear so serious as that which had occurred in 1783 and the three subsequent years[2].

It was these epidemics which led to the problem being tackled seriously in a practical manner. In 1783 special fever wards were established in the Chester Infirmary by Haygarth, and in 1790 "regulations to prevent the spreading of fever" were adopted at Bury and Ashton-under-Lyne[3]. Under the stress of the 1794–5 epidemic a Board of Health was set up at Manchester, evidently under the influence of Percival, fever wards were established, and in 1796 a House of Recovery was opened[4]. In this matter of fever hospitals it is interesting to note that Manchester was the first really important place to open one and to set the example to London[5]. In the next few

---

[1] With reference to changes in the methods of treating fever cases see Roberton, p. 47; Lettsom, *Medical Memoirs*, 1774, p. 17; Blane in *Reports*, 1816, III. p. 45. In the typhus epidemics in Ireland it is said that it was very often the people who were given up as dying and put outside the cabins, so that the others inside could be looked after, who recovered as they got into the fresh air after the impossible conditions prevailing inside. (Conversation with Sir Clifford Allbutt.)

[2] Creighton, II. pp. 137, 153, 156.

[3] *Reports*, 1818, VII. p. 18. See also *S.B.C.P.* VI. p. 88.

[4] Percival, I. p. cci. Also *S.B.C.P.* I. p. 98.   [5] Gray, p. 140.

years a good many fever hospitals were opened; in Leeds we are told that in 1801, above £3000 had been subscribed for the purpose and that a House of Recovery was opened in 1804[1], but as a matter of fact this was not full until 1817 when the period of freedom from fever was over[2]. In Newcastle a House of Recovery was opened in 1804 as the result of a difference of opinion which arose when the infirmary was being enlarged as to whether fever cases should be admitted to the infirmary or not[3]. Percival seems to have considered that London was slow in adopting the policy of opening a fever hospital[4]—"In May 1801," we are told, "an institution for the cure and prevention of infectious fevers in the metropolis was established by the Society for bettering the condition of the poor; and in February 1802 a London House of Recovery was opened."[5] These early hospitals were on a very small scale, and in any case their sphere cannot have extended anything like as far as the need, but again they could have the effect of disseminating information[6].

At any rate from 1803 to 1816 there was little fever in the country and the death rate was low and falling during that period. Great things were claimed for the Manchester House of Recovery, but Percival's statistics on which they are based are not infallible; they deal in this case with the figures of one year only and in some respects they have been called in question[7]. The decrease was also partially due to or assisted by "mild seasons and good harvests."[8]

Fever is next mentioned as a serious evil in the various inquiries into the health of towns, the growth of which has been unaccompanied by the sanitary precautions which had been recommended in this earlier period, and therefore it is again probable that the most valuable contribution of this earlier

[1] *S.B.C.P.* III. Appendix, p. 135.
[2] Creighton, II. p. 171.   [3] Hume, p. 27.
[4] *S.B.C.P.* III. Appendix, p. 135.
[5] *Reports*, 1804, V. Report on the Fever Institution.
[6] *S.B.C.P.* V. p. 194.
[7] *Ibid.* III. p. 271. Manchester House of Recovery, numbers treated:
Sept. 1793—May 1796   1256.
May 1796—May 1797   26.
[8] *Ibid.* V. p. 183.

period, and the cause to which more than any other it owed the mitigation of fever mortality, was its more careful and intelligent attitude to all matters of cleanliness and hygiene.

VII

There were other classes of disease that had decreased during the eighteenth century and had had an effect on the rate of mortality:

(a) Blane says that plague was not seen in London after 1679, and Heberden, writing in 1801, takes occasion to say that plague is no longer a disease that occurs in England, and again the effect of cleanliness and ventilation is emphasised[1].

(b) In the Bills of Mortality there is not much discrimination between intermittent fevers and dysentery and kindred complaints, but Blane, writing in 1813, asserts that on the evidence of the Bills of Mortality the "annual deaths from bowel complaints of which dysentery was the principal" fluctuated, in the seventeenth century, between one and two thousand, sometimes amounting to upwards of four thousand; in the early part of the eighteenth century between one thousand and one hundred, and in the latter part from one hundred to twenty, while the average in the first ten years of the nineteenth century was 22·8. He then remarks that the Bills are "justly chargeable with great want of discrimination," but that in this case the movement is so pronounced that there can be no doubt of its general truth[2].

Heberden quotes figures from the Bills of Mortality demonstrating the decrease in various diseases of a dysenteric or allied character[3]. Creighton, while frankly agreeing that dysentery

---

[1] Blane, *Observations*, 1813, p. 93. Heberden, *Increase and decrease of different diseases*, p. 95.

[2] Blane, *Observations*, 1813, p. 93.

[3] Heberden, *Increase and decrease of different diseases*, p. 34.

LONDON. Decrease of diseases described as bloody flux, colic, gripes, etc. (dysentery)

1700–1710 annual average 1070	1750–1760 annual average 110
1710–1720 ,, 770	1760–1770 ,, 80
1720–1730 ,, 700	1770–1780 ,, 70
1730–1740 ,, 350	1780–1790 ,, 40
1740–1750 ,, 150	1790–1800 ,, 20

did decrease in the century, does not agree with the evidence adduced by Heberden, and says that the decrease was not of the remarkable extent that Heberden's figures would lead one to believe. He further says that there were epidemics of dysentery in 1762 and again in the years 1779 to 1785, when there was also an epidemic of fever and some aguish years; then during the period in which the death rate fell and the remarkable increase of population took place dysentery was not prevalent and its great period in the nineteenth century coincided with and followed the two hot summers of 1825 and 1826, the latter of which was probably the hottest and driest summer of the century, and at this time the death rate was rising again[1].

(c) Ague is one of the intermittent fevers, but we are told that until the beginning of the eighteenth century it was blended in the Bills with continued fever, and again, therefore, one has to be careful of comparisons[2]. Ague is associated with fens, marshes and undrained land, and as drainage proceeds it tends to decrease, and herein lies the close connection between the agricultural improvements of the eighteenth century, the health of the people and the decline in mortality. Both James I and Cromwell died of ague in London, and London in those days was surrounded by country as marshy as the fens of Lincolnshire now are and in 1801 Heberden definitely associated ague with "putrid moisture" and the "marshy parts of the country."[3] Sydenham is quoted as the authority for the statement that agues were epidemic in London from 1661 to 1664 and from 1677 to 1685, though it must be remembered that there may be some confusion at this date with continued fevers. Blane declared that the mortality from ague had been declining throughout the eighteenth century. In 1728 the deaths within the Bills were forty, in 1729 twenty-seven and in 1730 sixteen, while in the first ten years of the nineteenth century the average was four. This decline he attributed largely to the use of

---

[1] Creighton, II. pp. 774–785.

[2] Blane, *Observations*, p. 94: "With regard to agues the bills of mortality do not afford us satisfactory information, this disease being blended with continued fever, till the beginning of the 18th century."

[3] Heberden, *op. cit.* p. 73.

Peruvian Bark[1]. Whatever the Peruvian Bark may have had to do with it, the important point is that the mortality decreased, and if this was due to the Peruvian Bark, then this was a factor in the technical treatment of the disease that is worth mentioning.

Elsewhere he quotes an example of this decrease in the mortality from ague at Portsmouth where the disease was very prevalent until efficient drainage in 1769 led to its disappearance, whereas Hilsea and other parts of the island of Portsea retained their aguish tendencies until a drainage scheme was carried through in 1793. He also stated that "numberless other examples might be adduced in proof of this" (the decline of the aguish tendency) "derived from the general improved state of health in various parts of the kingdom, in consequence of the inclosure of commons for the purpose of agricultural improvements, of which drainage is one of the principal."[2] Drainage, as we have seen, was a very considerable factor in the agricultural improvement that is associated with the inclosure movement. It is pointed out that among the counties which in 1811 showed a rate of mortality above the average, all those subject to ague are included with the exception of Lincolnshire, that Lincolnshire is divided pretty definitely into fenny and non-fenny, and that in Stamford, which is high and dry, the mortality is 20·0 per thousand, whereas in Boston, which is fenny, it is 37·0 per thousand[3]. The Vicar of Spalding, writing in 1813, said that the health of the flat country had been greatly improved "by the late Acts of Parliament for draining all the neighbouring fens,"[4] and a modern work says that it is owing to the almost universal drainage and cultivation of the soil that ague has largely vanished from the country[5].

(d) Heberden, again harping on the topic of cleanliness, refers to the practical extermination of scurvy, though in this case to cleanliness and ventilation "may be added, especially

---

[1] Blane, *Observations*, 1813, p. 94.
[2] Blane, *Select Dissertations*, p. 113.
[3] Blane, *op. cit.* p. 171.
[4] Milne, *Annuities and Assurances*, 1815, p. 456. Bateman, *Reports on the diseases of London*, 1819, p. 31.
[5] Murchison, p. 8.

with regard to the disorder immediately under consideration, the increased use of fresh provisions, and the introduction of a variety of vegetables among all ranks of people."[1] This was a disease which particularly attacked the navy. Creighton, speaking of the navy, says that various remedies had been adopted to improve its health; to guard against the introduction of jail fever men were not pressed immediately on being released from prison, new crews were not mixed with old, the allowance of soap was increased, the bilges were kept cleaner and the diet improved[2]. Blane dates a new era in the health of the navy from 1798, for a perfectly definite reason which does not appear from the writings of Creighton, for in 1796 "the sickness, instead of decreasing gradually, fell per saltum as it were. This is satisfactorily accounted for by its being the first year in which the general supply of lemon juice took place."[3]

(e) It should, however, be pointed out that certain diseases were on the increase in the period, although there can be no reasonable doubt that on the whole the gain in curative measures far outweighed the loss. Blane declared that "all those diseases of which the brain and the nerves are the seat" had increased and he

---

[1] *R.C.P. Med. Trans.* IV. p. 69. Heberden on Scurvy.

[2] Creighton, II. p. 119.

[3] Blane, *Select Dissertations*, pp. 4–22: "It appears...that during nine years of war preceding the general supply of lemon juice, the annual average of sick sent to hospitals was 1 in 3·9 of the whole men in the navy, but that in the nine succeeding years, the proportion was 1 in 8·4. Other causes, particularly the improved methods by which fevers were diminished, contributed greatly to this decrease of sickness, so that it may be difficult to assign precisely what is due to lemon juice. But what admits of no ambiguity, is that, ever since the year 1796, scurvy has almost disappeared from ships of war and naval hospitals." "The principal diseases which constitute sickness and cause mortality on board of ships in all climates are scurvy and fevers."

The table below shows the number of seamen and mariners, annually voted by Parliament, for two distinct and equal portions of war, with the numbers annually sent sick on shore, and to hospital ships on the home stations, during these periods:

(SUMMARY)

1778–1783 } 1793–1795 }	Voted	745,000	Sick	189,730
1796–1801 } 1804–1806 }	Voted	1,053,076	Sick	123,949

It is now known that fresh vegetables or, failing that, lime juice, are more important in the prevention of scurvy than any consideration of mere cleanliness.

considered that the reason was that a much greater proportion of the population lived independently of bodily labour than in previous times[1].

VIII

Another very important branch of medicine in which there were notable improvements during the period we are discussing was midwifery, the importance of which to the growth of the population has already been touched upon. During the early part of the eighteenth century, the practice of midwifery was chiefly in the hands of ignorant women[2] who combined it with callings which were often incongruous and who were grossly superstitious and dominated by prejudices which, like their art, had descended as ancient traditions. The other occupations of these women do not suggest that cleanliness would be among the qualifications they were likely to possess[3], and in their practice they seem to have combined a needless and, considering their small amount of technical skill and knowledge, an unwarrantable interference with the course of nature with a total disregard of the most elementary attention to cleanliness and ventilation[4]. In 1739 Smellie began to teach midwifery in London before which date there had been no systematic instruction, in the same year Sir Richard Manningham established a ward in Westminster Infirmary for lying-in women, and in 1747 the Middlesex Hospital made arrangements for taking such cases[5].

Lying-in hospitals began to be founded in London about the middle of the century; the first of these, the British Lying-in Hospital, was founded in 1749, the City of London Lying-in Hospital in 1750, Queen Charlotte's Lying-in Hospital in 1752, the Royal Maternity Charity in 1757 and the General Lying-in Hospital in 1765. The provinces followed rather later; the Newcastle Maternity Hospital was founded in 1760, the York

---

[1] Blane, *Observations*, p. 97.
[2] C. Cullingworth, *Charles White, F.R.S.*, 1904, p. 23.
[3] *Econ. Journal*, Sept. 1922, p. 340.
[4] Cullingworth, p. 24: "The old plan had excluded all ventilation and fresh air." See also p. 240, n. 1.
[5] Chaplin, p. 54. *Econ. Journal*, Sept. 1922, p. 340. In this 1741 is given as the year Smellie began to teach.

Dispensary and Maternity Hospital in 1788, St Mary's Hospital
at Manchester in 1790, the Liverpool Maternity Hospital in
1796 and the Chester Benevolent Institution for Lying-in
Women in 1798. By this time also small societies were being
founded in country places; at Tottenham a society for giving
assistance in the form of linen and money was founded in 1791,
in 1794 a similar society was founded in Buckinghamshire, and
in 1798 another for the benefit of the wives of the artillerymen
at Woolwich. As it is this kind of society of which records are
not kept with any care it is probable that there were a good many
others of which there are no traces[1].

If it be true that Smellie "must be regarded as the father of
modern midwifery" an honourable place must be assigned to
Charles White of Manchester. White was a friend of John
Hunter's, and the two studied under and attended the lectures
of William Hunter; by 1752 White was established in Manchester and was instrumental in that year, in conjunction with
the merchant Joseph Bancroft, in founding the Manchester
Infirmary, while in 1790 he was the moving spirit in the foundation of the maternity hospital, and in De Quincey's Auto-
biography he is styled "the most eminent surgeon by much in
the North of England." In the early years of his practice in
Manchester he was in charge of the parish poor both there
and in certain neighbouring places, and was much impressed
by the disastrous effects on lying-in women of the methods of
treatment then in vogue. He studied the subject for some time
and in 1773 published his observations in a work entitled
A treatise on the management of pregnant and lying-in women.
His biographer said that few medical books had been pro-
ductive of more important reforms in medical practice, and
modern authorities applaud White's views and practice as
startlingly modern and far in advance of his time.

White attacked the old methods of treatment and laid great
stress on the necessity for fresh air and ventilation—two things
neglected in the old treatment—and the necessity of keeping
the room as sweet and as clean as possible and free from any
disagreeable smells; "the patient should often be supplied with

[1] *S.B.C.P.* I. p. 163; II. p. 179; IV. p. 192.

clean linen, for cleanliness, and free, pure and in some cases cool air are the greatest necessities in this situation."[1] Nature was to be allowed to do as much as she would herself before any artificial assistance was given. Under these principles "the miliary fever almost entirely disappeared, and the puerperal fever soon became of comparatively rare occurrence." White declared that he himself, in a large experience, had never lost a single patient from this class of fevers—a boast to be proud of[2].

White's principles, as Adami has pointed out, were given a full trial with very successful results some years later during the mastership of Robert Collins at the Rotunda of Dublin. When he took over the mastership in 1826, puerperal fever prevailed to a great degree; a system of fumigating the wards and scrubbing the floors, painting, whitewashing and rotation of wards was inaugurated. Puerperal fever continued until March 1829 when these measures were taken, and then he says "from the time this was completed, until the termination of my mastership in Nov. 1833, we did not lose one patient by this disease."[3]

It will be noticed that the series of improvements on which White and later Collins lay stress was the need of fresh air, ventilation and cleanliness, just the things which others had been inculcating in the treatment of other complaints. All this goes to suggest that in this age the really big thing that people learned was the necessity for cleanliness and fresh air; they were following the principles of asepsis without knowing it and consequently making possible an improvement in health and a decline of mortality that they were unable to explain on strictly scientific grounds.

---

[1] White's description of the old method: "As soon as she is delivered, if she is a person in affluent circumstances, she is covered up in bed with additional clothes, the curtains are drawn round the bed, and pinned together, every crevice in the windows and door is stopped close, not excepting even the key hole, and windows are guarded not only with shutters and curtains but even with blankets, the more effectually to exclude the fresh air, and the good woman is not suffered to put her arm or even her nose out of bed, for fear of catching cold."

[2] For the account of White and his work see *D.N.B.*, Cullingworth's *Life*, Adami's *Charles White and puerperal fever*, 1922, and White's own book.

[3] Robert Collins, *A practical treatise on midwifery*, 1835, pp. 380–390.

Improvement is also shown by some figures of the mortality in the British Lying-in Hospital in London. It is not, of course, suggested that the figures of one hospital are by themselves any very sure guide as to what was going on all over the country, but when it is remembered that the principles of White had been started in another part of the country some years before the great decrease of mortality in this hospital is seen, it is possible that this does represent a general movement, even if not on the same scale[1]. The figures are remarkable and some of the short period figures would be creditable for the best institutions of to-day. Probably, however, these figures may be misleading and, being based on the averages of short periods, it is possible that they are not representative of the real state of affairs which is illustrated better by those of longer periods in the table. Even making this allowance it is obvious that a great improvement took place in this branch of medicine towards the end of the eighteenth century, the period when the death rate was falling, and that this improvement brought about an important saving of life.

IX

The question of infant mortality is very important and the saving of a young life is of great value from the point of view of an increase of the population. The question in the absence of official and reliable figures is very intangible; a certain amount of evidence is afforded by the London Bills of Mortality and some isolated pieces of information from other towns, but there is nothing in the way of detailed information for the country at large.

[1] Mortality in British Lying-in Hospital:

	Women	Children
1749–59	1 in 42	1 in 15
1759–68	1 in 50	1 in 20
1769–78	1 in 53	1 in 42
1779–88	1 in 60	1 in 44
1789–98	1 in 288	1 in 77
1799–1800	1 in 938	1 in 118
1799–1809	1 in 216	—
1806–1808	1 in 501	—

See Heberden, pp. 40–41; Highmore, *Charities*, p. 191.
Willan, *Diseases of London*, p. 410: "This table shows to what an extent the lives of infants may be preserved by proper attention and management."

During this period there were two great sources of infant mortality, one of which has already been dealt with, namely smallpox and deaths at or about the time of birth, and there can be no doubt that in the middle of the eighteenth century the infant mortality was very high.

In this section some attempt has been made to collect certain pieces of information which bear upon the question more or less from the numerical standpoint, to show the extent of the decline in infant mortality during the period and to deal shortly with other sources of infant mortality.

In 1772 or thereabouts Percival, expatiating on the "peculiar degree" in which towns were fatal to children, said that "half of all that are born in London die under two; and in Manchester under five years of age; whereas at Royton, a country township not far distant from Manchester, the number of children dying under the age of three years is to the number of children born only as 1 to 7."[1] It is interesting to note also that the remarks about the infant mortality in Manchester follow a description of the improvements that had recently been wrought in the health of Manchester[2].

In a lecture on the preservation of health in 1797 we find that the same proportion of deaths among children in London was maintained as that given by Percival for 1772, though it appears that if the age is extended to five there was a diminution of the mortality[2]. From 1730 to 1749 the burials of children within the Bills of Mortality were 74·5 per cent. of all the children christened, from 1750 to 1769 it was 63 per cent., from 1770 to 1789 it was 51·5 per cent. and from 1790 to 1809 it was 41·3 per cent.[3]

During this period it is doubtful to what extent institutions were contributing to the saving of infant life. The Foundling Hospital, which had a bad name from the moral lapses it was supposed to encourage, was not looked upon as much of a success in that way. Its infant death roll was little if any

---

[1] Percival, IV. p. 41.   [2] *Ibid.* III. p. 6.
[3] T. Garnett, *Lecture on the preservation of health*, 1797, p. 42: "It is a melancholy fact that above half the children born in London, die before they are two years old."
[4] *Econ. Journal*, Sept. 1922, p. 346, quoting McCulloch, *Account of the British Empire*, 4th ed. II. p. 543.

better than the general infant mortality at any rate in London; but it must be remembered that the class of children it took in were those whose chance of life without its assistance was of the smallest, and the rate of mortality which it did show may actually have been an improvement[1].

In an inquiry into the conditions of children's labour in 1816, Sir Gilbert Blane, commenting on the decline in the general death rate, is clear that "the great difference has arisen from the diminished mortality of children," which he attributes to the better treatment they receive[2].

In 1808 Heberden, writing of the mortality of London, said that the principal decrease of burials had taken place in respect of children under two years of age. In the inquiry into Friendly Societies in 1825, which is dealing chiefly with the poorer parts of the community, it is stated that in London "not half the children live to be four years old."[3] Finlaison, in evidence before the same Committee, gave an account even less favourable than this of the conditions among the lower classes in London, in which he stated that as a general rule during the child-bearing age births were constant and regular at the rate of one every two years, while only 542 children out of every 1000 born survived the period of nursing[4].

Bateman, writing in 1819, gives figures to show that the mortality among children had steadily decreased in London since the middle of the eighteenth century, which he attributed to "giving up the fatal system of hardening children."[5] The figures given by Percival for 1772 or thereabouts for London and Manchester make out that from the point of view of infant

---

[1] Hawkins, *Med. Stat.* p. 129: "Foundling Hospitals have done very little towards the preservation of infant life." Malcolm, *Manners and Customs of London*, IV. p. 14: "From 1770 to 1797, 1684 children were received, of which number, 482 died under the age of twelve months."

[2] *Reports*, 1816, III. p. 45: "This diminished mortality, I apprehend, has arisen from children being brought up in a purer air, with more cleanliness and greater warmth."

[3] *Reports*, 1825, IV. p. 52 (W. Morgan). [4] *Ibid.* p. 90 (Finlaison).

[5] Bateman, *Reports on the diseases of London*, 1819, p. xi:

1760	Total deaths	19·830	under two	6838	or 1 in 2·7 ...	370·4 per 1000
1789	,,	20·749	,,	6933	,, 1 in 3·0 ...	333·3 ,,
1810	,,	19·893	,,	5851	,, 1 in 3·4 ...	294·1 ,,
1818	,,	19·705	,,	5381	,, 1 in 3·7 ...	270·3 ,,

mortality Manchester was better than London. In 1833 and 1844 some figures are given on rather a different system, which show that by then London had a better record in this respect than many other big towns. This is an interesting commentary on the theory that of the large towns London was the only one which improved with anything like steadiness throughout the period with which we are dealing; and that other and more definitely manufacturing towns, as they grew more rapidly and without adequate regulation and control, also became less healthy[1]. There are, however, many statements to the effect that factory children are as healthy as those in other industries[2], that they do not show a higher mortality and that they recover from illnesses as quickly as other children[3], although it is confessed that they do not look so well as those who live in the country[4].

The general improvements in the conditions of life must have had a greater effect on infants and young children than on adults. At the beginning of the period the conditions under which children were brought up were not favourable to health. Infantile diarrhœa, mistaken methods of looking after children, spirit drinking on the part of the parents and the habit of giving spirits to the children all had an unfavourable effect on the mortality. Creighton says that the history of infantile diarrhœa is a continuous and uniform one with indications of greatest severity in the first half of the eighteenth century, and that though there is little positive evidence, it is unlikely that there was as much of it anywhere as in London[5].

Mistaken treatment with the neglect of fresh air and fresh food among the more fortunate classes of the community—the

---

[1] *Reports*, 1833, XX. p. 133: "On comparing the number of deaths under two years of age in Manchester, Liverpool and London, they appear to be far more numerous at Manchester than in the latter two places. Of 1000 persons buried in one year in those three places, 424 die at Manchester under two years of age, 362 at Liverpool, and 308 at London." *Reports*, 1844, XVII. p. 13:

Deaths per 1000 under *five* years of age

London	408	Manchester	510
Birmingham	482	Liverpool	528
Leeds	480		

[2] *Reports*, 1833, XX. pp. 802, 804, 861, 862.
[3] *Ibid.* p. 869.   [4] *Ibid.* p. 802.   [5] Creighton, II. pp. 755–756.

things against which Charles White worked in effecting his improvements in midwifery—and total neglect among the poorer classes of the people, combined with an orgy of spirit drinking in the middle of the eighteenth century, account for the heavy toll of infant life. But also, as Creighton points out, the broken constitutions of the parents were probably a more potent cause of the poor stamina of the children than close nurseries, injudicious food and even total neglect.

All the improvements we have seen in other connections would have their beneficial effect on infant life, and by the time Blane was writing in the early period of the nineteenth century the views as to the treatment and upbringing of children had improved. The places in which the old faults would be the most likely to continue would be the ill-regulated and unhealthy manufacturing towns which, as they grew, would probably be the places which, in the early nineteenth century, most resembled London in the middle of the eighteenth century, when it was the only really large town in the kingdom and as little controlled as many of the manufacturing towns were in the early nineteenth century. A suggestion of the revival of the earlier conditions is found in a medical report on the mining population in Shropshire in 1842 which states that, although the men and boys are healthy, there is an extraordinary mortality during infancy and childhood owing to the quantity of gin and opium given to the children—"those who survive are strong because the weak soon perish."[1]

Fresh food is an important factor in the health of childhood and in the reduction of infantile mortality; during this period agricultural improvements, which we have noticed, were having an important effect on this aspect of the subject. The system of the new husbandry and the careful cultivation of root crops as a substitute for the uneconomical fallows of the old system, provided the population with a greater supply of fresh vegetables than they had been used to before, and it is probable that the chief benefit of this would fall on the children. It is difficult to be certain how far the use of vegetables would permeate the population and particularly the town populations, but there can

---

[1] *Reports*, 1842, xv. p. 681.

be no doubt that the greater use of fresh vegetables was one of the advantages of the agricultural improvements, and is pointed out as one of the causes of reduced mortality. Heberden, writing in 1807, speaking particularly of scurvy but also generally of the improvements that have taken place, mentions "the increased use of fresh provisions, and the introduction of a variety of vegetables among all ranks of people."[1] With the picture of Ireland before their eyes, and the general reason always given for the increase of the population of Ireland, namely the use of potatoes, there was some reluctance in England to hail potatoes with too great enthusiasm[2]. Patrick Colquhoun, writing in 1815, however, emphasises the "regularly increasing culture and use of potatoes, particularly in the counties north of the river Trent and in Wales and Scotland," and goes on to say, "it is evident to demonstration, that but for potatoes, there must have been many famines not only in Scotland and Ireland but in the more sterile districts of England and Wales, where potatoes have constituted a large portion of the food of the people."[3]

In 1832 Sir Gilbert Blane was much impressed by the effect potatoes had played in the increase of the population in Ireland, and says also of them, "a valuable accession has been made to our stock of farinaceous food in the last hundred years by the introduction of potatoes. In the degree in which they have been cultivated in Great Britain, there can be no doubt of their having added to the comfort of the people, and even to their numbers." Having made that statement, he guards himself by drawing a warning from Ireland and concludes with the reflection that there is not the same risk in using potatoes in England as in Ireland, "potatoes not having been introduced into England till an age of high civilisation."[4]

Potatoes as an addition to a diet, provided they do not play too large a part, form a very valuable article of food, and it is

---

[1] Heberden, *R.C.P. Med. Trans.* IV. p. 69.
[2] Colquhoun, *Resources of the British Empire*, II. (1815): "Perhaps to this cause alone (the abundance of potatoes) is to be ascribed the rapid and growing population of Ireland."
[3] *Ibid.* pp. 10–11.
[4] Blane, *Reflections on the present crisis*, 1831, p. 39.

probable that the use of them referred to in these extracts was an improvement in the fresh vegetable food of the country.

With the cultivation of root crops came more animal food, and particularly more fresh animal food, as the difficulty of winter feed which led to much salt meat being used was got over. With the improvement of stock probably there also came an improvement in the milk supply, although it is interesting to note that the improvements which Bakewell introduced rendered the Dishley cattle a strain which the "grazier could not too highly value."

All these improvements in fresh food are particularly calculated to have an effect on the health and mortality of children, for fresh milk and vegetables and indeed food generally are of more immediate importance to children than to adults. The lack of them will have disastrous consequences sooner than in the case of adults, and in addition to this all the more general improvements which have been noticed were having an important influence on infant mortality.

x

In England in the eighteenth century smallpox was one of the most terrible evils which the population had to face; it is difficult now to realise the horror in which it was held and the distress it caused; contemporary literature is full of references to it[1]. It is stated on credible evidence that the total annual mortality from the disease in the eighteenth century amounted to forty or forty-four thousand, though it is not quite clear whether this is for England or for the United Kingdom; more probably it was for the United Kingdom, but in any case it is a guess, though it shows the kind of scale on which the disease prevailed[2].

In addition to this, smallpox derived its importance and also the fear in which it was held from the fact that it is a disease

[1] E.g. John Galt, *Annals of the Parish*, pp. 22–23, ravages in 1762. Macmichael, *Gold Headed Cane*, II. p. 65.

[2] *Reports*, 1802, XIV. p. 175: 45,000 for the U.K.; Highmore, *Charities*, p. 420: 40,000 for the U.K. Sir Anthony Bowlby, *B.M.J.* 6th February, 1923, p. 206: "At a time when the population of England was only seven millions the deaths from smallpox were said to amount to 44,000 a year."

to which there is very little natural immunity, and one which chiefly attacks children and has a very high mortality, being one in six or even higher[1]. Men would not marry until or unless the lady had had smallpox[2], servants were advertised for who had had it, people who had not had the disease were spoken of as "to have the smallpox,"[3] and ladies who had not had it or were not marked were at once regarded as beauties[4].

The incidence of smallpox in the eighteenth century was on the whole very great; greater, it would appear, than in the seventeenth century. In London it was, relatively to other diseases, more prevalent towards the middle and the end of the century[5], at least it was responsible for a greater share of the recorded deaths though the actual numbers of deaths from all causes including smallpox declined during the century. This provides additional evidence that the mortality from other causes was declining, and was doing so at a more rapid rate than the mortality from smallpox[6].

In the eighteenth century there were attempts to modify the severity of the scourge, especially by the practice of inoculation, which was introduced from the East in 1722 by Lady Mary

---

[1] Allbutt, II. Part I. pp. 484, 776.
[2] *Report of R.C.P. on vaccination*, 1807. Heberden, *op. cit.* p. 34.
[3] Allbutt, *ibid.* p. 768.
[4] *She stoops to conquer*, Everyman ed. Act II. p. 245.
[5] *Stat. Journal*, 1833, p. 404. Epidemics (an arbitrary level of 100 deaths in 1000 counting as an epidemic):

17th century (48 years)	10
18th century (100 years)	32
19th century (72 years)	0

"The 18th century showed a marked excess of epidemics."
[6] Blane, *Select Dissertations*, pp. 356–7. London, ratio of smallpox mortality to total mortality, total smallpox deaths in the periods and total deaths from all causes:

1706–1720	78·7 per 1000	27,557	Total deaths	350,530
1745–1759	89·3 ,,	29,895	,,	332,826
1785–1798	94·3 ,,	26,579	,,	293,350
1804–1818	52·9 ,,	14,716	,,	279,404

Heberden, *op. cit.* pp. 1–6. London smallpox deaths per 1000 deaths:

1700–1710	56·6	1751–1760	102·7
1711–1720	80·4	1761–1770	102·7
1721–1730	84·0	1771–1780	96·3
1731–1740	77·1	1781–1790	92·2
1741–1750	72·0	1791–1800	94·2

Wortley Montagu, and was used with varying persistence throughout the rest of the century. The question of the value of inoculation is a technical one which it is not within our province to discuss. Opinion is sharply divided, as it was divided in the days before it had ceased to be a practical issue. The mortality from inoculated smallpox was very much smaller than that from the natural variety and is given as about 2·5 per thousand[1]; but the disease which was the result was natural smallpox and was as infectious as the disease taken in the ordinary way, with the difference that the patient was only slightly indisposed and was therefore not kept indoors, and so was a fruitful source of infection to his fellow men[2]. For immediate purposes the fact to keep before our eyes is that, throughout the eighteenth century, smallpox remained one of the most serious evils to which the population was liable and that there was no startling diminution in its mortality, if indeed there was any. The contemporary authorities were not agreed as to the efficacy of inoculation; Heberden and Blane, for instance, said it increased the mortality, but the *Treatise on Fevers* of 1788, to which reference has been made before, was favourable to it, as was also a writer in the *Gentleman's Magazine* for 1796[3].

Modern authorities are cautious; there is a careful inquiry into the effects of inoculation in a volume of the *Statistical Journal*, which is inclined generally to be favourable to the practice though with no very generous support. It would appear that, although the century was one of many and severe epidemics,

[1] Heberden, *op. cit.* p. 34.
[2] Lettsom, *Medical Memoirs*, 1774, p. 182. He supports inoculation but says that smallpox has increased and that patients are exposed in the open air. "How far this free communication is culpable is not the subject before me; but as the increased deaths appear in part to arise from hence, a more guarded intercourse would be equally humane and politic."
[3] *Gentleman's Magazine*, Feb. 1796, p. 112: "The increase of people within the last 25 years is visible to every observer. Inoculation is the mystic spell that has produced this wonder." Before that time "it may be safely asserted, that the malady, added to the general laws of nature, did at least equipoise population....It is now 30 years since the Suttons and others under their instructions, had practised the art of inoculation upon half the kingdom and had reduced the chance of death to 1 in 2000. Hence the great increase of people."

the practice of inoculation reduced the mortality in the period between the epidemics to a lower figure than it would have been had there been no inoculation, but it is added that there were other causes to decrease the mortality in that general movement towards greater cleanliness which has been emphasised before, and the summary is cautious[1].

A modern authority is of opinion that our knowledge does not justify a definite conclusion as to whether the practice was or was not an advantage, and states that in the eighteenth century and for many previous centuries smallpox was one of the most fatal scourges to which mankind was subject[2].

The great change came in 1798 and subsequent years with the discovery by Edward Jenner of vaccination. The story has been told many times. By the vast majority of mankind the value of the practice is fully recognised and the debt which the world owes to Jenner is fully acknowledged. All that is necessary is to show the effect which the introduction of vaccination had on the reduction of mortality from smallpox in this country. We must remember that it was a disease which chiefly attacked children and young people, and that, while the chances were that they would contract the disease in their early years, if they escaped, it was very unlikely that they would do so permanently. This makes it clear that a reduction in the mortality from smallpox was a very important contribution to the causes of the increase of the population, and the introduction of vaccination came in the middle of the period when the death rate was declining. At first it was not realised that re-vaccination after a certain lapse of time was desirable, and it may be that when the death rate again began to rise about 1820, this was due to a failure to recognise this necessity.

In 1812 the National Vaccine Establishment reported that previous to the discovery of vaccination the average annual mortality within the Bills of Mortality had been 2000, whereas in 1811 it was only 751, in spite of an increase of 133,139 in the population during the previous ten years. The Report added that throughout Great Britain the increase in the same period had

[1] *Stat. Journ.* 1883, p. 425 (Guy).
[2] Allbutt, II. Part I. p. 769.

been 1,609,000 to which "augmentation the practice of vaccination has probably much contributed."[1]

The mortality in London from smallpox in the last thirty
years of the eighteenth century had ranged between seventeen
and twenty thousand per decade; in the first decade of the
nineteenth century it was 12,534, and for the two following
decades 7858 and 6950 respectively[2]. The rate of the decrease
of smallpox was slower in the decade 1821–1831 than it had
been in the two previous decades; in this decade the death rate
rose, and it is clear, therefore, that the decline in smallpox was
not having the beneficial effect it had in the first two decades
of the century[3].

In the navy and army, where the uniformity which can be
obtained makes them valuable experimental grounds, the introduction of vaccination did great things. It appears that in
the navy, although the practice of vaccination had not been
universally adopted, the mortality from smallpox had been very
greatly diminished, while in the army the results as reported
in 1812 were even more satisfactory[4].

The alteration in smallpox mortality in the nineteenth century
is said to exhibit "numerical phenomena which no sanitary
reform can explain, and which vaccination alone appears com-
petent to account for."[5]

In more general accounts of the increase of the population
written at the time, vaccination is given a very prominent place.

The Report on the 1821 Census, in a discussion of the causes
of the increase, lays stress on the "improved treatment of
disease—especially the substitution of vaccination for the
smallpox."[6] Roberton, writing in 1827 of infantile mortality,
says, "so great an increase in the value of infantile life does not

[1] *Accounts and Papers*, 1812, x. p. 168.
[2] Allbutt, ii. Part i. p. 770. London smallpox deaths:

1771–1780	20·923 in the decade.
1781–1790	17·687 in the decade.
1791–1800	18·477 in the decade.

[3] *S.B.C.P.* vi. Appendix, p. 114 (1813): "In consequence of mischievous
Publications it (mortality from smallpox) has again risen to near 1200."
[4] *Accounts and Papers*, 1812, x. p. 167.
[5] *Stat. Journ.* 1883, p. 424.
[6] Prelim. Obs. 1821, p. xxvi.

depend alone on vaccination, but upon many causes, of which, nevertheless vaccination is the most important."[1]

We may conclude this discussion of the increase in medical skill, the movement for greater cleanliness and fresh air and the important reduction of mortality which resulted, with a quotation from Macmichael's *Gold Headed Cane*, a work originally published in 1827:

In thus approaching modern times, we cannot fail to be struck with the great change that has taken place in the general character of the systems of physic, which has been effected by the gradual substitution of observation and experiment for learning and scholastic disputation. No one will deny that the result of this change has been the improvement of the practice of our art; hence the rate of mortality has decreased nearly one-third, within the last forty years, referable to the more temperate habits which prevail almost uniformly through all orders of society, to the utter disappearance or mitigated severity of many fatal diseases, and, above all, to the substitution of vaccination for the smallpox[2].

[1] Roberton, p. 47.   [2] Ed. of 1915, p. 241.

CHAPTER XI

Conclusion

H UMAN progress may be rapid or slow; the changes in the general conditions under which different generations live may also be rapid or slow, and it is almost certain that a greater change has been wrought in the state of this country between the early days of our great-grandfathers or our great-great-grandfathers and the time in which we are now living than in any other period of similar duration. A man who was born in the early years of the reign of George III and who lived to be an old man, is well within the memory of old men living to-day. He lived through the great age of road making and canal making and well into the railway era—he may even have had a flutter in railway stock in his declining years. He lived through that period in which the almost medieval system of industry was replaced by the modern factory system and in which he saw hand-power superseded by water and steam. In the realm of theory he saw the old mercantile system attacked by Adam Smith; he saw the system of individual and industrial freedom, to which this system inevitably led, proclaimed and practised by the Utilitarians, and the free trade movement, its child, inaugurated by Huskisson. On the other hand, as English legislation is rarely theoretically consistent, he saw the beginnings of collectivism in the Factory Acts; a collectivism, however, which was based on obvious calls for decent treatment and which commended itself more to the Tory landowner than to the Whig manufacturer.

There was one other change which he saw, as far-reaching and as important as any of the others, and one of which he was thoroughly afraid. He lived through the great period of the increase of the population. In decennial periods, although we are now adding greater numbers to our population than were added in similar periods about a hundred years ago, the percentage increase, which is the only sure criterion, has diminished. The centre of our Georgian gentleman's life, from 1780 to 1820, covered the period of the most remarkable increase in the population of this country. Whatever his walk in life, he would be brought face to face with this phenomenon. If he were a countryman and a landowner he would be concerned with the effect of inclosure, with the housing arrangements on his estates and with the administration of the Poor Laws, either as a magistrate or merely as a ratepayer. If he were a town dweller and a manufacturer, he would be concerned with the conditions of the new towns, which were growing to sizes of which his forbears had never dreamt, with the supply of workpeople for his mills and with the useful though trying bands of Irish who kept coming in search of work. If he had a turn for theory and political economy the menu provided for him was most tempting. In his young days men were quarrelling as to the size of the population. In his prime, a gloomy picture was presented by Malthus of the effects of a people increasing too rapidly, and the first Census showed that the population was larger than had been supposed even by many who had always maintained that an increase was going on. In his later years there was discussion in abundance as to the effect of this increasing population on the questions of wages and industry; the fear which it caused gave rise to inquiries into the conditions in Ireland and to recommendations in favour of schemes of emigration. In this he would be quick to see difficulties, such as the necessity of its being accompanied with a restriction of housing accommodation, and the danger that the Irish would at once fill up the "vacuum" which emigration might cause.

This period of rapidly increasing population, following generations of very slow increase and followed by a period in which the rate of increase has declined, is very remarkable. The discussion of it has been made harder, though more interesting, by two facts. First, the information on which the estimates of the population can be based is very defective before the first Census; no reliable figures for the population were known to contemporaries and it is impossible even now entirely to remove the uncertainty. As a result of this uncertainty there existed a very widespread feeling that the population was decreasing, and this gave rise to many discussions and to the advocacy of many measures, and was the historical background of Malthus and of the general attitude he attacked. Secondly, to explain the causes of the increase of the population further than by discussing general tendencies and favourable conditions would be to approach very closely to the exceedingly personal question of human motive or lack of motive. Just as there is a tendency to assume that man lives on employment, whereas he lives on the food which employment enables him to buy, so there is a tendency to ascribe the increase of population to favourable conditions which can only create a state of affairs in which the human motive may have greater or less play.

Before the Industrial Revolution began the population of England was practically stationary and conditions were changing but slowly. The maintenance of the apprenticeship and guild regulations prevented early marriages; the Corporation and Settlement Laws, assisted by the primitive conditions of communication, rendered movement difficult; the system whereby farm labourers lived in the farmhouses, the lack of cottages and, in certain cases, the policy of the landowners to check the building of cottages tended to keep the rural population stationary.

In industry to a considerable extent, and in agriculture to a very great extent, the demand to be supplied was local; this system, based on the needs of local subsistence, and the general watertight structure of society did not encourage the growth of a large population. There also existed in the lack of medical skill positive checks expressed by a high rate of infantile and general mortality.

In a recent work on *The Population Problem* it is stated that the great increase of population which began in this country with the Industrial Revolution was merely "the response to increase in skill."[1] If this is interpreted in a broad way, it was probably the primary cause. Behind all this increase there loom the advances in the industries of the country, which progressed in response to the increase of skill; in so far, therefore, as many

[1] Carr Saunders, *The Population Problem*, p. 308.

of the influences which tended to increase the population in this period would not have been called into operation but for the economic demand from our own people, and would all have been powerless to maintain a greatly increased population without the increase in the opportunities of employment which the growing industries supplied, to that extent the increase of the population *was* the response to the increase of skill. There existed features in the increase, connected with the economic organisation of the country, which are not necessarily bound up with the increase of skill, though they depend on the expansion of industry. Apprenticeship first of all declined and was then swept away by legislation, with the result that one great obstacle to early marriage was removed, while the change of housing arrangements in the country removed another. Trades and industries of a heavy unskilled kind which did not require apprenticeship as a training, and which for various legal reasons were outside these regulations, grew up, and these were mostly trades in which the full earning power was reached at an early age, with the result that there was no great inducement to postpone marriage. The watertight structure of society was destroyed both in the industrial and in the agricultural districts. The manufactures supplied an ever widening market, and improved transport and methods of agriculture enabled farmers to supply the wants of people other than their immediate neighbours. In addition to these changes in the economic organisation of the country, which tended to increase the population, the administration of the Poor Laws, with its system of allowances from the rates in aid of wages, was looked upon at the time as a fruitful source of the increase. In contemporary reports and literature it enjoyed more prominence than any other single cause, though it is probable that its actual effect was not so potent as was represented. These are all factors which would tend to raise the marriage rate and the birth rate; the marriage rate rose until 1790, and the birth rate rose steadily from 1710 to 1790.

The increase of skill and the greater opportunities for employment to which it led, encouraged another source of increase; the population of Ireland was increasing at a rate even more rapid than that which obtained in this country, and chiefly as a response to inadequate and unsafe encouragements; and the opportunities in this country provided many Irish with a livelihood in various more or less unskilled occupations, and by immigration added a considerable number to the population. The comparative absence of any increase of skill in Ireland during this period and the great increase in its population should act as a warning against ascribing too much in England to the influence of an increase in skill; that is, against ascribing without due consideration the increase to the Industrial Revolution.

In addition to these causes of increase which were connected with the industrial aspect of the country, another lay in the medical improvements of the time. The period saw the rapid development of the hospital movement, and the beginning and remarkable growth of the dispensaries. Medical education and scientific investigation were improved. Sanitary science and right principles in the treatment of such scourges as fever which thrived under insanitary conditions were advanced, though not necessarily for strictly scientific reasons. For our purpose, however, the important thing is the reduction in mortality which resulted whatever the scientific principles involved may have been. The practice of midwifery was greatly improved: certain diseases which in former times had been serious sources of mortality were reduced or abolished, and small-pox was greatly lessened after the middle of the period by the introduction of vaccination. Many of these improvements were based on empiricism; the greater care for cleanliness and hygiene which was displayed, was in unconscious harmony with the scientific discoveries which came later, and it may well be that this was the greatest single achievement of the medical improvements of the period. Many things may have contributed to this. Cleanliness is not cheap, and the growth of wealth may both have created the desire and enabled the ideal to be realised. The increased use of soap, combined with the substitution of easily washed cotton goods for the heavy and rarely washed woollen goods, which followed the com-paratively recent growth of the cotton industry, may have assisted[1]. The greater communication with India and the East where habits of cleanliness were enforced as part of the regulations of a caste system, and where in some cases the climate rendered them more essential, may have been an additional influence. The religious enthusiasm of the Wesleyans and the precept that "cleanliness is next to godliness," may also have had their share, and in his Constitutional Code Bentham outlines a Ministry of Health of a very elaborate kind, which reflects the attitude of the Benthamite group to the question[2].

The increase of medical skill, combined with such things as a decline in the consumption of alcohol and an improvement in the food supply resulting from certain phases of the agricultural revolution, which led to a decline in the death rate and to a prolongation of life, worked hand in hand with the increase of industrial skill, with the increased opportunities of employment to which this gave rise and with the changes in the economic organisation tending to encourage early marriage, to increase the population. Either of these would have been seriously handicapped without the other; the increased wealth of the country and the increased opportunities of employment afforded by the industrial development were at once the bedrock on which the medical improvements were built and the justification for the demand for a large population, and the industrial improvements were enabled to take effect with less strain on the country than would have been the case had there been no medical improvements.

For about thirty years, from 1780 to 1810, the birth rate was rather higher than either before or after. From 1780 to 1800 the marriage rate was high and with the fall in the marriage rate the fertility of marriage rose from 1795 to 1815. It has been noted that Malthus gave no support to the imposition of any check on the number of children once marriage had been contracted. But in spite of Malthus's view and the view of others at the time that marriage once contracted children will be procreated up to the physiological limit, we have seen that

[1] Blane, *Select Dissertations*, p. 126: "Average yearly consumption of soap, 1787–88, 292,006,440 lb. Ditto, 1819–21, 643,000,963 lb. The soap used in manufactures not being taxable is not included in this statement."
[2] Bentham, *Works*, IX. 443.

before Place and others began the neo-Malthusian movement the fertility of marriage did show considerable fluctuations, and it is therefore not easy to believe that the fertility of marriage is a constant apart from such modern methods. The breakdown in the restrictions on marriage, followed by the reduction in the age of marriage, with the increased opportunities for employment and the medical skill in preserving the lives of children, led to a higher birth rate, a higher survival rate, the large families which we associate with this period and an increase in the population. Deliberate care seems to have been taken in the early part of the nineteenth century to secure the certainty of having families, and it was the prevalence of early marriages, combined with the large families which followed, that gave rise to neo-Malthusianism[1].

During the period from about 1780 to 1810 the increase in the population demanded by the industrial growth was being provided by a high birth rate and a falling death rate; rather later—from 1795 to 1815—the fertility of marriage rose. For some time, then, owing to the economic demand which was the cause, backed up before the opening of the nineteenth century by the fear that the population was decreasing, the population was growing owing to a rise in the birth rate and a fall in the death rate. The warnings of Malthus probably checked the rise in the birth rate, but that was partially counteracted by a rise in the fertility of marriage until, after 1815, it in turn was checked when as a matter of fact—from 1850 to 1880—the birth rate again rose. The death rate fell from 1780 to 1810 and had

---

[1] Gaskell, *Manufacturing Population*, p. 29: "Some surprise may be excited probably by the assertion, in those whose attention has never been directed to the subject, but it is none the less true, that sexual intercourse was almost universal prior to marriage in the agricultural districts. This intercourse must not be confounded with that promiscuous and indecent concourse of the sexes which is so prevalent in the towns, and which is ruinous alike to health and to morals. It existed only between parties where a tacit understanding had all the weight of an obligation—and this was that marriage should be the result. So binding was this engagement that the examples of desertion were exceedingly rare—though marriage itself was generally deferred until pregnancy declared itself." Cowell's evidence in the Poor Law Report: "I appeal to the experience of all overseers in rural districts, whether instances of marriage taking place among the labouring classes are not so very rare as to constitute no exception to the general assertion that 'pregnancy precedes marriage.'" Carr Saunders, p. 319, note.

been showing a falling tendency since 1730, marred by a rise from 1760 to 1780, and this fall is the most important factor in the growth of the population. The birth rate had started to decline some ten years before the death rate started to rise owing, probably, in addition to Malthus's warning, to the feeling, possibly unconscious, that population had increased sufficiently. If this was really the case and if some check was required, it was clearly better that the aim should be to lower the birth rate rather than to raise the death rate, for this is a course which obviously no one would advocate. The increase depends on the rise in the birth rate relative to the fall in the death rate; if the fall in the death rate supplies the necessary increase the rise in the birth rate will be checked. If, when the economic demand for people was being supplied, an extension after marriage of the moral restraint which Malthus recommended before marriage could not be relied upon to secure this limitation, some other check had to be found, and this began in the neo-Malthusianism which was gaining support in the twenties of the nineteenth century. Thus it came to pass that certain accompaniments of the Industrial Revolution, the changes caused in the social and economic arrangements of the country coupled with the increase of medical knowledge and skill, broke down one series of checks on the growth of the population and led to a period of very rapid increase. To the minds of many this demonstrated the necessity for some other means of lessening the growth of the population and finally gave rise to the movement to promote certain checks of a more direct character than had previously been in existence.

The Malthusian controversy has inevitably focussed attention very considerably on the questions of birth and marriage. In conclusion it should again be observed that the emphasis appears to have been somewhat misplaced. The birth rate rose from 1710 to 1790 but the rise was not as spectacular as the fall in the death rate from 1730 to 1810. The birth rate was contributing in an important way and as it can be controlled by the action of the ordinary member of the community in a way in which the death rate cannot, the importance of its movements is enhanced. The really important factor, however, is the fall in the death rate.

Mortality Tables for Ireland

(Reference Ch. III. p. 73)

Reports, 1824, XXII. Preliminary Observations to the Irish Census, p. xvii.

PARISH REGISTERS

"From the title of the Population Act it appears that the object of the Legislature in enacting it was not only 'to take an account of the population of Ireland' but also 'to ascertain the increase or diminution thereof.' It therefore becomes necessary to add a few observations under this head. In the Act there are no provisions for obtaining returns from the officiating Ministers of Churches and Chapels throughout Ireland as in the case of the Population Act for Great Britain, from which such valuable data have been obtained, for ascertaining the increase and diminution of the population in that part of the Empire, during the preceding century. This omission has doubtless arisen from a knowledge of the very defective state of parish registers in Ireland."

(The Report then goes on to say that in 1810 an inquiry was addressed to the several diocesan registrars, to ascertain the state of the parish registers. The result of this inquiry was not so satisfactory as could have been wished, and the Commissioners recommended that the bill at that time before the Legislature "for the better regulation and preservation of the Parish and other Registers of births, baptisms, marriages and burials, and for establishing general repositories for all such registers in England" should also be established in Ireland.)

Reports, 1843, XXIV. Report on the Irish Census of 1841 (Surgeon Wilde's Report), p. viii.

"None of the ancient Irish writers attempt to enumerate the diseases of this country, to catalogue their names or describe their symptoms or fatality. The same deficiency in medical nosology is apparent in those of more modern times, and in no instance has any effort been made to draw up a general table of mortality for this kingdom until the present. The only conception of this kind arose with Sir William Petty who in 1683 published a small tract of *Observations upon the Dublin Bills of Mortality*, MDCLXXXI, *and the state of that city*."

(From that time in Dublin and with various defects Bills of Mortality seem to have been continued for some time.)

P. xi.

"These Bills continued to be registered till 1772, from which period I have been unable to obtain any account of their existence; and Prof. Barker, for so many years Secretary to the Board of Health in this country, has informed me that a similar result has attended his inquiries upon the same subject. They certainly have not been kept since the commencement of the present century."

APPENDIX II

Extracts from Reports on the Poor Laws

(Reference Ch. VI. p. 146)

Reports, 1818, v. p. 166. Rev. W. H. Grey. Hunts and Beds.

"I think it [the increase in population] depends in some measure upon the persons marrying earlier now, without having provided for a family, which they were in the habit of doing formerly, now depending on parochial relief."

See also pp. 217 (Exeter), 248 (Manchester), 229 (Marriages not early in Scotland).

Reports, 1824, VI. pp. 404, 429. John Dennis. Hunts.

"Then in fact your opinion is that the Poor Laws are a premium upon matrimony?"

"Yes, and for this reason; I have known many young men perhaps because you would not give them more than 3s. a week, they will say we will marry and you must maintain us."

P. 460. Rev. Anthony Collet. Suffolk.

"Pray is it your opinion that it is advantageous that unmarried men should be paid less wages than the married men?"

"Certainly not, not to the extent that they now practise it, because the prospect of additional wages is a bounty on marriage and they marry for the sake of a greater allowance. That circumstance tended materially to increase the population of the country."

Reports, 1831, VIII. (Lords, Poor Laws), p. 63. Thomas Partington.

"Does not the present administration of the Poor Laws tend to the encouragement of early and improvident marriages?"

"I have no doubt that it does, if a man can marry and be sure that all his family will be provided for by the parish, it naturally has that effect."

On the other hand, p. 191. John Barton. Sussex.

"Do you consider that [over-population] to have arisen from the prevalence of early marriage?"

"I think the proportion of marriage relatively to the population has not increased for the last seventy years, nor are they earlier than they used to be."

Reports, 1833, v. (Agriculture), Q. 941. Wilts.

"Has the increase of population been considerable in these parishes?"

"Very considerable."

"Is the system of early marriages prevalent?"

"Too much so a great deal."

"With a view to getting the allowance from the parish for children?"

"I do not think that that is the inducement."

Q. 1340.

"The Poor Laws hold out every encouragement for that population to be increased. It has been too much the practice to throw young single men out of employment in preference to married men, and that is a great inducement for a young man to marry."

Reports, 1834, xxvii. p. 46.

"As the farmers have under the scale system a direct inducement to employ married men rather than single, in many villages particularly in the southern districts, they will not employ the single men at all. In others they pay them a much lower rate of wages for the same work in the hope of driving them to seek work out of the parish."

P. 73.

"The first and most prominent [result of the allowance system] is, that from the neglect of single men, and the lower place to which they have been and are forced in the scale, a series of early marriages has ensued, for the avowed purpose of increasing income, until a generation of superfluous labourers has risen up."

Reports, 1834, xxix. p. 39. Villiers' Report, Worcestershire.

"The greatest fault which was committed in the present administration of parish relief and of the other charities was that of practically teaching the people that they would obtain a larger share of their advantage by early marriage and large families."

P. 91. Henry Pilkington's Report, Castle Donnington.

"It is quite a common thing for mere lads to get married in order to get families, and by this means get the benefit of parish allowance."

P. 177. Stephen Walcot, Wales.

"The effect of thus placing the married and unmarried men on a different footing as to relief, is clearly to encourage early and improvident marriages, with their consequent evils. Of this there is no lack of evidence."

Reports, 1836, VIII. (Agriculture), Q. 13,266.   Sussex.

"Do not you consider that there has been another very injurious thing which has led very much to improvident marriages, the system of paying a strong, young and healthy labourer lower wages than a married man, merely because the married man had encumbrances upon him?"

"Certainly, there can be no question but that that has been the practical result in the neighbourhood in which I reside."

"And they have been married in consequence?"

"I know instances where they have threatened to do it....I have no hesitation in saying that marriages have constantly occurred from the fact of the single men being paid much less than the married man....I believe that the difference of the wages of married and single men has had the effect of inducing men imprudently to marry."

Letter to the magistrates, 1828, p. 6.

"Few farmers are probably so completely blind as not to see that by employing the married men in preference to the single they offer the latter a direct premium to marry."

BIBLIOGRAPHY

MOST of the works which have been consulted in the preparation of this thesis have been included in this list, though not all the works are actually cited in any part of the thesis. Certain official publications from which figures used in the compilation of some of the tables were taken have not been included as detailed information is attached in all cases to the figures or diagrams.

In this bibliography, with the exception of section (*B*), certain works which are of special interest or importance have been starred; in the case of the modern publications (that is in part of section (*A*) and in section (*C*, 3)) an attempt has been made to star a series of works which shall be representative of most of the main subjects touched upon.

(A) PERIODICAL PUBLICATIONS AND WORKS OF REFERENCE

American Economic Review. 1911. Field: Early propagandist movement in English population theory.

Annals of Agriculture.

Annual Register.

Burdett's Hospitals and Charities.

Contemporary Review. 1883. Rae: Why have the Yeomanry perished?

Dictionary of National Biography.

*Economic Journal. Sept. 1922. M. D. George: Some causes of the increase of population.

Edinburgh Review. Vol. xxxviii. Cobbett's Cottage Economy. Vol. xxxix. Restraints on Emigration.

Encyclopædia Britannica.

Gentleman's Magazine.

Historical Manuscripts Commission Reports.

Monthly Magazine.

Parliamentary History.

Quarterly Review.

*Reports of the Society for bettering the condition of the Poor. 1798–1814. 6 volumes.

Statutes at large.

Victoria County Histories.

ARTICLES FROM THE STATISTICAL JOURNAL

Vol. ii. 1839. Condition of Leeds and its inhabitants, First Report of the Registrar General.

Vol. IX. 1846. Wm. Farr: Influence of scarcities and of the high prices of wheat on the mortality of the people of England.

Vol. XLIII. 1880. R. Price Williams: On the increase of the population in England and Wales.

Vol. XLV. 1882. Dr W. A. Guy: 250 years of smallpox in London.

Vol. LIII. 1890. Dr Wm. Ogle: On marriage rates and marriage ages.

Vol. LX. 1897. Sir Robert Hunter: The movement for the inclosure and preservation of open lands.

Vol. LXIII. 1900. Rubin: Population and the Birth Rate.   F. A. Welton: Distribution of population in England and Wales and its progress in the period 1801–1891.

*Vol. LXXVI. 1913. E. C. K. Gonner: Population of England in the eighteenth century.

(B) OFFICIAL PUBLICATIONS

Reports, vol. IX. 1795. Committee to consider several laws which concern the relief and settlement of the Poor.

Reports, vol. IX. 1795. Committee to examine into the state of Parish Children.

Reports, vol. IX. 1795. Waste Lands.

Reports, vol. XIV. 1802. Report from Committee on Dr Jenner's petition respecting his discovery of vaccine inoculation.

Journals of the House of Commons.

Reports, 1802–3, v. Report from the Committee on the Woollen Clothiers' Petition.

Reports, 1802–3, VII. Evidence taken before the Committee on the woollen trade.

Reports, 1804, v. Report on the petition respecting the Fever Institution.   Report on petition of manufacturers of woollen cloth in Yorkshire.   Evidence on Calico Printers' Petition.

Reports, 1806, III. State of the woollen manufacture of England.

Reports, 1812, x. Report on the National Vaccine Establishment.

Reports, 1812–13, IV. Apprenticeship.

Reports, 1814–15, VI. Parish Apprentices.

Reports, 1816, III. State of the children employed in the manufactories of the United Kingdom.

Reports, 1817, VI. Employment of boys in sweeping chimneys.   Watch makers of Coventry.   Poor Laws.

Reports, 1817, VII. Police of the metropolis.

Reports, 1818, v. Poor Laws.

Reports, 1818, VII. Report on the contagious fevers in London. Report on contagious fever in Ireland.

Reports, 1819, VIII. Report on Steam Engines and Furnaces.

Reports, 1819, VIII. First and Second Reports on the state of disease and condition of the labouring poor in Ireland.

Reports, 1820, IX. Correspondence respecting paupers sent from England to Ireland.
Reports, 1821, IV. Laws relating to Vagrants.
Reports, 1822, XXI. Report from the National Vaccine Establishment.
Reports, 1823, VI. Employment of the Poor in Ireland.
Reports, 1824, V. Artisans and Machinery.
Reports, 1824, VI. Labourers' Wages.   Report of Committee on Poor Rate Returns.
Reports, 1824, XXII. Report on the Irish Census.
Reports, 1825, VI. Friendly Societies.
Reports, 1825, VII. Disturbances in Ireland.   Lords Report on the State of Ireland.
Reports, 1825, VIII. Commons Report on the State of Ireland.
Reports, 1825, IX. Lords Report on the State of Ireland.
Reports, 1826, IV. Emigration.
Reports, 1826–7, V. Emigration.
Reports, 1828, IV. Poor Laws.   Scotch and Irish Vagrants.
Accounts and Papers, 1829, XXI. Abstract of the returns of numbers of poor persons.
Reports, 1830, VII. State of the Poor in Ireland.
Reports, 1830, X. Report on the Sale of Beer.
Reports, 1830, XXIX. Emigration. (Figures.)
Accounts and Papers, 1830–31, XI. Poor Law Expenses.
Reports, 1831, VIII. Lords Report on the Poor Laws.
Reports, 1833, V. Report on Agriculture.
Reports, 1833, VI. Report on manufactures, shipping, and commerce.
Reports, 1833, XV. Public Walks and Places of Exercise.   Report on Sale of Beer.
Reports, 1833, XX. and XXI. Report of the Factory Commissioners.
Reports, 1834, VIII. Intoxication among the labouring classes.
Reports, 1834, XV. Sewers of the Metropolis.
Reports, 1834, XXVII–XXXVII. Reports of the Poor Law Commission.
Reports, 1835, XXXII. Poor Law in Ireland.
Reports, 1835, XXXV. First Annual Report of the Poor Law Commissioners.
Reports, 1836, VIII. State of Agriculture.
Reports, 1836, XXIX. Second Annual Report of the Poor Law Commissioners.
Reports, 1836, XXXIX. State of the Irish Poor in Great Britain. (G. Cornewall Lewis.)
Reports, 1837, V. Lords Report on the State of Agriculture.
Reports, 1837, XVII. Commons Committee on the Administration of the Poor Law.
Reports, 1837, XXV. Third Annual Report of the Poor Law Commissioners.
Reports, 1837–8, XXVIII. Fourth Annual Report of the Poor Law Commissioners.   Supp. I. Arnott and Kay: On the prevalence

of certain physical causes of fever in the metropolis.   Supp. II.
Southwood Smith: Physical causes of sickness and mortality to
which the poor are particularly exposed.
Reports, 1839, x. Railways.
Reports, 1839, xx. Fifth Annual Report of the Poor Law Com-
missioners.
Reports, 1840, xi. Health of Towns.
Reports, 1840, xlv. Railways.
Reports, 1840, xxiii–xxiv. Reports from the Assistant Hand Loom
Weavers Commissioners.
Reports, 1842, x. Interments in towns.
Reports, 1842, xv. Employment and condition of Children in Mines.
Reports, 1843, vii. Committee on Smoke Prevention.
Reports, 1843, xii. Employment of women and children in Agriculture.
Reports, 1843, xiv–xv. Children's Employment Commission. Ap-
pendix to Second Report.
Reports, 1843, xxiv. Irish Census Report.
Reports, 1844, v. Report on Commons' Inclosures.
Reports, 1844, xi. Railways.
Reports, 1844, xvii. First Report on the state of large towns and
populous districts.
Reports, 1844, xx. Scotch Poor Laws.
Reports, 1845, xviii. Second Report on the state of large towns and
populous districts.
Reports, 1846, xiii. Condition of labourers employed on railways.
Reports, 1847–8, xxv. Eighth Annual Report of the Registrar General.
Reports, 1857, Sess. I, iv. First Report of the Commissioners of Inland
Revenue.
Reports, 1870, xx. Account of the quantities of malt charged to duty
in England.
Reports, 1884–5, xxii. 28th Report of the Inland Revenue Com-
missioners.

(C) HISTORIES AND ARTICLES

(1) ANONYMOUS

1680. Britannia Languens, or a discourse on trade.
1772. The advantages and disadvantages of inclosing waste lands
and open fields.
1780. An inquiry into the advantages and disadvantages resulting
from bills of inclosure.
1785. A political inquiry into the consequences of inclosing waste
lands and the causes of the high price of butchers' meat.
*1788. A treatise on fevers.
1795. Hints for the relief of the Poor.
1817. A Picture of the Royal College of Physicians.

1820. On the means of retaining the population within any required limits.

*1828. Letters to the magistrates of the south and west of England on the expediency of correcting certain abuses in the Poor Laws.

*1828. Parish Settlements and Pauperism.

*1833. Extracts from the information received by the Commissioners on the Poor Laws.

1836. Report of the Committee appointed by the Medical and Surgical Association on the new Poor Law.

(2) WORKS ARRANGED IN ALPHABETICAL ORDER OF AUTHORS,
PUBLISHED BEFORE 1850

Aikin, John, M.D. A description of the Country from thirty to forty miles round Manchester. 1795.

Alcock, Thomas. Observations on the defects of the Poor Laws. 1752.

Bailey, J. and Culley, Geo. General view of the agriculture of Northumberland. 1794.

Bateman, Thomas. Reports on the Diseases of London. 1819.

Baxter, G. R. Book of the Bastiles. 1841.

Bell, William. What causes principally contribute to render a nation populous. 1757.

Bentham, J. Observations on the Poor Law Bill of 1796.

Bland, Dr. Midwifery Reports of the Westminster General Dispensary. Phil. Trans. vol. LXXI. 1781.

Blane, Sir Gilbert. Facts and observations on the Walcheren fever. Trans. of the Royal Med. and Chir. Soc. vol. III. 1812.

* — Observations on the prevalence, mortality and treatment of different diseases. Trans. of the Royal Med. and Chir. Soc. vol. IV. 1813.

* — Select Dissertations. 1822.

— Reflections on the present crisis. 1831.

Champney, T. A Review of the healing art. 1797.

Cobbett, William. Rural Rides. (1886 ed. used.)

Collins, Robert. A treatise on midwifery. 1835.

Colquhoun, Patrick. Resources of the British Empire. 1815.

Coxe, William. Historical Tour in Monmouthshire. 1801.

Davenant, Charles. Political and commercial works. Ed. 1771.

Defoe, D. Giving alms no charity. 1704.

Duncombe, John. General view of the agriculture of Hereford. 1805.

*Eden, Sir F. M. State of the Poor. 1797.

Fielding, H. An inquiry into the causes of the late increase of robbers. 1751.

— A proposal for making an effectual provision for the Poor. 1753.

Garnett, T. A lecture on the preservation of health. 1797.

*Gaskell, P. The manufacturing population. 1833.

*Gaskell, P. Artisans and Machinery. 1836.

Hanway, Jonas. Letters on the importance of the rising generation. 1767.

Harrison. Description of England, printed in Holinshed's Chronicles, vol. I. 1807.

Hawkins, Dr F. Bisset. Medical Statistics. 1829.

*Heberden, Wm. Junr. Observations on the increase and decrease of different diseases. 1801.

* — Some Observations on the Scurvy. 1807. On the mortality of London. 1808. Both in the Med. Trans. of the Royal College of Physicians, vol. IV.

Highmore, A. Pietas Londiniensis. The history, design, and present state of the various public charities in and near London. 1810.

Kay Shuttleworth, J. Manchester in 1832. Reprinted in Four Periods of Public Education. 1862.

Lettsom, T. C. Medical Memoirs. 1774.

Lewis, G. Cornewall. On local disturbances in Ireland. 1836.

McCulloch, J. R. Statistical account of the British Empire. 2nd ed. 1837.

Macmichael, Wm. The Gold Headed Cane. First published 1827. (1915 ed. used.)

Malcolm, James. A compendium of modern husbandry, principally written during a survey of Surrey. 1805.

Malcolm, J. P. Anecdotes of the manners and customs of London. 1810.

*Malthus, T. R. Essay on Population. (1817 and 1872 eds.)

Marcus. On the possibility of limiting populousness. 1838.

Milman, Francis. An inquiry into the sources from whence the symptoms of the scurvy and putrid fevers arise. 1782.

Milne, Joshua. A treatise on the valuation of annuities and assurances on lives and survivorships. 1815.

*Newenham, Thomas. Inquiries into the population of Ireland. 1805.

* — View of the circumstances of Ireland. 1809.

Pearson, John. Life of William Hey. 1822.

*Percival, Thomas. The works of Thomas Percival, M.D. 1807.

Place, F. Illustrations of the Principles of Population. 1822.

Plymley, Joseph. General view of the agriculture of Shropshire. 1803.

Roberton, John. Observations on the mortality and physical management of children. 1827.

Smith, Adam. Wealth of Nations. 1776. (Everyman ed.)

Starkey's Dialogue, c. 1538. Early English Text Soc. 1878.

Stone, Edmund. Willow Bark to cure ague. 1763. Phil. Trans. vol. LIII.

*Strickland, George. A discourse on the Poor Laws. 1827.

Tucker, Josiah. Advantages and disadvantages of France and Great Britain with regard to trade. 1749.

— Instructions for travellers. 1757.

Ure, A. Philosophy of Manufactures. 1835.
Wakefield, Edward. Account of Ireland. 1812.
Wales, William. An inquiry into the present state of the population in England and Wales. 1781.
*White, Charles. A treatise on the management of pregnant and lying-in women. 1773.
Willan, R. Miscellaneous works. 1831.
Young, Arthur. Farmers' Letters. 1771.
— Political Arithmetic. 1774.
— Tour in Ireland. 1780.

(3) Published since 1850

*Adami, J. G. Charles White and puerperal fever. 1922.
*Allbutt, T. C. and Rolleston, H. D. System of Medicine. 2nd ed.
Arber, E. A transcript of the registers of the Stationers' Company of London. 1875.
Bonar, J. Parson Malthus. 1881.
— Malthus and his work. 1885.
*Brownlee, J. The history of the birth and death rate in England and Wales taken as a whole from 1570 to the present day. Re-printed from 1916 Public Health.
Bryce, Viscount. Two Centuries of Irish History, 1691–1870. 1888.
Cannan, Edwin. A history of the theories of production and distribution in English Political Economy, from 1776 to 1848. 1903.
*Carr Saunders, A. M. The Population Problem. 1922.
*Chaplin, Arnold. Medicine in the reign of George III. 1919.
Cox, Harold. The Problem of Population. 1922.
*Creighton, Charles. History of epidemics in Britain. 1894.
Cullingworth, Charles. Charles White, F.R.S. 1904.
*Cunningham, W. Growth of English Industry and Commerce.
Daniels, G. W. The early English cotton industry. 1920.
Dunlop, O. J. English Apprenticeship and child labour. 1912.
Ernle, Lord (R. E. Prothero). Pioneers and Progress of English Farming. 1888.
— English Farming, Past and Present. 1922.
Fawcett, Henry. Pauperism, its causes and remedies. 1871.
Fay, C. R. Life and Labour in the nineteenth century. 1920.
Garrison, F. H. History of Medicine. 1917.
*George, M. D. London life in the eighteenth century. 1925.
*Gonner, E. C. K. Common Land and Inclosure. 1912.
Gray, B. Kirkman. A history of English Philanthropy. 1905.
Hammond, J. L. and B. The Village Labourer. 1911.
— — The Town Labourer. 1917.
— — The Skilled Labourer. 1919.
Hasbach, W. History of the English Agricultural Labourer. 1908.
Heaton, H. Yorkshire Woollen and Worsted Industries. 1920.
Hume, G. H. History of the Newcastle Infirmary. 1906.

Jephson, Henry. The sanitary evolution of London. 1907.
Jevons, W. S. Investigations in currency and finance. 1909.
Jewitt, L. The Wedgwoods. 1865.
Johnson, A. H. The disappearance of the small landowner. 1909.
Johnson, S. C. A history of emigration. 1913.
Lecky, W. E. H. History of England in the eighteenth century. 1882.
Lindsay Steven. Morgagni to Virchow. 1905.
Longstaff, G. B. Studies in Statistics. 1890.
*Mackay, Thomas. A history of the English Poor Laws, 1834–1898, being a supplementary volume to Sir G. Nicholls's History. 1904.
McVail, J. C. The prevention of infectious diseases. 1907.
Murchison, Charles. A treatise on the continued fevers of Great Britain. 1884.
Newton Pitt. Hunter and the medical societies of the last century. Hunterian Oration, 1896, continued in the Lancet, 1896, vol. 1.
*Nicholls, Sir G. History of the English Poor Law. 1854. History of the Scotch Poor Law. 1856.
Porter, G. R. Ed. F. W. Hirst. Progress of the Nation. 1912.
*Scrivenor, Harry. History of the Iron Trade. 1854.
Slater, Gilbert. The English Peasantry and the inclosure of Common Fields. 1907.
— The making of modern England. 1919.
Smiles, S. Lives of the Engineers. 1862.
Smith, Frank. Life of Sir James Kay Shuttleworth. 1923.
*Stangeland, C. E. The Pre-Malthusian Doctrines of Population. 1904.
Tawney, R. H. The agricultural problem of the sixteenth century. 1912.
Thorold Rogers. Six centuries of work and wages. 1884.
Toynbee, Arnold. The Industrial Revolution. 1884.
Trevelyan, G. M. British History in the nineteenth century. 1922.
Wallas, Graham. Life of Francis Place. 1918 ed.
Webb, S. and B. English Local Government. IV. Statutory Authorities. 1922.
* — — History of liquor licensing in England. 1903.
Williams, Orlo. Life and Letters of John Rickman. 1912.
Wright, Harold. Population. 1923.

INDEX

Abernethy, J., 215
Account of Ireland, Wakefield, Edward, 51
Ague, 235
Alcohol, 198–207
Allowance system, 142–169
American War, 22, 33, 59, 176, 177
Annals of Agriculture, 144
Annual Register, 64
Apprenticeship, 112–120, 256
Arnott and Kay, *Report on fevers in London*, 183

Baillie, Matthew, 213
Bakewell, Robert, 174, 247
Baptisms of Nonconformists, 29
Bastardy, laws of, 138–139
Bateman, Thomas, 243
Beaufort, Dr, estimate of Irish population, 47
Bedfordshire, affected by the allowance system, 150
  increase of population in, 155–159
  Poor Law expenses in, 152–155
Bentham, Jeremy, 258
Birmingham, birth rate in, 196–197
  death rate in, 186–187
Birth rate, 27–33, 72, 97, 98–100, 104, 105, 180–181, 196–197, 159–160
Blane, Sir Gilbert, 215, 234, 237, 243, 246, 249
Boerhaave, Hermann, 212
Bradford, increase of population in, 22
  apprenticeship in, 115
Brighton, increase of population in, 22
Bristol, birth rate in, 196–197
  death rate in, 186–187
Britannia Languens, 114
Buckinghamshire, affected by the allowance system, 150
  increase of population in, 155–159
  Poor Law expenses in, 152–155
Burials of Nonconformists, 36, 186
Bushe, G. P., estimate of Irish population, 47

Cardiff, increase of population in, 22
Cattle, improvements in, 174–175, 247

Chadwick, Edwin, 211
Cheshire, increase of population in, 25
Child labour, 101–105, 191–193
Chippenham, apprenticeship in, 115
Cholera, 183, 206–207
Civil Registration, introduction of, 15
Clarke, Sir Ernest, 1, 9
Cobbett, William, 3, 96, 195
College of Physicians, 216–217
Collins, Robert, 240
Colquhoun, Patrick, 246
Common Land and Inclosure, 3, 170
Cornewall Lewis, G., 5
Cottages, and the Poor Law, 107, 143–145
Counties, badly affected by the allowance system, 150
  not badly affected by the allowance system, 150
Coventry, apprenticeship in, 118
Cox, Mr Harold, 94
Creighton, Charles, 234, 237, 244–245
Cumberland, increase of population in, 155–159
  not affected badly by allowance system, 150
  Poor Law expenses in, 152–155

Darlington, apprenticeship in, 119
Death rate, 35–42, 72, 99–100, 180–186, 193, 204–207, 208–252, 259–260
Devonshire, increase of population in, 25
Diabolical Handbill, 95
Discourse on the Poor Law, Strickland, G., 152
Dispensaries, increase of, 224–226
Dobbs, Thomas, estimate of Irish population, 46
Domestic system, 189–191
Dorset, affected badly by allowance system, 150
  increase of population in, 155–159
  Poor Law expenses in, 152–155
Drainage, of fens, 174, 236
  of towns, 185, 210
Dublin, Bills of Mortality, 73
Durham, birth rate in, 104–105
  increase of population in, 25

CAMBRIDGE: PRINTED BY W. LEWIS, M.A., AT THE UNIVERSITY PRESS

For EU product safety concerns, contact us at Calle de José Abascal, 56–1°,
28003 Madrid, Spain or eugpsr@cambridge.org.